WE WANT SOME TOO

UNDERGROUND DESIRE AND THE REINVENTION OF MASS CULTURE

Hal Niedzviecki

PENGUIN BOOKS

PENGUIN BOOKS
Published by the Penguin Group
Penguin Books Canada Ltd, 10 Alcorn Avenue, Toronto, Ontario,
Canada M4V 3B2
Penguin Books Ltd, 27 Wrights Lane, London W8 5TZ, England
Penguin Putnam Inc., 375 Hudson Street, New York, New York 10014, U.S.A.
Penguin Books Australia Ltd, Ringwood, Victoria, Australia
Penguin Books (NZ) Ltd, cnr Rosedale and Airborne Roads, Albany,
Auckland 1310, New Zealand

Penguin Books Ltd, Registered Offices: Harmondsworth, Middlesex, England

First published 2000

1   3   5   7   9   10   8   6   4   2

Copyright © 2000 by Hal Niedzviecki

Author representation: Westwood Creative Artists
94 Harbord Street, Toronto, Ontario M5S 1G6

Printed and bound in Canada on acid-free paper ∞

CANADIAN CATALOGUING IN PUBLICATION DATA

Niedzviecki, Hal 1971–
We want some too: underground desire and the reinvention of mass culture

ISBN 0-14-029172-5

1. Popular culture. 2. Subculture. I. Title.

HM621.N53 2000   306   C99-932524-8

Visit Penguin Canada's web site at **www.penguin.ca**

CONTENTS

WE WANT SOME TOO

UNDERGROUND DESIRE AND THE REINVENTION OF MASS CULTURE

FRIDAY NIGHT WITH BRAINO

AN INTRODUCTION

You got tires for eyeballs, you got the concrete blocks for ears, you got the brain cells made of jello pudding, you got a backbone made out of beer, you got one foot on the throttle and the other on the brake and if they offer you a better job, ya'll would move down to the States . . .

— "Tires for Eyeballs," words by Soon, sung by Braino in an off-key a cappella

It's Friday night. Braino takes the stage like they've got nothing to prove. Five guys you wouldn't look at twice if you passed them on the street. They file in, pick up their instruments, tune up, stare down at their shoes. Chris bleats into a horn. The drummer, Ben, takes a tentative swipe with his sticks. Maybe someone mutters something into a muted microphone. Or, more likely, no one bothers saying anything. It's taken them four years to get to this stage, and the moment before the band starts playing is a long one, swollen with the kind of anticlimactic significance that's as difficult to express as it is to let go of. The crowd is restless, attentive to the idea that something is about to happen, though they don't know what that something might be and—in a way—they don't particularly care.

For us, it could be any Friday night in any big city. A suf-
focating bar, smoke swirling between bodies, small tables lit-
tered with ashtrays and empties. The sense that, for once,
we're in the right place at the right time. Or are we? There's
more to it than that. And less. Years of peripatetic effort; the
ghosts of ex-Braino band members who drifted away; a
century of pop culture. Then there's what it all comes down
to, which doesn't mean a thing: a night. Another night at
another downtown club at another CD launch party. I'm too
drunk, or I'm not drunk enough. My friend John has paid for
me to get in.

Finally, after what seems like hours, Braino starts playing.
They play loud, bursting into the bubbled pause that went on
for too long. They play weird. They play in staccato blasts
that unnerve the scattered chattering poseurs and scare the
unprepared. I'm glad for them. The music doesn't mean anything. We could be anywhere. They play like it matters.

■   ■   ■

The first thing that you should know about Braino is what
they aren't. They aren't the most original band; they
aren't the most exciting; they aren't the strangest, the sexiest,
the stupidest. Obviously, you're reading about them anyway,
conferring upon them an importance that, from the stand-
point of pop musicology, is ill deserved. What have they
done? What do they look like? Not much. Years of practices
and a handful of gigs culminating in a September Friday

night. "CD launch" promises the poster stapled to the door. The picture is the same as on the cover of their disc: a Victorian doctor-gentleman puffing into what looks to be a didgeridoo fashioned out of plastic drainpipe. In the background, a vaguely Tibetan monastery. "Braino" written across the top in flaming letters. A B-movie name, a silly name, what you call the popsicle headache you get in the middle of your cerebral cortex. "Hideous!" screeches singer Soon in his high-pitched nasal falsetto. "Hideous!" Double horn rhymes pump up a chorus somewhere between maudlin and innovative. You can't escape it, and you don't dance to it. "Hideous!" Is he addressing the band's performance, or some other aspect of the multifarious Braino world?

Which brings me to the second thing you should know about Braino: the band functions—for me, for you, for the purposes of this book—somewhere between representative and ambassador. These are wary diplomats reluctantly inviting us into their country, though they doubt we'll understand their customs and are pretty sure we'll leave gum wrappers and Styrofoam cups on their pristine beaches and hallowed monuments. Braino's struggle to experiment, to innovate, to continue to exist—coming as it does at a time when the forces of corporate hegemony and common-denominator shlock appear to have gained a near-complete victory—is the story of individual possibility in the shadow of the impossible. Braino is a band working out what can still be done when everything's already *been* done. Braino is a testament to the muted optimism that runs through this book like a stream under asphalt. Their music—a self-conscious, ironic mélange of avant-jazz, rock, punk, soundtrack, and barbershop—is, in some odd way, a celebration. If Braino can be said to be special (and I'm not saying they are), it's because, as individuals and as a collective unit, they believe in the celebration of art: they believe that it's still possible to live in imagination, to navigate the terrain between popularity and obscurity, to reassess their pop heritage in such a way that their lives, and the lives of those around them, are reaffirmed.

Like most of the people you will meet in this book, the boys of Braino are not brilliant innovators or radical revolutionaries. What they do is made possible because of the great experimenters who have gone before—from Ornette Coleman to Yoko Ono—but their purpose is not to extend that search for new forms. Instead, Braino is engaged in the simple, desperate process of keeping their footing in the cultural eddies swirling all around us. So Braino is a synecdoche, a stand-in for any number of musicians, zinesters, artists, theorists, and slackers I could have chosen to focus on from across the industrialized world. People who are, consciously or not, finding that their mental environment is 1 percent inspiration and 99 percent pop perspiration.

■   ■   ■

Toronto-based quintet Braino was founded way back in 1992 by filmmaker/nerd-jazz-enthusiast/trumpeter Chris Gehman and the long since AWOL Gary Dawson (a.k.a. Uranea 235, a.k.a. Roscoe Dogbone). Part of what's interesting about the band is its longevity. Two years is generally considered the lifespan of your average unknown indie rock band, but Braino has weathered its disputes and defections, maintaining its core of Gehman and singer/bassist Soon and replacing those who decamp with a steady influx of fledgling Braino enthusiasts. The two older members of the band have something like careers—steady jobs that pay more than minimum wage. They are settled in their lives, as sure of their direction as any of us will ever be. They know that they will never make their living playing music. At the same time, they aren't just pretending to be in a band, guys getting together in the garage to drink a case of beer and play the same three Stones songs over and over again. For the elder members, Braino is a crucial outlet, one that makes the more ordinary and mundane world tolerable.

In contrast, the younger guys are barely rooted: they don't have real jobs, they don't know what they'll be doing or even where they'll be next year. All the Braino youngsters plan to make a living—some kind of living—as musicians. Not to doubt their commitment, but one gets the sense that their plans might change. At age twenty-five, bass player Dave still lives in his parents' suburban home, keeps a drum kit in the basement, rocks out when nobody's home. For the three junior members of the band, all in their mid-twenties, playing in Braino is an experiment, a chance to learn and explore and expand their pop heritage by challenging everything they know about how to make music.

Throughout Braino's various incarnations, the band has been decidedly uninterested in "progressing" as it is generally understood in the music industry—getting their name out, putting out recordings, becoming known and commercially viable. Braino is fun, loose, crazy in a good way. "Cathartic giant noise," enthuses Dave, the most obsequious cello-playing punk rebel you'll ever meet. "And it hangs together and it's fast and crazy and nobody really gives a shit."

In the increasingly rigid, bottom-line world of indie rock, however, a band, like any small business, needs a manager, someone whose job it is to give a shit. In the pre-CD-launch months of mid-1998, it was clear that nobody was taking charge, nobody was the ego, nobody deliberately stood out, nobody was willing to look after the day-to-day operations of Braino. "It comes down to the wonderful democracy we've got going on," drummer Ben tells me, displaying just a hint of bitterness at the Braino collective's collective deficiencies. "We're an equal-sharing program, which works well for making music, but it doesn't work for selling CDs." The closest thing Braino has to a leader is their singer and bass player, the aberrant father-figure Soon, whose weird mixture of shy insecurity and belligerence, of idiot-savant and enthusiastic acolyte, makes for an engaging musical mentor but does nothing for the band's commercial prospects. In conversation, Soon reveals a boyish desire for Braino's work to have an audience, but he doesn't seem nearly as interested in finding an audience willing to pay for that work. "The argument has been entered into," he says, "whether the work that we do is—[laughs]—I don't think it's a money-making thing, it's a money-spending thing. I don't have a lot to put in, mind you . . . Well, let's say that some members in the group have the opposite opinion . . . though I couldn't speak for them."

Still, the CD comes out, and the launch, as promised by one of the ugliest posters ever made, happens. Sort of.

I mean, it was the best show Braino ever played. And probably the best attended. At the same time, even on the miniature scale of the Toronto indie scene, the launch was a non-event, barely noticed. The CD itself, coming so many years after the band's inception, seemed to Braino and the few fans who bought it more like an echo than a noise—time and money and hope and dreams pressed into a shiny disc. "It just stalled," Ben explains, speaking to me several months after the CD release. "You've created the product, you've done all the musically interesting things now. It's there, it's done. Everything after that is a sort of anti-music."

And so the five-headed creature Braino is willing to stick its collective snout out of the earth, willing to crawl from point to point, but unwilling or unable to stand up straight, stake out its territory, and, in doing so, announce its intention to subvert the paradigms of mass culture in North America. To truly surface, the members of Braino would have to decide that the conventional, relatively comfortable lives they lead aren't worth the charade we all perpetuate from day to day. It's one thing to make subversive music—which Braino does only too well. But it's another thing altogether to live the subversive life that music inspires. There are those who take up that mantle. Those who, literally, live and die through the courage of their cultural convictions. Nevertheless, it's the boys of Braino—their desperate hold on a fast-eroding normalcy, their more familiar struggles—who inspire this book.

■　　■　　■

"**B**eing in Braino," says Soon, "is a chance to do something. It should be. It should be an act of—I don't know—an act out of—I don't want to say revolution, but otherwise, what's the point?"

Soon's reluctance to proclaim the Braino revolution connects to the band's artistic and managerial difficulties. How do you sell yourself, how do you woo an audience used to careful stratifications of genre, when the only original thing you are doing is proclaiming your originality? And so Braino worms along just beneath the surface, existing almost entirely in an "underground" that doesn't actually exist. Like so many creators growing up in the shadow of pop culture and struggling to fashion something new, Braino's half-reluctant tussle with pop suggests the paradox of independent culture in North America: entire generations of young would-be creators trying desperately to find that place where aesthetic freedom marketed as a commodity can lead to a validation of their lives as something other than consumers. As Soon suggests with his hesitancy to use clichéd words like "revolution," this redemption through culture is a murky, subjective goal. Can it ever be attained? Or is it always one step ahead of us, an illusory pop culture concept, a TV construct that allows us to deceive ourselves, convince ourselves that through uncompromised creativity we can lift our lives out of the quicksand of mass culture conformity that's been sucking us down since birth no matter what we do? Braino, like so many of us, walks the balance beam of pop, determined to perform singular gymnastics, yet eager to be rewarded by the bemused judges, who look in vain for Braino's moves on the score sheet. In preaching distinct underground creativity as the key to happiness and individuality in a cookie-cutter world, are we not just fooling ourselves, buying stock in a mass culture get-happy-quick scheme that doesn't exist? The desire that Braino has—our desire—is to craft something completely new out of our pop culture legacy. At the same time, we see in Braino something that we feel in our own frustrating lives—the inability to go all the way, to truly challenge the conventions of the everyday.

In the mediocre world of top-forty crapola, in our made-in-Taiwan-product-ridden universe, there is little room for Braino, precious little room for the individual as anything other than a buyer. We want to participate, to give meaning to the pop culture we live with, but how do we do that? For Braino, the answer is to make music that uses genre ironically for comic effect, clinging to the possibilities of pop while experimenting just for the sake of it. This urge to reinvent mass culture is where our difficulties begin and where they always seem to end. The various members of Braino call the band "rock," they call the band "punk," they want to be free of the conventions of pop music, but they also want an audience in their hometown. They want the trappings of success; they don't just want to be weird. For Braino, as it is for an increasing number of us, the urge to reinvent society starts with the struggle to go against the grain, to apply oneself in unrewarding enterprises. And yet, the building blocks we use to identify and understand ourselves are almost entirely a construction of mass culture.

"For me, it's a personal quest," says cellist Dave on his participation in the band, "a personal challenge. And if you know the influences of Braino, everything kind of refers back to some other kind of music, and then you can argue maybe that the only originality that you get out of something is how things will be combined in different ways." As with many of the creative acts you'll be introduced to in this book, what starts with the natural tendency to rebel through originality ends with the conundrum of accessing an audience for what is, essentially, an elaborate parody of pop culture conventions. And so we return to Soon's muted howl of rebellion: a mournful, elegiac articulation of inner despair, as opposed to a public attempt to overthrow the government. Braino's revolt is the revolt of the everyday. It's the revolution we invoke when we spend two hours flipping through the TV channels before turning off the set and proclaiming, as we do almost every night, "Why am I wasting my time? There's nothing on." How do we turn our force-fed mass culture into something bold and true and life-affirming for each of us? Braino wants to rebel against the mundane, the pacified, the buy-and-sell of art. This isn't so uncommon. We all want to cast off the shackles of TV, of fast food, of prepackaged snacks and predetermined outfits. We all want to take control. But how? And of what?

■   ■   ■

So much has happened so quickly. In less than a hundred years, almost every possible rule pertaining to aesthetic culture has been broken. The notion of the specialist, the professional artist, the genius creator has been irrevocably challenged. Suddenly, we are all artists, filmmakers, musicians, thinkers. As a result, we must all take on the responsibility the artist has—of accepting nothing, relying on nothing, questioning everything. No wonder even our experts seem confused, subject to a cultural dreamscape where everything matters and nothing seems to make a difference. Like Braino, we struggle to accept pop's conflicted legacy of individual responsibility married to passive acceptance. We want to refuse to descend into the "anti-music" of commerce, without negating the legacy of a pop culture we are so desperate to validate—a legacy that includes locking the fetters of commercialism onto every cultural endeavour. As anyone in Braino can tell you, it is one thing to put out your own CD—to record it, design it, pay for it, launch it—and quite another thing to promote it and distribute it and market it as if it were just another style of jeans.

"How does the music get into the world and get heard by people?" trumpeter Chris wants to know. "Once you start thinking about it, you realize you are trapped by the structures that have been set up. So there develops a pervasive irony because we won't take the surface value of any of the forms that we deal with seriously. The irony is to look at every available form ironically, whether we dislike or like it.

You can't take anything as being sacred, because you can't put yourself in the position of being inferior."

Braino's nonconformist approach to music represents our collective future in a world where we find our individual memories and lives influenced and shaped by mass culture. It's a world in which the everyperson artist must create an identity out of a generic mass by employing the kind of ironic refractions that Braino struggles with and against. Here we are now, living in that brave new world of mass culture in which nothing is sacred, nothing is superior. Entertain us, we demand. But, as Braino makes all too clear, what we really want is to find a way to entertain ourselves.

Braino's story is the story of underground desire and mainstream ambition—the story of how pop culture has come to reinvent our lives. We're live in concert with Braino not just because they make a big, painful, awkward noise that's worth sitting through at least once, but because the new kind of life Braino testifies to has to do with producing new ways of making and understanding culture. As we come to understand and witness our lives and world through the precepts of mass culture, we are demanding novel ways to participate and articulate who we are in the mass culture sphere. In our search for a way to make pop culture's generic promise of personal salvation and individual validation par-ticular to our lives—a half-hour sitcom for each of us!—we are changing how our society understands what it is to work, to go to the mall, to read the newspaper, to play in a band. These changes point to a larger, fundamental shift to be explored in this book—a shift that challenges how we will understand "reality" in the twenty-first century. Like it or not, the story of Braino is our story, the story of the many people all over the world who struggle to imbue their lives with a dignity and validity that, increasingly, we seem to find only through the cultural participation we have come to understand as our birthright. Braino uses our legacy—accents of rock and punk and Saturday morning cartoons and blues and jazz and jingles and noise experiments—to refer to something that is none of those things. The band is, effectively, doing what we are all doing in our lives: reordering mass culture, interpreting it to have a meaning that allows us to stand defiant in the face of the generic anonymity we are otherwise doomed to.

■   ■   ■

So it's Friday night. You were at home watching "Millennium," but I dragged your ass off the couch and out to the club. I wanted you to see Braino. Well here they are. They don't look like much. In fact, they look pretty normal, they look an awful lot like you and me. And yet they have been branded rebels, weirdos, underground freaks. The boys on stage are just another demonstration of how our attempts to make sense of mass culture collapse the "ordinary" into the strange. Today there can be no underground, no revolution, because in the process of finding meaning in our lives, we—with our hockey or teddy bear or Elvis obsessions—all seem a little strange, a little out of kilter. Whether we affix a stamp in our album or we take the stage dressed in a jumpsuit and shades, we are yelling out the facts of our lives as we see them. We are reinventing our truth, and, in the process, asserting that we will not continue to be the passive consumers that mass culture requires, even as we attempt to use pop to express our most individual and private lives.

Now it's getting late and you want to go. All the same, I think we should stay just a little longer, lean into the cigarette-butt air, thick like a wall, and fall over the creeping cacophony of Braino's late-night symphony to vulnerability and improbability. Part hobby, part passion, part compromise, part steadfast stubbornness, the band, and the people who make up the band, and even the people who made up the band before we knew there was such a thing as Braino, are a promise that can't be delivered, what happens when the legacy of a mass, transcendental pop culture for the people meets the reality of a rigid, profit-obsessed market economy that would turn all creative expression into widgets rolling off the assembly line. Braino is what has happened, what is happening, to the possibilities of creativity. It is what we long for, what beats in turgid chest thumps, a music so crammed with the ether of life it is as difficult to listen to as it is to ignore. "Yeah, sure, it's a hobby," says drummer Ben, "but my hobby is ten times more important than my job. Because we're making music. Because I'm putting a hell of a lot of myself into this."

It's annoying music. You want to walk out. But you don't.

It's too late. You're stuck in place, staring at the spectacle even as it disintegrates. Like that strange, fragmented entity mass culture, the song has dissolved—not into pop song jingles, but into something deeper, something that worms under the skin of your scalp and gives you pain on the cold spot of your brain.

GOING UNDERGROUND, GOING NOWHERE: THE STRANGE TALE OF LIFESTYLE CULTURE

PART ONE

"THIS SUCKS! CHANGE IT!": TOWARD A LIFESTYLE CULTURE

CHAPTER ONE

> My earliest childhood memory is sitting on the couch on an early weekday afternoon with my mom. We were watching "He-Man," which was my favourite show, and I remember the afternoon sun coming through the thick yellow curtains that used to cover the big sliding window, warming my skin.
>
> — Jennifer Brook, *Under the Stars* zine

I t's three days before the concluding episode of the moron cartoon "Beavis and Butthead." I'm sitting in a radio studio waving around my Beavis and Butthead pseudo-remote-control with sound effects (a present from my brother) and listening to a professor of Media Studies from Ottawa's Carleton University explain why the show is ugly, stupid, violent, and, worst of all, morally bereft. That's when it hits me: culture is dead.

At least, culture as this particular academic knows it is dead, buried, reincarnated only to walk the earth as a movie remake based on the original sitcom. So when it gets to be my turn, I can't help myself. First thing I do is hit the *"Shuddup! Assmunch!"* button. I follow this with the key that vomits up Butthead's *he-he-he* laugh. There's a brief moment of stunned silence. Then I tell Avril Benoît, co-host at the time of Canada's flagship morning current affairs radio show "This Morning" (who looks on with an expression somewhere between bemusement and horror), that our dear professor's concern with the values of "Beavis and Butthead" reveals a larger, more endemic problem that is crucial to cultural consumption in the late twentieth century. The problem isn't dumbed-down television or the proliferation of immoral pop culture, or even a house-of-mirrors assembly-line media. The problem resides in the inability of the majority of those who comment on the arts—journalists, academics, professional artists, producers, editors, information-age cultural critics— to come to terms with new ways of living with and through mass culture.

The truth is, no member of the TV generations (roughly anyone born in the 1960s, '70s, and beyond—"the electronic generations" Marshall McLuhan called us) watches television for its advocacy of family values and societal rectitude. We do not watch television to be informed, instructed, or otherwise educated. Though we might turn on the television believing that we are seeking information, we are quickly, willingly, knowingly drawn into a medium that can flash up to one hundred images a minute into our brains. And what a minute! Sixty seconds pulsing with the kind of artifice that makes life interesting. Style and attitude, colour and glamour, nonsensical truisms and completely sensible lies. So let's face it: we—and though I speak of the TV generations, this also holds true for large swaths of the population in general—

watch television for its capacity to disgust, horrify, reveal, and penetrate the thin veneer that covers up the heart of darkness deep in the jungles of the post-industrial experience. We don't watch the tube to see the way our lives should be reflected back at us, but to extend our self-serving perception of life's hilarious inadequacy when measured against life on television, which, accordingly, must be ever more gorgeous, disturbing, over the top, violent, disgusting, depraved, distant, dubious, and oh so close to home. We're watching not to adhere to some moral code but to take part in the media universe, an unreal world we, ironically, apply to and compare against our own confused, fractured, bored lives.

To put it simply, we watch TV because it is the easiest way to take part in an entertainment continuum that is fast becoming the most important element of our personal and collective experience. Once, politicians, priests, and parents frightened of the immoral impetuosity of pop culture railed against it, rejected it out of hand. But rejecting pop is no longer an option. For us, choosing this brand and this channel and this pair of jeans and this superstar has become far more than the casual lifestyle choices we fit into our weekends. Instead, these commonplace practices have become our way of making sense of ourselves and the world around us. It's the one thing we all share, and it's the thing we do—watching TV, listening to music, surfing the web, arguing about the new *Star Wars* movie over mochaccino lattes—more than anything else.

The collective delirious obsession we all share when it

comes to mass culture represents a significant shift in the way we live our lives: the TV generations are replacing the traditional values of country, work, religion, and family with a slavish dedication to pop. I call this phenomenon "lifestyle culture." Lifestyle culture isn't just watching a lot of TV; it's a new way of understanding TV, and all the other manifestations of an impersonal world. What we do in lifestyle culture is simple: we make the stuff that isn't supposed to matter— movies, bands, fashion, toys, TV shows, and an endless world of possible products—matter. We give that stuff prominence in our lives. We elevate the meaningless because we have grown up believing, being taught, that through mass culture we can find meaning. In lifestyle culture, things that do not of themselves have direct relevance to our lives—the vagaries of thousands of formulaic plots, for instance— become somehow crucial and important. Lifestyle culture, like television, is the triumph of our leisure lives over the things we are supposed to be paying attention to.

The pat promise underlying almost every formulaic plot and pop song is that of the individual's triumph over the forces of homogeneity and conformity. "Be yourself," "Go for broke," "Seize the day," "Just do it," scream our sitcoms, our movies, and our billboards. But, in fact, this promise is delivered to us via the mechanisms of a mass culture that depends on our silent acquiescence and conformity. The pop promise, then, is a false one—or, rather, it's an allegory not meant to actually confer upon us the capacity to announce ourselves as autonomous individuals free to pick and choose from the offerings of commercial society, of organized religion, of family and heritage. And yet, however gradually, this bogus promise—the ironic contradiction at the heart of mass culture—has become a central precept by which we organize and evaluate our lives.

So we come to lifestyle culture as a way to validate the promise we want to believe in and accept as true. By elevating pop culture's (fraudulent) promise of freedom and individuality over many aspects of our lives, we are using our lifestyle culture as an unheard battle cry that announces our engagement in an invisible war: we want to be part of the entertainment confluence; it is real to us; it is important and fundamental to our lives; we refuse to be shut out of it, to be deemed passive consumers and willing dupes whose chronic leisure pursuits are indicative of society's complete moral collapse. At the same time, we also want to recognize that we are separate from the trappings of pop culture—we have been affected by TV characters and celebrity personas, but that doesn't mean we have become them.

I'm not trying to say that lifestyle culture is a good thing or a bad thing. Lifestyle culture is a response to a world increasingly dominated by an all-pervasive entertainment industry—it's a way to deal with a world in which everything is subsumed by mass culture, even our own lives. So lifestyle culture by its very nature is a paradoxical idea. It's a reflection of our general ambivalence toward an entertainment industry that promises us freedom and power through media that actually induce passivity and impotence. Most of us don't announce that from now on we will be actively engaged in creating and commenting on mass culture in order to hold the media to their as yet unfulfilled promise. We don't set out to become practitioners of lifestyle culture any more than we set out to become regular TV watchers. It just happens. Some of us, like the members of Braino, take the urge to be involved in pop culture to the next level—we start bands, produce zines, stage plays in the backrooms of bars. These are our lifestyle culture pioneers, taking the risks we all wish we could take but don't. And yet, we are ambivalent about what these lifestyle culture pioneers—often our friends and family members—represent. There's just something about paying six bucks to sit on a sticky milk crate and watch our brother's girlfriend's "Happy Days" takeoff skit performed on the stage of the local tavern. In a way, we'd rather be at home, watching the "real" Fonz, instead of some pomaded thespian fresh out of acting school. Though we recognize the urge to intervene in the way we are force-fed our pop culture, we are also embarrassed by what that urge says about us, about the culture we believe in. This, too, is lifestyle culture: we are ashamed to admit that we get through the day by thinking about sports, or movies, or our collection of antique tea cosies. We don't want to admit to anyone, even ourselves, just how much time we spend in the amoral, reflexive Beavis and Butthead world.

The half-hour cartoon show "Beavis and Butthead" was one of the first pop outlets to recognize how much we are coming to value and order our lives around the precepts of mass culture. For those of you who haven't had the pleasure, this dynamic portrayal of a drooling duo combines a lampoon of the suburban geek teen and a fond portrait of our own endless capacity for vapid, mind-numbing entertainment in the form of videos, giant-size sodas, and non-stop mental masturbation concerning that which might be attainable if only we could ever leave the living room. "Beavis and Butthead" embodies the lifestyle culture attitude in which we have almost unconsciously and accidentally come to relate to TV not as an information source but as a way of life. "Beavis and Butthead" is, in fact, essentially a clever parody of lifestyle culture. It shows how we turn to mass culture to find meaning in our lives, only to find that we are chasing our own tails. "Beavis and Butthead" is as good a place as any to highlight the irony of lifestyle culture: we turn to that which shouldn't matter and make it matter in order to give our lives a meaning in a world where individual lives are diminished by the spectacle of pop culture. We use the very elements that demean and reduce us to try to find dignity in our lives.

■ ■ ■

Most of us are aware of the banality of what comes out of the "culture industry." Since birth, we've navigated the highways of mass culture. We know how to communicate and interpret these conventions, and we are coming to realize that we can use them, rather than be used by them. In lifestyle culture, we try to manipulate the conventions of pop, we try to superimpose that world on our own standards and beliefs—on our world. Only, even as we attempt to do this, we discover that many of the standards and beliefs have, in fact, been supplanted by a mass culture that teaches us to hate our bodies, hate our parents, hate our jobs, hate our homes. Ads and polls conspire with sitcoms and pseudo-sarcastic homages to our disaffection (*Fight Club*, *The Truman Show*) to leave us reeling, confused, anxious. Who are we? What do we want? We want to be part of this, all of this going on around us, happening for us but not on our behalf. We want a role in the mass culture play—a play in which we are at once the director, the writer, the actors, and the audience, just as Truman, trapped in the world's largest set, is forced to play, unwittingly, the character of himself. We too want to play a character, and we want it to be ourself—only without the soul-deadening tedium of Truman's sitcom life. How can we do this? We don't know. We just know that when we figure it out, our lives will have the meaning and direction we are made to feel they lack.

Our confusion, the ambiguity of our values, comes from the strange, unreal world of mass culture. Each day, we are asked to reinvent ourselves, choose among stations, products, outfits. It is up to us to confer upon each object of entertainment, each aspect of mass culture, a moral status—good or bad, true or false. Assured by the false promise of pop that we can set our own standards and values, we no longer look for the moral truth of a TV show, a song, or a trip to IKEA. We are liberated by the covenant of individualism, but we are also left in a void where everything is subject to the fluctuating standard of the TV movement, a void where it is all too easy to be manipulated by the demands of mass culture. As Michael O'Neill, a former editor of *The New York Post*, has written: "The culture of entertainment is turned to emotional stimulation rather than information . . . In a climate of moral relativism, there are few scruples about perverting the public's view of society, government, and the world beyond."

Put in less alarmist language, this says that among the ever-growing numbers of people who search for meaning via mass culture, there is a significant level of shoulder-shrugging confusion. We, collectively and individually, don't know what our values are, what our culture represents, beyond a desire for self-validation. So we take our culture into us and regurgitate it in forms that attempt to return to us the privilege of speaking for and to ourselves. And this, in turn, requires that we find a way to tell the story of life in the pop void without denying the importance of pop culture in our lives. Lifestyle culture rejects any belief system that seeks to demean those things that are, after all, the very stuff of our lives; we lifestyle culture adherents reject those who long for the days when there was a central moral authority that could authorize art and rein in our slavish devotion to entertainment culture; we reject the cultural capitalists who see us as nothing more than numbers, consumers tricked into buying what we supposedly don't need, and adopting viewpoints that often run counter to our interests and our experiences. Through lifestyle culture, we reject all of them by attempting to reshape the cultural forces swirling about us.

It might help to understand it this way: TV makes a deep and permanent and real impression on our psyches, despite the fact that the medium's narratives are considered to be completely fabricated and more than a little superfluous. Television affects our lives. It changes the way we are, that is, the way we live and the way we think we live. Similarly, in lifestyle culture, what shouldn't matter, what appears to be frivolous amusement, becomes extraordinarily important. All we have to do is look around us to know this is true. Each and every one of us knows people who have devoted themselves to what we consider a hobby or pastime. These hobbies are becoming bigger and better parts of our lives, the parts of our lives over which we have at least some illusion of control. And so there are magazines for the collection of almost every mass culture artifact. There are list-servs, websites, clubs, zines, and innumerable ongoing daily discussions in which we, quite seriously, discuss everything from "The Price Is Right" to the latest teen sensation.

When did this stuff become so real, so important? It was when TV, our portal into the many manifestations of lifestyle culture, became integral to the fabric of our lives. The moment TV became something we could not and would not live without, all our other lifestyle culture antics were validated. Life became unreal and entirely subjective—a dream-scape world without standards. We can now look forward to those artificially manufactured, totally fabricated genuine experiences we have every day. Watching TV becomes as real as a trip to the mall or the zoo or the theme park or the workplace. In each case, we are controlled, told what to see and where to go. Life becomes a carefully constructed narrative enacted for the purpose of leading the greatest number of people down the same path. Frustrated, disgusted, we nevertheless accept our new environment. We search for a way of living, a lifestyle, that will allow us to become part of the fake-real environment we live in but cannot control. We begin to demand the opportunity to shape our own malls, theme parks, zoos, offices. We don't reject these things. On the contrary, we admit that we can't live without them. It is this admission that makes lifestyle culture so possible, so terrible. It's our collective understanding that mass culture has now seeped into our brains. "There's plenty of bad art and entertainment in the world," a reporter once noted while commenting on the short-lived Magic Johnson talk show, "but these don't pervade our lives the way television does, don't create a kind of constant alternative consciousness in which we are all forced to dwell."

This increased reliance on mass culture to validate and order our lives has many implications. Ever-increasing numbers of us are finding that nothing other than some fundamental connection to mass culture will give our lives meaning. We find solace in the bizarre minutiae of pop. And yet, celebrity worship becomes celebrity stalking; flirtations turn into obsessions that leave us empty, compromised, cheated into confusing passions with hobbies or vice versa.

When I suggest that we are using the tools of mass culture to create our own rhetoric and provide a representation of our lives within the flux of passive mass entertainment, I am also saying that this can be a dangerous thing: in uplifting that which doesn't matter as a way to reinvent our lives, we are also in danger of forgetting who and what we once were. We lose hold of even the tenuous structure that a reality made up of artificial environments allows us. When we realize that we will not become the superstar or even minor, momentary celebrity we are told we should be, we all too often turn upon ourselves and others, the move from flirtation to obsession to addiction accomplished with breathtaking, agonizing speed, often with breathtaking, agonizing results.

■ ■ ■

The dangers I'm alluding to seem to be similar to the ones that the middle-aged intellectuals who regularly hold forth on cultural doings in North America like to expound on. These are the people who, like my opponent decrying "Beavis and Butthead" on the radio, tell us that our mass culture is evil, an aberration imposed on us, an alien invasion of surface values and hollow principles that we must resist through vigilant defence of the ballet and subscriptions to the correct periodicals of high-minded thought. It's true that much of mass culture is disseminated through the auspices of giant corporations whose billionaire executives and millionaire lackeys seek to undermine our capacity for free thought by preaching to our fears and playing to our senses. But what our vaunted critics fail to recognize is that it is too late to reject mass culture. Movies and TV shows and magazines and newspapers and rock stars and models do not compose the essence of an aesthetic experience in the late twentieth century. It is us, our lives, the world we live in, the air we breathe—all of it—that gives mass culture its force. At this point, to try and turn back the clock, to try to reject or moralize about mass culture, is to try to reject the food we eat, the buildings we live in, the things we do every day, the people we have become.

When our critics rail against pop culture and mass media, they are doing so on our behalf, arguing that we have allowed ourselves to be duped, to be taken in. And yet, to us, pop isn't just another way to replace the money from our wallets with proxy wisdoms and pseudo-plots that, unlike the great artworks of yesteryear, have no intrinsic moral or aesthetic value. We struggle to make mass culture real and meaningful and important to our individual lives and communities. We search for ways to participate and to subvert the seeming autonomy of industry not only by buying (or not buying) but also by wresting the reins away from both the faceless bottom-line corporations and their inaugurated elite of journalists, cultural critics, publishers, TV faces, movie celebs, and so on. Still our critics dismiss us, reserving their harshest criticism for cultural creation taking place outside of the industry, without official sanction, by the people and for the people. The result, they warn, of ever more people making their own websites, movies, "Happy Days" satires, comics, zines, books, and commentaries will be information overload. And anyway, our critics tell us, we have nothing to say; we're far too busy "amusing ourselves to death."

Preferring to hide behind simplistic equations, our critics ignore the way we are attempting to subvert the mass culture status quo by becoming our own critics and creators. They see this as further evidence of society's grand perversion at the hands of entertainment. They ignore how we actually bring mass culture into our lives, and instead regurgitate watered-down versions of the dour ideas pioneered most notably by the Frankfurt School thinkers Theodor Adorno and Max Horkheimer. In their much-revered (at least by beady-eyed grad students) essay, first published in 1947, called "The Culture Industry: Enlightenment As Mass Deception," Adorno and Horkheimer lay the sophisticated groundwork for what later becomes an increasingly unsophisticated argument against mass entertainment:

> This bloated pleasure apparatus adds no dignity to man's lives. . . . The culture industry perpetually cheats its consumers of what it perpetually promises . . . the promise, which is actually all the spectacle consists of, is illusory: all it actually confirms is that the real point will never be reached, that the diner must be satisfied with the menu.

With a sweep of their bitter, brilliant pens, these critics savage popular culture, leaving us to flounder in a nexus of empty impulses and purposeless desires. At least, that is what most of the subsequent thinkers who latched on to the Horkheimer–Adorno essay would have us believe. An endless parade of critics cite this essay, usually to argue quite simply that mass culture in all forms is intrinsically bad. But Adorno was more concerned with the way mass culture could or would be used to delude and pacify. One thinker in the burgeoning field of Cultural Studies—itself a de facto argument for lifestyle culture's primacy—summarized Adorno's main point against mass culture as: "If there is no aesthetic autonomy, there will be no moral and/or political autonomy. (There will be no freedom.)"

Adorno's philosophy is a response to Hitler's fascist regime, a monstrous propaganda machine that banned modernist manifestations of what it called "degenerate art" and utilized the popular mass culture of the time—everything from Wagner to film—to present the deadly myth of a pure, uncorrupted Aryan nation on the march to world domination. Adorno and Horkheimer were right to group creative autonomy with the wider range of freedoms most of us take for granted—particularly within the context of a war-torn world where mass propaganda constantly threatened to replace mass culture (as it still does, to some extent, today). And yet, in lifestyle culture at its most penetrating, we all become artists and thinkers. So the illusory spectacle may still liberate us from the propaganda of consumerism.

Mass culture as a method of communication could still approximate the McLuhanesque global village in which we are all equals, creating and consuming and living on our own terms.

Despite the possibilities made evident by the movement that is lifestyle culture, it is the notion of a soul-deadening, dangerous mass culture which offends on its own terms—a perversion of Adorno's criticism of the culture industry—that endures. We can trace the Horkheimer–Adorno critique of culture, in its increasingly bastardized and unsophisticated form, through the next fifty years of indignant commentary on the popular arts. I could fill an entire tome with the ridiculous evils that middle-aged pundits have accused pop culture of perpetuating. The 1933 book *Movies, Delinquency, and Crime* sets the tone when its authors argue that "pictures of excitement, adventure and daring seem most likely to induce emotional possession, and, in doing so, to give impetus to delinquent tendencies." It is easy to see how this kind of opinion appeals to politicians speaking out against violent television and pundits interviewing video-game creators to discuss their moral culpability for teen rampages. One hilarious, if slightly offbeat, example centres on a 1954 book, *Seduction of the Innocent*, written by a psychiatrist treating juvenile delinquents, Dr. Fredric Wertham. This guy got it in his mind that the then-burgeoning comic book industry was a moral travesty and a danger to young people. His text's tenor presages what is now a mini-industry of books bemoaning the state of such pop culture evils as the Internet, television, rap music, video games, romance novels, etc. Wertham goes so far as to portray the then hugely popular, and famously benevolent, Superman as "a symbol of violent race superiority." (This attack on the comic book industry of the 1950s, now just another squeal in the upper registers of deadpan invective, was surprisingly influential: the book led to Senate hearings, public outrage, and the near demise of an industry that, compared to today's version, seems a bastion of good taste and traditional morality.)

Those who would brand mass culture responsible for all our ills have had ample attention paid to their arguments. Dwight MacDonald's classic 1950s essay "A Theory of Mass Culture" sums up their approach to pop: "Mass culture is imposed from above. It is fabricated by technicians hired by businessmen; its audience are passive consumers, their participation limited by the choice between buying and not buying."

Tepid and fussy, even archaic, and yet MacDonald and Wertham could just as easily be preaching their pseudo-philosophy in the year 2000. Indeed, today's critics are continuing their peers' work with a steady onslaught of hyperbolic assaults on what they figure is a pretty safe bet: the sheer crass meaningless materialism that hides behind the mask of culture. Writes technology critic Neil Postman:

When a population becomes distracted by trivia, when cultural life is redefined as a perpetual round of entertainments, when serious public conversation

becomes a form of baby-talk, when, in short, a
people become an audience and their public business a vaudeville act, then a nation finds itself at
risk; culture-death is a clear possibility.

Yet another professor is on hand to reiterate this end-of-
the-world mantra, citing, as usual, the evils of mass culture
and the inevitable moral erosion of the citizenry. Writes Tom
Henighan:

> We should not assume too quickly that elegies must
> be spoken over "the arts as we knew them"; we
> should not, without a struggle, allow ourselves to be
> deprived by "progress" of some precious experiences,
> of values that give our lives real meaning and pur-
> pose, not to mention of pleasures that speak to the
> senses in the old ways.

However much this line of thinking has to recommend
it (and there's much truth to it, as we'll see), such arguments
are also sadly retrograde. They are betrayed by this yearning for, as Adorno put it in a later book, "what an artwork
once was." Evoking "the old ways" becomes the ace up the
sleeve of our latter-day moralists. Nostalgia seems to be the
only rhetorical solution some critics find permissible when
faced with the crisis of meaning that is at the heart of
lifestyle culture. As Marshall McLuhan notes in his brilliant
Understanding Media: "Some feel keenly that speed-up has

impoverished the world they knew by changing its forms of human interassociation. There is nothing new or strange in a parochial preference for those pseudo-events that happened to enter into the composition of society just before the electric revolution of this century."

We are condemned for living in the age of mechanical production, and are looked at with disdain for trying to make that age our own. The anger of our pundits harnesses the puritan energy that lashed out when Elvis made the scene, when the Beatles were more popular than Jesus, when the Sex Pistols said "fuck" on the BBC. Of course, mass spectacle is hardly a new development. Yesterday, the Romans gave us religious deviants ripped apart by wild animals in front of large audiences; today, the Fox network gives us "When Animals Attack." Did the Roman Empire collapse when the upper classes of its society reached the point at which they were "amusing themselves to death"? And if it did, who do we blame? The gladiators? The Christians? The emperors? The screaming fans?

Many of our critics fight not just against mass culture but against the process whereby we try to make that culture stand for something other than multinational profits and millionaire celebrities. In response to our lifestyle-culture-fuelled insistence that we be allowed to function as our own creators, consumers, and critics, the pundits have begun turning away from condemning the various media of mass culture—television, newspapers, movies, pop music—and toward condemning the way we embrace and try to use that culture. With the needs of a hyper-aware, culturally addicted, generally confused populace in mind, editor and producer and reporter and writer, people just like us, try to stand outside this unprecedented explosion of cultural consumption and specialization—what I postulate is a new form of living, of being alive, an actual lifestyle with what used to be understood as "fringe" culture at its very centre—by offering up a profusion of pundit/thinker/writer personalities who will organize our frenzied desire to have "real" cultural experiences into poignant commentaries and shocking new theories. Predictably enough, with a few exceptions, the result is to add to our sense that we are at sea in aestheticism, tossed by the stormy waves of artistic temperaments, marketing forces, and cultural analysis open twenty-four hours a day. The vast majority of the media's experts and pundits do nothing more than actively reinforce our own sense of helplessness and lack of "information." In trying to account for our wacky antics, the pundits do little other than reorder information we already have—mind-boggling statistics randomly employed, newspaper articles, commentary on TV shows—into apocalyptic rhetoric. Thus our pundits endlessly jog in place on the cultural treadmill while following this simple formula for success: predict fearsome circumstances and dire results (or the opposite); quote McLuhan, Plato, and/or Faith Popcorn; assert that society's moral centre is spiralling out of control; make the talk-show rounds and leave the public wondering what it all means and why it has to mean anything at all.

Of course, I'm hardly the only cultural thinker to excoriate this kind of retrograde thinking. There are hundreds of less populist scholars whose contradictory position is, like mine, to defend mass culture without, somehow, defending the monopolistic conglomerates that produce it. There is something unsatisfying about much of the argument we find in this kind of social analysis—high-minded theories that put our cultural interventions on a pedestal they do not deserve. Lifestyle culture isn't a cry for help, it isn't the beginning of an age of more serious dissent—it is an end in its own right. This book takes up many of the ideas these more obscure thinkers put forth—thinkers who remain marginal and relatively unknown because the big corporate culture producers are, generally, less willing to entertain complicated ideas about how mass culture actually shapes the way we live. It's so much simpler to market a book whose main argument is "TV is going to kill your children" than one that takes a more ambivalent stance, such as "TV is bad, but not always, depending on how we watch it, and nobody really knows anyway but, hey, it sure does pass the time."

■   ■   ■

Evidence of the increasing prevalence of people using pop culture as a way to order their lives is everywhere, from your earliest memory involving "He-Man" to ongoing relationships with the constructs of pop that afford us a pathos we might otherwise lack in our mundane lives. "Oh

my God. She's dead. I can't believe she's dead!" a man was
reported to have screamed while browsing through the
weekly edition of *Soap Opera News* in a Toronto bookstore.
There are countless other examples, sometimes embarrassing
moments that underscore the power of pop culture to alter
us. "The Album That Changed My Life" is the title of poet
Jeffery Conway's tribute to his juvenile discovery of the
record *The Pleasure Principle* by Gary Numan. It's 1980 and
New Wave is splashing into the suburbs. Writes Conway:

> Within a week I had a crewcut
> and was bleaching my hair blond with
> a bottle of hydrogen peroxide I found
> in the hall closet. I started
> to shop at thrift stores, buying only black.
> Mom screamed, "Christ, what are you doing
> to yourself!" I'd stare blankly and answer
> in a monotone, "Am I a photo? I can't remember"
> a line from "My Conversation," one of
> my favourite songs on Gary's album.

Now we can say these are weirdos and freaks, or we can
understand that they are expressing something not generally
understood within the constraints of our one-sided dialogue
with pop culture. The experiences of our budding New
Wave poet and our anonymous soap opera fanatic are
common to all of us in various degrees. The more our lives
revolve around alienating cultural precepts, the more we

have the desire and need to manipulate those precepts. In other words, the more mass culture there is, the more we are forced into becoming active participants in mass culture just to make sense of it all. In an unreal world, where we can pick and choose who we are, we will all end up as virulent lifestyle-culturites—just to survive.

Today, we are beginning to recognize the subjective nature of mass culture and use it to validate our lives the way pop has always said we could. Like the boys of Braino, we struggle with our intention to reshape mass culture so that it exists on our terms. This process—in which passive consumers become semi-active hobbyists and then, finally, full-blown creators—challenges the gatekeepers of culture by asserting the power of the everyperson to be his or her own critic and creator. In this scenario, the hierarchy of critics and academics and experts exists to prevent us from becoming what pop promises us we can all be. Only experts, geniuses, the lucky, get to be writers, actors, celebrities. We need to be selective. We need to pare down. We need to maintain a system of experts because, without experts, who will be the arbiters of good and bad, right and wrong, beautiful and ugly? We'll return to this pressing point later in the chapter and throughout this book. For now, suffice it to say that when I argue that most of us watch television not to be preached to or even entertained but because—like eating and shitting—it is part of the fabric of our life, I'm really trying to broach the much larger issue of how it has become suddenly very necessary to reassess the experience of culture at the turn of the century. I'm really trying to say: "Welcome to lifestyle culture." Or, as I used to mutter when I worked as an usher at Toronto's Massey Hall: "How are you this evening and may I show you to your seat?"

■　■　■

Like it or not, the process of personal redemption that lifestyle culture suggests has already begun. When did the pop culture revolution start? When the first kid stuck a safety pin through his nose and formed a band without ever playing a musical instrument? When the first home movie cut through a dark room? When technological advances— from the home tape-deck to the home video-recorder to the photocopier—made it possible for the individual to ape and exploit the conventions of mass culture? We might not know when the lifestyle culture movement began, but we do know that it continues to evolve, with thousands of zines—self-published photocopied periodicals—produced all over North America, in which people of all ages pronounce their own lives and opinions worthy to be published and read, lives serialized like a soap opera, but without the stereotypes and the preformed expectations. It reasserts itself in a big way when a movie like *The Blair Witch Project*, shot for next to nothing by a couple of aspiring filmmakers with little experience, becomes not just a huge blockbuster but also an answer to those who would tell us that only society's sanctioned experts can sell our stories back to us, leaving us perpetually in the margins of our narrative in the process.

In fact, it is family and religion and other cultural structures that are in the margins—social traditions that, if not absent, are in a disarray that effectively renders them absent. Religion, which, as T. S. Eliot told us, "provides the framework for a culture, and protects the mass of humanity from boredom and despair," has failed us. In its absence, we have "boredom and despair" and our various attempts to express, even overcome, that emptiness. In lifestyle culture, traditional conceptions of depression, rebellion, employment (or lack thereof), irony, advertising, shopping, and reality itself are called into question. In a world where everything is for sale, in a world where mass culture has subsumed and consumed our capacity to understand and appreciate what used to be called "art," everything is changing, everything is possible (though nothing is also a likely outcome).

The British novel *Stickleback*, by Birmingham writer John McCabe, shows us lifestyle culture in its purely paradoxical state, as it is found in the dying days of the twentieth century. Here, desensitized booze-hound Ian rants at his Trekkie office-mate:

> Look, any programme made in the sixties is bound to
> look dated sooner or later, usually sooner, right, and
> as soon as it looks dated, it becomes kitsch, and as
> soon as it's become kitsch it becomes cultish . . .
> which only encourages sad bastards like you to
> believe you're a member of some special club, so you

huddle in anoraked groups and discuss the missing episodes or whether Shatner wore a corset, or the physics of travelling at the speed of light like you're doing something secret and important because it's as close as you get to even appearing to be doing anything remotely interesting or furtive.

We exist in this perpetual state of ironic servility primarily due to the incongruous nature of the culture industry, an industry that is at once thrilled with our compliance, overwhelmed by our fanaticism, and destroyed by our rejection. When trailers for the fourth Star Wars film, *The Phantom Menace*, began showing in Fall 1998, more than half a year before the release of the "prequel," New York theatres were crowded with people who paid the full admission price just to catch a glimpse of the preview. Most people didn't even stay for the featured movie. Twenty-six-year-old Chris Bergoch took the day off work and spent it watching the trailer. He'd seen it twenty times by 8:00 p.m. Jude Lane, who was three when the original *Star Wars* came out, told *The New York Times* that the movie was her first memory. "No matter what the color, race, background or religion of the people watching the trailer, for two minutes and five seconds everyone feels the same," she said. Not for the first time, crass mass fanaticism, the need of individuals to believe, and pure capitalism met, in all their quasi-religious splendour. A zine dedicated to B-movie culture celebrates the release of *Menace* with a special issue. Big deal, you're thinking, so did

getting arrested for doing nothing more than putting up an unsanctioned billboard in the land of free speech.

Why are we so hungry to hear our own voices? Is it because of the mass culture pap we're fed every day? After years of hearing how "we can make a difference" and how "our opinions matter" and then being proffered, as per usual, the typical array of predetermined choices, we have decided to offer up our own recipes. Those who adapt dishes to suit their dietary needs survive despite everything; those who do not find that malnourishment of the soul is complete and total. Increasingly, consuming a nutritious cultural meal involves doing the cooking, not just picking out the frozen dinner. The vagaries of predictable tunes and plots might be the meat and potatoes, but the way we roast, boil, and fry makes the recipes our own. We become fanatics and collectors, enthusiasts and apprentices, chefs and wine-tasters. Suddenly, we're all gourmands, website creators, publishers, and dreamers living in a mental environment that bears only the slightest relationship to what is conventionally understood to be "real life." But lifestyle culture, the howl of voices speaking outside of the corporate entertainment structure, is almost never reported on, discussed, or validated in the mainstream media on anything but a self-referential basis—open a Star Trek–based tourist centre in your small town, as they did in Vulcan, Alberta, and you'll get a mention in *People*. ("Live long and prosper, eh," goes the headline.) Otherwise, according to the cartography of corporate news, Vulcan's a planet in Hollywood.

We have moved away from considering anything we read in the papers, hear on the radio, see on TV, as being educational or meaningful in any substantial, moral way. We watch TV, Beavis and Butthead TV, to remind ourselves of the irony not just of television-watching but, more important, of the overarching paradigm of mass culture in post-industrial North America: a culture that gives us plenty to think about and say and even the time to think and say it, but looks upon the majority of our attempts to participate in the cultural sphere as either pathetic representations of their conviction that we are idiots (Star Trek conventions, for example) or parodies of cultural paradigms best left to the experts (amateur beauty pageants, zines, underground film and video).

A *Ryerson Review of Journalism* feature on independent publishing has a telling comment from talk-show host Evan Solomon, decrying the zine genre's lack of objective standards. "If there's no self-regulating force that checks that the news source is held accountable," says Solomon, "then you're endangering your news source and the zine is held accountable to no one except the author." That is, within the confines of the for-profit media we can rest assured that what is being said is said honestly and in our best interests because it is, somehow, accountable not to its creators but to you, the customer who always "buys" the information you believe to be the most true and unbiased. "If your newspapers can say what they like," retorts that caustic English activist Matthew Arnold, "you think you are sure of being well-informed."

Beyond the info industries, gathering size and speed like

tumbleweeds in the desert, there are only those whirling grains of sand that get in our eyes and blind us with their self-serving, special-interest whining. If it isn't product it isn't trustworthy—it lacks the accountability of product, with its customer service reps and managers and publicists and lawyers all situated to ensure that no words of boycott or dissent come between us and our pocketbooks. Of course, this is the naive assumption the media always rely on: the public believes them, trusts them, because they have the standards and ethics and expertise that can be held accountable. In a world where a handful of giant corporations own the majority of our mass media—from book publishers to record companies to movie studios to distribution companies to movie theatres to newspapers, magazines, and TV networks—there can be no such thing as unbiased arts reporting. Only those products that can be integrated into the entertainment continuum will be reported on, distributed, and made available. Kalle Lasn, founder of the anti-consumer magazine *Adbusters*, puts it this way:

> The great power of the media megacorporations lies in their vertical integration. They can produce a film and distribute it through their own partially or fully owned theater chain, promote it through their own TV network, play the soundtrack on their own radio stations, and sell the merchandising spin-offs at their own amusement parks. . . . What does freedom of speech mean in this kind of mental environment?

49

Not, in itself, a particularly new argument, but there's something interesting in the way Lasn evokes a "mental environment" as if he understands and appreciates that we live in a dreamscape of multiple "reals," where it is perception, not actuality, that gives us our assurances. Lasn's "mental environment" represents his understanding of the way mass culture allows for near-complete subjectivity—in lifestyle culture, there are shared perceptions, but no shared values. Freedom is the illusion that we propagate when we obsess over seemingly trivial matters, when we tour Alberta with our klezmer-hardcore trio whose gimmick is to play only show tunes—these are the things that have to pass for free speech in the "mental environment" of monopolistic entertainment megacorps, where self-determination and collective morality are just focus-group formulas designed to maximize profits. As Jean-Paul Sartre said in a 1970 interview: "This is the limit I would today accord to freedom: the small movement which makes of a totally conditioned social being someone who does not render back completely what his conditioning has given him."

Though we are constantly exhorted to be leaders and individuals, the subtext of mass culture sends a very different message. From the golden age of Hollywood to the bullet-ridden twilight of gangsta rap, our hero/celebrities have represented the success of the little guy, the outsider who wins against all odds. The most moral—and immoral—of messages are delivered to us through media that assume and demand our rapt attention, our silence. So we watch film after film exhorting us to stand up and be heard, protest, run for office, rob a bank, kill a cop, expose a scandal. Go ahead and watch all you want of the terrific, moving films about taking control of your life; but try interrupting the show with even a simple catcall of disagreement and you'll be out on your ass. We passively imbibe endless plots and reruns, recycled plots, which serve to demonstrate to us that our individual lives are lacking that "higher cause"—a profundity easily suggested in everything from movies to pop songs to serial-killer trading cards. As a result, we become pent up with something analogous to desire: our need for a higher calling. What is the proper expression of our desires? How can we be like the people on TV, whose everyday lives seem suffused with purpose? If you report the weather on the street corner, you're crazy. If you call for rain on ten thousand TV screens, you're a celebrity.

■　■　■

T. S. Eliot identified culture as "all the characteristic activities and interests of a people: Derby Day, Henley Regatta, Cowes, the twelfth of August, a cup final, the dog races, the pin table, the dart board, Wensleydale cheese, boiled cabbage cut into sections, beetroot in vinegar, nineteenth-century Gothic churches, the music of Elgar." Like the pronouncements of Adorno and Horkheimer, Eliot's famous analysis of culture as the embodiment of people's lives comes out of a post–World War II period. But unlike the Frankfurt

School thinkers, German Jews forced to flee their homeland, Eliot wrote from the ideology of victory—culture is what the people want, as opposed to what the industrial-fascist complex instructs us to want.

As we've seen, however, the predominant understanding of culture today is not Eliot's. The emergence of lifestyle culture, coupled with massive technological change, has left us with an understanding of the interrelated pastimes known as leisure and art and entertainment that is at times frightening and confusing, both meaningless and pregnant with all kinds of insidious interpretations. Eliot wrote at a time when the entrenchment of cultural studies was yet to occur, and semiotics—the study of symbols—had not yet taken hold as the best way to make everything mean something like nothing. One can't help but be jealous of Eliot's confident supposition that it will always be the will of the people that shapes a culture, and not the bewildering forces of capitalist cultural innovation that shape the will of the people. Eliot probably never imagined the forces that have led cultural production to, at least on the surface, supersede the wants and needs of "the people." Eliot did not envision that cultural doings would turn into an unreal construction so complex and overwhelming that we struggle to live side by side with it, to prevent it from running us over like a rogue eighteen-wheeler plowing through a school crossing. "The reader can make his own list," he naively predicted.

I'm a mass culture love child. I grew up with the Beatles' *White Album*, with "Love Boat," the Ponderosa Steak House, tattered Isaac Asimov paperbacks, *X-Men*, Linda Carter as Wonder Woman, and Leisure Suit Larry (a seedy interactive hero I guided via the mouse pad into repeated bouts of

The original Leisure Suit Larry Adventure Game.
When my brother and I finally got Larry laid,
we thought we had won—until he died of an
unspecified STD. Good clean family fun!

gonorrhea). For me, mass culture was cool, fun, meaningful. It was superheroes and movies I wasn't allowed to watch—though I could read all the smutty paperbacks by John Irving I wanted. I grew up inundated, accessorized, used my first computer when I was ten or so. Like others in my generation, I matured with a somewhat misguided sense of control over my culture. I could pick and choose. I could change everything by the simple act of putting up or tearing down my Echo & The Bunnymen poster. I made mass culture my own, assuming it was my right as a snot-nosed, overprivileged kid in the suburbs to slavishly follow the music of the post-ska supergroup Specials and spend my afternoons drinking Löwenbräu (the beer brewed in America by permission of the Danish king) while systematically microwaving my Han Solo action figure. I never felt this thing, culture, looming large over me. I never thought that what I was acquiring was a body of knowledge so vast and all-encompassing that it would one day replace history and consolidate entire new perspectives of self-determination.

Many of us came of age confidently aware of our power as cultural interlocutors. But, as I've pointed out, the legacy of mass culture—of rebellion, of creating a timeless record, of thinking for yourself—was always in contradiction with the emerging beast that is the culture industry we know today. It's Eliot versus the Frankfurt School. It's the people's capacity to own their culture versus the demands of a faceless conglomeration of money-grubbing power brokers. While I was learning how to work the record player, the record industry was learning how to inject pop music into every aspect of my life. By the time we were ready to live, to be, to rebel through art and give our lives the lasting legacy of tortured creativity, we were faced with the monolithic culture industry of the 1980s, an industry so pervasive it could take a song like Bruce Springsteen's protest jingle "Born in the U.S.A." and make it into a patriotic hit; an industry so dominating it could replace the black vinyl disc once known as the record with the silver ring known as the compact disc (also slated for demolition from the cultural map) in just a few short years. By the time I was old enough to take up the guitar, MTV was reinventing the whole standard of stardom and, hey, look at that, it has nothing to do with musical ability or even shock value. So what does it have to do with?

We came of age when we realized that our desire for genuine transcendent experiences was contrary to the way we saw such experiences literally manufactured all around us. Essentially, we were—and continue to be—caught between two primary conceptions of the role of the aesthetic experience—of "consuming" art—in capitalist society. Confused, we assumed a jaded distance, went to film school, found ourselves adopting the mantra of the disgusted columnist who claims to long for the days when having a culture experience was tantamount to having a moral experience. We put our disenchanted mark on an entertainment industry that could consume and regurgitate everything from Frank Zappa to Abba. We no longer believed in the pop promise, and yet we had to believe, because our pop iconography was, perhaps, the single most prevalent aspect of our childhood and our adolescence. Take all the movies and TV shows and video games and shopping malls out of our minds, and how many hours, days, weeks, and months are left empty? To negate pop culture is to negate the very foundation of our lives—a foundation that is no longer found in religious instruction, in the moral precepts of the state, in the bosom of the family, but in the frantic embrace of a pop emancipation we crave despite—and because of—who we are.

In the wake of this complete integration of pop into our lives, how do we respond to those who would reject and defy the importance of mass culture? Right now, as we enter the twenty-first century, we must believe in the capacity of pop culture to provide us with meaning; to do anything else would be to challenge everything we grew up with, bought into, dreamed of. Along with our grudging admission that consumer culture does manage to take care of most of our material comforts comes our primal, once enthusiastic, now somewhat muted embrace of art as the only possible conduit to meaning in our otherwise perfunctory lives. Having grown up believing in rock as rebellion, art as truth, for us to now accept that the mass culture we were raised by is nothing more than a chimera would be tantamount to admitting that the stuff that makes up our lives and dreams is no different from the effluvia flowing ceaselessly from the evil empire of megacorporations. We might as well get jobs.

In the zine *Radio Free Elvis*, Michael Comeau talks truthfully about the process whereby we have to accept the extent to which our cultural needs, our culturally instilled pseudo-mini-rebellions, give way to a deeper longing to reassert ourselves not just as consumers but as creators:

> My youth was spent inhabiting an insular world focused on my teenage kicks. That veneer has become outdated and growing up is done with a twinge of loss. Smoking and drinking are way cooler when you're criminally underage. The realities of our actions come crashing down around us. Fingers begin to yellow, kisses taste like ashtrays and drinking gin before AA meetings doesn't have the same thrill as in the closet before high school.
>
> As my friends scatter themselves all over the land, I can take heart in the knowledge that age has proved the knocking of opportunities. Opportunities to form bands, record labels, produce magazines, movies; to take back the media and reclaim our culture. This development can make for something as bold as a revolution, or as simple and sweet as a kiss blown across the country.

So goes the spirited, disjointed optimism of a reborn lifestyle culture. Left to fend for ourselves in the steel-cage mud-wrestling Jell-O-pit spectacle that is mass culture, we have fragmented and spread out, moved from punk jazz to rap poetry. We have zines like the popular *Infiltration*, an obsessively detailed chronicle dedicated to "going places you're not supposed to go" that encourages us to take back public spaces from urban centres divided into gated communities and guarded office towers. The way we live informs our cultural appetite, and what we read and watch and buy informs the way we live (the fake oil painting of Kramer from "Seinfeld" hanging in living rooms and bars all over the place—wallpaper? art?). We have flocked to Syracuse University's Center for the Study of Popular Television and signed up en masse for the University of Alberta course "Reading Oprah." We've turned political sex scandals into movies and movies into political sex scandals. In lifestyle culture, the role of the aesthetic experience in our lives is taken seriously, but only in so much as we find a way to make it our own—at which point its value is automatically diminished. We arrive at the heart of resuscitated mass culture furious and defiant; lifestyle culture is our vital outlet, our universally understood fuck-off gesture. Our participation in reinterpreting pop instantly asserts our own tenuous, dogmatic affiliation to free speech, to cultural freedom, to the shaping of a new kind of mental environment—a climate that does not include an understanding of ourselves as the huddled little people Postman calls "easy targets." All this in our search for a reinvented mass culture that might function as the thing that the boys of Braino long for and Eliot describes: a culture that is the only thing we can ever truly and wholly own.

But the lifestyle culture process of reflecting our independence and our needs through reinterpretations of mass culture (as opposed to having mass culture express our desires) means that we must reluctantly leave Eliot's matter-of-fact analysis behind us. That's not to say that we are capitulating; if it's anything, lifestyle culture is our last, desperate, pervasive attempt to rebel against those who seek to reduce us to cogs in the machine. At last (alas) we have entered the world of lifestyle culture: a strange twilight zone where profit-making agendas meet myth-making irrationalities.

■ ■ ■

We North Americans spend a staggering amount of time watching television, listening to various forms of music, flipping through magazines, reading billboards, wandering through subterranean Muzak malls. We watch an average of seven hours of television a day. No wonder: by the end of the shopping decade (also known as the 1980s), 98 percent of our households owned at least one television. But appliance ownership isn't a story, it's a market fact, like the number of countries where you can buy a can of Coke. No statistic can tell us any other story than the one we want to hear. "It is not statistics we are after," wrote theatre critic Walter Kerr in his jovial classic *The Decline of Pleasure*, "we are after some reassurance that we are not statistics."

Not that I'm in any way above bandying around numbers I've gratuitously stolen from other authors who do, in fact, think they can cite statistics as evidence for their theories. So: fifty years after the printing press was invented, more than eight million books had already been printed.

These days, the United States alone cranks out 40,000 new book titles every year (300,000 are published worldwide, with Canadians contributing something like 11,400). Or how about this: every day in America, 41 million photographs are taken (more pictures than there are people living in Canada). The United States, our cultural ground zero, boasts something like 260,000 billboards, 11,520 newspapers, 11,556 periodicals, 27,000 video rental outlets, 500 million radios, 100 million computers. Since 1994, the number of movie screens in the United States has risen by 40 percent. In Canada, movie attendance is reported to be at a thirty-six-year high, with the construction of giant mega-plexes shifting from urban centres to untapped small and medium-sized "markets." Meanwhile, a commercial for nothing particularly identifiable as a product tells us that a population the size of the United Kingdom joins the Internet every six months. I've got 700 independently published underground periodicals on my database of Canadian underground zines, and there are probably another 700 or so that I haven't come across yet (not to mention the ones that will come into the world between the time I write this book and when it gets published). There are roughly fifty independent record labels in Canada. Canadians buy—and presumably consume—some 90 million boxes of Kraft Dinner a year. I could go on. I could tell you how many art galleries there are in Saskatchewan, cite the ratio of ads in bar bathrooms to live bands in bars. But these numbers are just a smoke screen. Just as relevant are the number of oranges grown in Florida, how many shoes there are in the Bata Shoe Museum, how many nose jobs it would take Michael Jackson to return to his original face.

Still, all these "facts" mean something to us in the sense that they are—like the constant mass culture bombardment sometimes mislabelled "information"—present in our lives. The primacy of statistics tells us something about what is an unparalleled explosion in the quest for entertainment, the quest for meaning through the illusion that is lifestyle culture. My father, who buys bargain compact discs with titles like *The Top Twenty Greatest Classical Hits of All Time*, painted a bizarre picture when describing his trip with Mom to tour the Van Gogh exhibit visiting Washington's National Gallery of Art. Lining up beginning at 7:00 a.m. for upwards of four hours, dealing with scalpers, engaging in banter with the upscale crowd, all for the opportunity to shuffle past the great master's works. His tale brings to mind novelist Joseph O'Connor's evocation of attending a Beatles concert in Dublin, or Don DeLillo's description in his novel *Underworld* of the crowds lining up outside Yankee Stadium to get a ticket to the World Series. In other words, there is a sense of pilgrimage and privilege to have been present at these great events that, however subtly, has helped shape world consciousness. Only, as my father's trip to see the sunflower king demonstrates, all culture is now presented to us as if it were a rock concert or a sporting event. And so one wonders to what extent we can now appreciate, believe, commune with the world Van Gogh conjured. For Dad, and the many others who drove from as far away as Florida to see the exhibit, and who have helped spawn an incredible industry of Van Gogh T-shirts, posters, postcards, puzzles, even a "Great Artists" series Barbie doll in a sunflower dress, the exhibit is just another notch in the belt. It's cultural consumerism at its finest. It's high art for the masses, and no one—not me, not my parents, not the 215,000 people who obtained advance passes—has any real sense of what we can possibly hope to find when pursuing these kinds of inexplicably generic mass cultural experiences.

And yet, how many of us are prepared to admit that the fabric of our life lacks substance? That we consume aesthetic experiences the way we snack on our favourite brand of chips? Culture is insidious because it is, at some pure level, inherently contrary to capitalism. Lifestyle culture isn't about ownership—though it is about what we collect, what we value, what we assimilate, what we discard, what we cast away, and what we want to dismiss but find ourselves storing in our minds like endless reruns of our most precious memories. You can't own our memories, can't charge us two dollars every time we resurrect a scene over a couple of pints or cover the "Love Boat" theme song while soaping up in the shower. Similarly, value is impossible to assign. The Mr. T puzzle I bought at a yard sale somewhere in the middle of nowhere cost a mere thirty-five cents. In the city where I live, I could get at least five dollars for it. In fifty years, it could be worth five hundred dollars. Or nothing.

The value of mass culture lies in its endless repertoire of cultural reference points that we use to define who we are and what we believe in. Fictional characters refer to their favourite movies. Sixties psychedelia, '80s grunge and '90s trip-hop define decades, ages, entire sensibilities. Lifestyle culture is possible because of the way our experiences are increasingly collective, the personal interspersed with shared snippets of our favourite Pacino dialogue in *Scarface* ("You stupid fuck! Look at you now! Now you dead!") and where-were-you-when moments of space shuttle explosions, celebrity murders, hung juries, and ice storms. These moments corrode our sense of having personal experiences; they shore up our collective memory, allow us to make friends quickly and easily with the person sitting next to us at the airport bar, while never having a single conversation with our next-door neighbour. The extent to which our minds store sound-bites of culture which are then associated with personal events is evidence for the entrenchment of mass culture in our minds. At the same time, there is a certain disingenuous confusion about the way we use these manu-factured memories. Our shared pop world exists at the brink of a collective abyss in which we're not individuals, we're sales units, ratings, profit margins. Precisely because of this trend to devalue the individual, we shape our communal ref-erence points—the day the Blue Jays won the World Series, the opening night of *The Empire Strikes Back*, the fabulous Van Gogh retrospective—into personal experiences that can validate our culture, our sense of who we are, while ensuring us a manner of communication that redeems our anonymity by making it our most important asset.

The generic essence of cultural space is celebrated and confronted in the short stories, TV shows, zines, paintings, and songs of the new generations of creators who regularly portray pop culture happenings in a fictional context. Montreal poet David McGimpsey includes titles like "I, Urkel" in his oeuvre. The nasty cartoon series "South Park" revives obscure TV characters from the 1980s such as an aging Tina Yothers (once Alex Keaton's baby sister on "Family Ties") and an aging Sally Struthers ("All in the Family" star turned TV psychic hotline spokeswoman). References to our communal TV memories predominate in the works of young writers publishing zines. They are so ubiquitous, and so earnest, that it is difficult to dismiss every passing reference as mere satire. In the same week, I find the poem "Watching The Simpsons on Drugs" in Kevin Pearce's *Orgasm Death Gimmick* zine and read the lines "Charlie's Angels try to Get Smart in The Wonder Years/Inner city life Welcome Back Kotter and Good Times/John Travolta is an adult now/Jaclyn Smith clothing on sale at K-mart" in Jeffrey Mackie's aptly titled zine *Junkfood Architecture*. Much more than the sum of their parts, these zines articulate our collective sensibility, our struggle to find ourselves in a world of Charlie's Angels outfits for fatsos (with the Charlie's Angels movie on the way!).

The zine *Heinous* devotes itself entirely to the legacy and exploits of the 1970s icon Evel Knievel.

The zine for
stunt-jump
enthusiasts and
Evel Knievel
fanatics
everywhere.

Writes Steve Mandich in the introduction to issue five:

I've amassed a wealth of information not only on Evel, but also on nearly 80 other motorcycle jumpers from the last fifty years. I've been at work compiling all this stuff into what I'd like to be a single definitive volume, both on Evel and motorcycle jumping in general. My goal is get it published some day, and better still, become required reading for Oprah's Book Club.

Magazines run lengthy essays on the meaning of malls; staid literary journals solicit material for their pop culture issues. Someday soon Steve will not just fulfil his goal, he will become an international star, a hero, an art god, surpassing Warhol. He might win the first Nobel Prize for pop. Or maybe Steve will lose out to rural Pennsylvania's Phil Petra, who, safely approaching middle age in his parents' basement, has amassed over 40,000 items dedicated to Tarzan, Lord of the Apes. Says Phil: "But I'm not some weird fan, like a Trekkie." Personally, I don't see the difference, except that Phil, with less chance of finding people who share his obsession, is more of a romantic loser, whereas the Trekkie is just one of many, a conference participant and autograph hound lacking the fundamental solitude of the Tarzan fan or, even, the Knievel acolyte. Where did Phil get the idea that he could be a Tarzan expert in the first place? Or that anyone cared? Motorcycle jumping is a sport, sort of, and Star Trek fans, well, they're at least the recipients of reruns and movies and novels and conventions. But Tarzan? Like Steve, Phil dreams of opening a museum, publishing a book, being recognized as an authority. Of course, Phil already is an authority, he has the museum collection, all he needs to do now is put up a website and send out a press release and he's in business. Or he's a laughingstock. Either way, it's no accident that increasing numbers of individuals are announcing themselves—however tentatively—as experts on all manner of incredibly bizarre esoterica.

Collecting is just one of the many ways we attempt to shape mass culture. There is a group of skydivers in Florida who try to jump every time a space shuttle is launched. Somehow, their hobby seems more real to me than the blastoffs taking place at Cape Canaveral. Space is all right, if you can afford it. The rest of us jump out of planes for kicks, devote ourselves to slavish rituals that defy analytical understanding, that speak, like love, to our deepest desires, our most base terrors. To identify, to understand, to make the big picture of mass culture ours, we seek ways to participate.

Consider the Museum of Bad Art. Located in the placid Boston suburb of Dedham, Massachusetts, the place is part feverish dream, part civic duty (the directors are all volunteers), part joke, and part serious undertaking. The MOBA provides a pithy example of what happens when lifestyle culture tries to address our urgent need to participate in—create and elevate—the world of pop. Much more than a museum, the MOBA is a contradiction, where the idiosyncrasies of postmodern mass culture confront the "old ways" of art-world stereotypes and, in the process, crash headlong into our society's inability to deal with creation outside of the context of the marketing machine. It is here, in this seemingly innocent suburban vortex next to a basement bathroom (and in so many other self-proclaimed venues of the independent arts) that the struggle to validate our everyday lives of pop, product, and person gains ground inch by inch. "In fine arts museums people are silent," Marie Jackson, volunteer "Director of Aesthetic Interpretation," tells me over the phone. "People don't feel powerless when they come to the MOBA. We don't empower them, but they are given power by being able to comment on the art. It's a very egalitarian experience to go to the MOBA. We're an ongoing force for the celebration of art. We encourage people to make art, not bad art—but if it comes out in a very spectacularly wrong way, we would love to have it and show it to people. The fear of making art is one of the saddest things."

The MOBA shows us that anybody can paint a picture, anybody can start up a museum. According to Jackson, visitors

Lucy in the Field with Flowers, *the flagship painting of the Museum of Bad Art's permanent collection.*

to the MOBA leave encouraged to make their own art, assured that in a world where museums are arbitrarily erected by the average joe, art is subject only to the individual—which is another way of saying that so compelling is our pull toward ordering our lives through the precepts of lifestyle culture that standards of "good" and "bad" no longer exist.

I do not, personally, consider myself an obsessive whose life revolves around meaningless risks or meaningless collections. And yet, I've accumulated more than five hundred tapes and CDs, and at least two hundred books. I've watched TV religiously since I was old enough to escape my parents' rules against binge viewing, and, of course, like so many of us, I've taken in thousands of movies, whose plots I am more familiar with than the history of the Roman Empire. My brother and my father collect stamps. My mother has a closet full of shoes that would put Imelda Marcos to shame. Meanwhile, our media pundits seem to collude to perpetuate the myth of the homogenized culture of non-participants, casting us as dazed fans who spend hours in line-ups for tickets to the show without a thought in our heads.

We have at least some inkling about what we are doing. We are the North American version of Japan's *otaku*, young people "who trade tidbits of information on arcane topics as if they are commodities of value." Which they are.

■   ■   ■

At the critical juncture where desire meets style, the ever-encroaching mythologies of cultural rebellion run over and reincarnate the best minds of my generation. Style may be our drug, but culture is our religion. At the cultural crossroads, there are both tragedies and near misses. Some of us slam headfirst into mass culture, and end up acting out the kind of violent, dirty-mouthed catatonia our aged politicians like to slap with a mandatory rating. Others of us are carving out new routes, driving down parallel tracks to places where there aren't any ambulances, police, lawyers and judges, agents and editors, to pick up the pieces, cast blame and praise, and assign value to our deeds. It's the no-man's-land of culture now, a place without maps or rules or boundaries, the sort of place where you can wander around forever, and end up exactly where you started. As the novelist Matthew Stadler said in discussing the lack of a cohesive art scene in his hometown, Seattle, "As a result, any hierarchy of cultural production falls apart in loose and sloppy ways. You can't really know what is broadly 'important' because there's no consensus or authority to make anything broadly 'important.' There's no venue to sanctify it, and no critic to anoint it."

Such cultural freedom can be frightening. Without a new way to approach and understand our lives as lived through mass culture (a culture of entertainment, a culture of often pathetic, slavish dedication to fleeting, forgettable moments), we become guilty of devaluing our lives, attuning ourselves to our culture's ethos of fragmentation and self-destruction as embodied in our celebration of drug addiction, depression, sexual deviance, insanity, and violence (a celebration that makes sense from a veiled ironic perspective, but can be extremely harmful to those who don't get the joke—try watching Todd Solondz's gross-out black comedy *Happiness* as if it were a TV movie and you'll see what I mean). So we end up lamenting, and somehow perpetuating, phenomena like online skinheads flogging Aryan hardcore music. We create kids blowing their heads off and kids sticking their veins, all in memory of any number of drug-addled, alcohol-hazed cultural icons (Jack Kerouac, Jimi Hendrix, Sylvia Plath, Kurt Cobain, Janis Joplin, Lenny Bruce, R. Crumb, Philip K. Dick, and William Burroughs, among the many we think we relate to). Alienated youngsters are turning to a celebration of mindless self-destruction as the only way they think they can get themselves heard. We have—as we shall see—those who look inward for a lifestyle of culture, not to rediscover and reinvent themselves in ecstatic opposition to the passive norm, but to give away their free will in a codified process of rituals and dress codes akin to collective madness. Or is it a cryptic sanity, a bold new vision of ordering the universe? Or is it just the same old thing, groupies and fanatic fans, safety-pin punks and the generic tie-dye druggie guy from high school who dropped out to follow Grateful Dead? When I read the level-headed, completely insane fanzine by Glendon McKinney wholly devoted to flamboyant Cape Breton fiddler Ashley MacIsaac, I think—well, no, this is

The obsessively well-written zine dedicated exclusively to Cape Breton fiddler Ashley MacIsaac.

something bold and beautiful, something right for our times, something creepy and pathetic and altogether new.

I'm not of the opinion that we are going to solve our problems just because we have a culture of communal reference points that allow us to engage strangers and make new friends by appealing to our enduring and frightening capacity to store mass culture trivia. Even though almost everybody in North America is part of this process to reclaim our culture for ourselves, paradoxically we still remain, collectively, a passive society. Despite our ever-mounting urgency to participate in and possess our own cultural paradigms, the vast majority of people in North America are still unconvinced that they have a say in their culture, or, even, that they deserve a say in their culture. In that respect, gloating executives and pseudo-liberal scholars who long for the old days are absolutely right. We are a duped majority, awestruck by the machinations of the culture industry. We are forever linked to the assembly line of stuff. We are developing a lifestyle that rationalizes and frees in one sense, but entraps and confines in another. Many of us go to the museum, but how many of us would presume to write an article about what we saw there, or, better yet, decide to start our own museum in the shed? Like Dad does, we might criticize the admission price, the long line-ups, the rudeness of the security guards, but rarely will we feel that we have the right to discuss the merits of the art itself.

Still, things change. Evidence of participation is growing. And I'm not just talking about the increasing number of courses offered in filmmaking and creative writing (though education is a factor). I'm talking about giant Star Trek conventions, and Star Trek theme towns, Madonna lookalikes and Madonna stalkers. I'm talking "Days of Our Lives" Day at the local mall, Gay Day at the Wonderland theme park, affordable karaoke for the home, and hundreds upon thousands of aspiring writer-editors publishing zines on subjects ranging from sex to bad jobs to commodity capitalism to high school to poetry.

Zines are particularly important windows into lifestyle culture. "What zinesters are trying to do," writes Stephen Duncombe, who has penned a rare worthy academic treatise on the subject, "—consciously or not—is to reforge the links between themselves and the world they buy." An exponentially proliferating form of writing/publishing, zines are "memos from the frontlines . . . produced in indecent haste" that create a place where we can validate our own subcultures (our lifestyles), our dreams, our pastimes. Zines are dedicated to pop culture, to entertainment, to sub-sub-genres of movies and music, to that which cannot be reduced to product—when you create your zine, you are the lord of your domain, you are in total control, you and your memories are not for sale. You enter a "space" where you can "escape from work and make [your] own world." Even the simplest, stupidest zines—I'm no apologist for the genre, many zines can be quite idiotic—illustrate the power of the conflict between us and the products we can't help but admit have become part of us.

Zines act as an implicit countervailing force that asserts the will of the populace, however deluded that will might be. "I don't want to sound insulting or dismissive," says Rick McCallum, producer of *The Phantom Menace*, in an article entitled "Even bad reviews can't stop menace,"

but I don't think the so-called print media can stop the film, you just don't have the power. If anything, you might make us look like an underdog. There are 1,400 Star Wars Web sites on the Internet, and they reach probably 30 to 40 million people worldwide. Put another way, one kid writes a review on the Internet, he can reach more people than *Time* and *Newsweek* combined.

Zines—and their electronic counterparts, e-zines—convey a message that is fundamentally important to the development of a genuine independent media serving the new lifestyle culture this book will explore. They exist to bridge the gap between our products and our lives, a gap that, if it is not closed, causes us either to live life like automatons, unwittingly aping the products we produce and consume in a rote daze, or to live lives of perpetual anxiety and longing and self-disgust, trapped in a world where we hate what we are.

The difference between a zine publisher and a letter-writer to the local paper is, in reality, slight. It's the recognition of our possibilities as individuals in a totally subjective lifestyle culture that allows us to validate who we want to become. Social scientist George Comstock writes at the beginning of his compendium of studies *Television and the American Child*: "One of the principal effects of television has been to enlarge dramatically the place of the mass media in [the lives of children and teenagers] and to heighten enormously the place of entertainment." Despite a book that references a full forty-two pages' worth of journal articles and research studies concerning the effects of television on kids, Comstock clearly lacks the capacity to tell us what "the place of entertainment" actually is in our lives. Statistics and studies can't give us a sense of how we make sense of our lives any more than so-called audience participation can give us a real voice in our cultural discourse. That so much energy should be expended to wriggle out of the car wreck of mass culture we have ourselves crashed is both amazing and sad. The more lifestyle culture—a way of using entertainment to define ourselves—becomes embedded in our minds, the more we will struggle to understand who we are amidst this alluring babble of images and stories. Ultimately, it is up to us invisible citizens of the unrecognized republic of mass culture to explain the way we have become confused, disengaged, fascinated, and obsessed.

So let's see if we can't dodge the cars long enough to make it past the twenty lanes of speeding traffic and into that overgrown grass strip where the hardy weeds flourish. Let's discover how we—whether we know it or not—make the everyday decisions that render understanding our relationship to mass culture one of the new century's most provocative challenges. At stake is the ability of individuals to create and consume their own culture, their own meanings. At stake is the capacity to reinvent reality as a precursor to reinventing individuality and, ultimately, society. Some of you won't like where I'm going. Needless to say, if at any point you wish to comment on our journey, feel free to press buttons on your Beavis and Butthead remote control. I don't mind the occasional *"That's cool"* or *"Don't make me kick your ass"* or even *"This Sucks! Change It!"* After all, if there's one thing lifestyle culture promises, it's the capacity for choice. Isn't it?

"Well," the Carleton professor spluttered.

"Thanks for that," Avril said. "Coming up next: the death of the underground!"

PASSIVE RESISTANCE: THE MYTH OF UNDERGROUND CULTURE

CHAPTER TWO

Once and for all: There is No Scene: There is no membership activity. We've all done our time with the punks, the Goths, the crusties, club scenes, art scenes. Galleries, grebos & factories. You name it. We've done the tattoos, the hairdos, the scars, and the steel till we all looked alike. Communist meetings, anarchist rallies, potlucks, back rooms, witch circles; all the underground credentials you could want. . . . Having now safely returned to the helm we can report: there wasn't really anybody there.

— Scott Treleaven, *Salivation Army* zine

I t's 9:00 a.m. Monday, and I'm being treated to an unlikely sight: a pack of dishevelled punk kids gathered in the yard of one of the ramshackle houses that make up this normally placid Toronto west-end neighbourhood. The punks are sleepy-eyed and motley, a crew of pierced Visigoths occupying unfamiliar terrain, called here to witness the opening ceremonies of the anarchist-oriented Active Resistance conference. I'm covering the event for *The Globe and Mail* and, along with the rest of the "corporate" media, am cooling my heels under a hot August sun, waiting for the proceedings to get under way.

When things finally do get started, the opening spectacle quickly takes on the trappings of street theatre. A CBC News cameraman nervously pans slouched teens nonchalantly sipping 7-Eleven coffees. A car alarm goes off and somebody jokes: "We had nothing to do with that." A stern panel of fresh-faced revolutionaries lectures the gaggle of journalists about displaying their "corporate media" passes at all times, warning them not to try to conduct interviews inside Symptom Hall. Symptom Hall is Active Resistance headquarters. It's a crumbling wooden structure consisting of a huge meeting room, a basement, a kitchen, and a warren of apartments, home to an ever-shifting group of organizers who use late-night booze-cans to subsidize the rent and keep the doors open to activists, theatre groups, and radical lefties of all kinds. Set in a working-class Portuguese area just off Dundas Street, it's an anomalous venue to say the least.

For the next week, the organizers tell us, the ramshackle hall is to be reporter-free, a "safe zone" where conference participants can meet informally over a free meal without being spied on by the self-serving media. One primly clad reporter steps up to ask for an explanation of the hostile attitude toward mainstream media. The kids in the crowd demand that the reporter explain why the press consistently distorts the opinions put forth by the radical left. The reporter contends that this is a press conference—he's here to ask questions, not to answer them. "This is an *anti*-press conference," an onlooker jeers. The back of my "corporate media" press pass offers the following "suggested question":

"What kind of spin can I put on this conference to maximize the sales of my commercial sponsors' products?"

So begins a meticulously planned gathering that, over the course of a sultry week in August 1998, brings to Toronto around five hundred young anarchists and activists from all parts of Canada and the United States. "Toronto Police are bracing for a 'radical gathering' of anarchists," warned a *Toronto Sun* article. "During a similar four-day meeting here in July, 1988, some 36 people were arrested, three cops were injured and public property defaced when anarchists ran amok through the city during a demonstration."

No wonder the savvy twenty-something organizers of this week-long affair have decided to engage in their own attempt at media spin. Stuffing my "corporate media" pass under my T-shirt, I slink away from the info-session parody. I'm betting that later in the afternoon the generally amiable conference participants will be willing to focus more on their goals as nouveau revolutionaries and put aside their not altogether unfounded theories concerning the poisoned world of the mainstream media.

So, some four hours later, I'm sweltering in the crowded, mildewed, concrete basement of flophouse/revolution headquarters Symptom Hall.

"We want you to be able to walk away knowing how to put together large-scale street theatre to take over your city," David from San Francisco is saying, addressing the roughly one hundred aspiring activists attending the first meeting of the Art and Revolution Core. (There are four Core groups that participants of Active Resistance can attach themselves to: Art and Revolution, Alternative Economics, Building Revolutionary Movements, and Community Organizing.) The gaunt, enthusiastic David—first name only—shows slides from the Chicago 1996 protest against the presidential elections, in which his giant puppets "confronted the ugly corporate power behind the U.S. government." The polite crowd breaks into applause when the "coffins of democracy" are shown being delivered to the Democratic and Republican campaign headquarters. "I've been involved in street actions for most of my adult life," David tells the rapt audience, "and street theatre is the most effective form of organizing I've done."

It doesn't take much to convince this crowd. The point of the Art and Revolution Core isn't to recruit and inculcate, but to educate and inform those who are already believers. By the same time the next day, this group will be hard at work building their own giant puppet images for use in the weekend downtown Toronto protest dubbed Hands Off Street Youth.

The speedy move from would-be radical to hands-on revolutionary is what AR is all about. Gone is the innocent fervour of yesteryear when it was believed that you could link arms, chant slogans, and make everything all right. Today's young radicals are turning away from traditional protests and sit-ins. Instead, they use concerts and readings and street performances to build a "scene" of like-minded peers and break through the apathy most people exhibit when it comes to leftist actions that threaten to disrupt the free-flowing profusion of goods representing our good lives.

Karen Manko came from Manitoba to listen and participate. "It sounded interesting," she says, shrugging off the distance she travelled to be at the event. She's part of a
radical-left youth coalition operating out of Winnipeg, and,
despite her affected aplomb, she seems to be getting a lot out
of the plans for the big protest, which include dancing,
singing, drumming, and chanting. "Street theatre is really
good to get the media's attention," she reluctantly tells me.
"Most people hear about demonstrations through the media,
so if you can get their attention . . ."

The new activism is all about repelling and attracting the
media. Billboards are defaced, half-joke communiqués are
faxed to the press, and protests are choreographed. In today's
highly politicized cultural atmosphere of punk collectives
mixing strict do-it-yourself (DIY) principles with people-
positive concerts, the message and the medium have never
been more in collusion. It's not enough just to give interviews
and attend protests. Unwilling to relinquish their power to
frame the context, the Active Resistance organizers turned
down a request from the now defunct CBC hipster activist
show "Big Life," hosted by Daniel Richler, to do a segment
on the event.

"It's getting across a homemade radical culture of people
doing for themselves," explains Maegan Willan, an Art and
Revolution co-ordinator and former Toronto resident on
break from college in Olympia, Washington. "Have art mean
something," she says. "Create something that isn't about
money. We're responding to mainstream culture by saying,

WE WANT SOME TOO

'This is our space. I don't acknowledge the authority of the corporation to own public space.'"

When Willan says "space," she means, of course, not just the literal space of streets and parks but the mental space of ads and jingles and candy-wrapper gutters we all have to share. Willan and her cohorts object to the fact that our physical and mental environments are becoming predominantly the property of the corporate sector. The Active Resisters want to put forward ways for us to "reclaim" our everyday. Younger activists have effectively called attention to the problem of diminishing public space by using the 1990s phenomenon of "culture jamming"—an anti-corporate movement in which activists across North America paint over billboards and spoof corporate logos and bumf. The kind of street theatre the Art and Revolution Core is planning takes its inspiration as much from culture jamming as from the stock 1960s protest images the TV generations have grown up with. For these nascent activists, culture jamming—the first concrete grassroots movement to galvanize young people by tapping into both their lifestyle culture ambitions and their increasing unease with a world run for profit by anonymous corporations—is an evolving phenomenon with as yet undetermined potential.

"I used to really enjoy culture jamming," says another Art and Revolution organizer, Toronto resident Dave Fingrut. "I think it's an interesting phenomenon, but you're focusing attention on the product you are opposing. The act of culture jamming is just a stepping stone to more radical action.

Spray-painting over an ad isn't going to change society. It's the difference between vandalizing a KFC ad or burning down a KFC, like they did in India."

In a nondescript T-shirt and sporting a bushy beard, Fingrut looks more like your typical middle-class 1960s revolutionary than his post-punk compatriots. But his vision of moving beyond culture jamming isn't revolutionary claptrap. Fingrut doesn't really advocate the destruction of fast food franchises—at least I don't think he does. What he's saying is that culture jamming is a good way to get attention, but it is limited by the fact that it can only refer to the corporate iconography that dominates life in North America. The Active Resisters want to own and create spectacle, not respond to the existing spectacle of imposed mass culture. As such, they are the radical fringe of our collective lifestyle culture movement.

The Art and Revolution planners didn't come to their ideas in a vacuum. They share head-space with a number of grassroots groups, including popular anti-consumer ad satire magazine *Adbusters* and the Guerrilla Media group in Vancouver, best known for its occasional spoofs of newspapers, including a funny summer 1999 anti–*National Post* satire featuring newspaper mogul Conrad Black as Conzilla. What

One of the many anti–Conrad Black
gags produced by Guerrilla Media

joins these diverse activist progenitors together is their search not so much for revolution as for reclamation. Whether they know it or not, their struggle isn't to enact anarchism as a system of (non)government in North America (most of the attendees have no idea how such a system might operate), but to enact a form of cultural anarchism whereby we feel that we can participate in our own cultural discourse on our own terms, and, in doing so, slip out of the trap of corporate culture that threatens to subsume everything from rebellion and individualism to collectivism and activism.

Rather than foster a renewed sense of the possibilities of the fringe or the underground, the Active Resistance conference's emphasis on reclaiming the aesthetic territory of spectacle from corporate culture is really an admission that the only way to manipulate the system is by aping it, that is, by making it relevant to individuals and communities in North America in the same way that pop culture makes itself relevant, by insinuating itself into the nooks and crannies of our everyday lives. This relevance doesn't have to do with intimidating protests, sects of balaclava-clad revolutionaries, and long-winded petitions. It has to do with appealing to our desire not to be created but to create. In asserting the difference between a press conference and an anti-press conference, Fingrut and his cohorts are figuring out ways to, as he says, "get away from the stereotyped protest done without creativity." In the process, they are reinventing cultural participation, restating the terms of so-called underground culture, and reconfiguring radical politics.

■ ■ ■

In *Media Virus! Hidden Agendas in Popular Culture*, Gen X/ cyber-guru Douglas Rushkoff offers a template for the kinds of books in which cultural critics nervously try to ascertain and assert control over the free-flowing, fragmented activities that characterize lifestyle culture and that the AR movement epitomizes. Rushkoff uses a pseudo-scientific computer-language term, "memes," to postulate that various people (radicals) employ info viruses (memes) to inject their agenda into an ever-receptive media. Rushkoff's text is notable because it at least attempts to recognize that there is an element to our aesthetic needs that supersedes the typical portrait of a passive, hypnotic mass culture. "The media web has neither captured nor paralyzed the American individual," he writes. "It has provided her with the ability to chart and control the course of her culture. She's been empowered."

Clearly, Rushkoff recognizes that the majority of the cultural activities he calls "underground" really have to do with authoring personal reactions to a "mainstream" culture— a mainstream beginning to buckle under the weight of so many voices. In a continent of shopping-addiction help groups, "Most Dangerous Teen Drivers" TV specials, suburban serial-killer celebrities, and oh so much more, the punks and socialists and drop-out miscreants of Active Resistance aren't trying to corrupt the system, they are just trying to find themselves in it, just hoping to stare, one day, into this dizzying mall of mirrors and see their own contorted faces staring back at them. That doesn't make them underground purveyors of dangerous, sweet-tasting viral confections. On the contrary, it makes them everyday standard-bearers of pop culture. They are the flipside of our passive longings, the ones who push the boundaries by normalizing our "underground" desire to make our lives as important as our pop culture. The only difference between the Active Resisters and, say, the Tarzan collector is self-perception. The Active Resisters have pronounced themselves experts capable of staging media events and conferences; the Tarzan collector lurks in his mom's basement, longing to do the same. In the meantime, our popular media, and even critics like Rushkoff, shrink from admitting that we all have the virus now, having long since been infected by a domineering culture industry.

Pop culture taught us—through the many, many texts that convey the myth of everything from the rebellious teen (*Rebel Without A Cause*, et al.) to the disenfranchised dad (*American Beauty*)—that it is our inalienable right to have something, anything, to rebel against. In search of this rebellion, we jump from tall structures attached to a giant elastic band, we surf the Internet masturbating to grainy pictures of naked, dead celebrities, we travel to distant war zones and take pictures. And in all these activities, the distinction between mainstream and underground becomes ever more suspect. Consider the celebrity-as-deity phenomenon. We don't just have pop stars and action figures of pop stars, we have magazines devoted to *the collection of* pop star action figures. In one of these glossy, hyperbolic magazines, I found an interview in which a Spice Girl talked about what it was like to have her likeness in the form of a doll. Collectibles catalogues merge with celebrity fascinations merge with us ordinary folks, who nevertheless are mainstream hobbyists, corporate-sanctioned and encouraged by savvy marketeers who see in these pastimes a way to reconcile the distance between us buyers and our mass culture of celebrity products and product celebrities.

British pop culture theorist John Fiske tells us that fandom and its incarnations can produce works of "art" that "rival, extend, or reproduce the original ones." He describes, for example, the 1987 MTV video competition in which people were asked to submit their own homemade Madonna music videos. The station got so many entries it ended up broadcasting a selection of them in one twenty-four-hour marathon. Within the sanctified space of an MTV contest, our wish-fulfilment fantasies—base expressions of our desires as lifestyle culturists—can be expressed without entering the pantheon of so-called underground culture. But if an arts collective conducted the same contest and displayed the homemade videos in a warehouse, they would be entering into the murky mythology of the underground.

Change your shirt from a polo to a tie-dye and you are changing not just your look but the outlook and lifestyle you broadcast to the world. What AR wants to propagate is the

idea that the only authenticity possible is that which we ourselves proclaim as authentic. In a world where jeans come out
of the factory newly ripped and faded, it's hardly surprising
that young people are searching for ways to assert the
authenticity of their culture, of their lives. Culture jamming is
one facet of this search—a post-industrial graffiti grappling
with the two central problems of global capitalism: identity
and consumption. But lifestyle culture demands that the
search for authenticity be taken to the next level. Forget
vandalism and graffiti; the time has come to reclaim the spectacle, not to deny it. It is in the space where our passive, near-
unconscious everyday lifestyle culture activities meet the
active reclaim-the-streets-in-our-minds resistance of our new
crop of young radicals that the underground ceases to exist.

■　　■　　■

Once upon a time, the project of underground culture was
not to be part of the spectacle but to reveal the spectacle
as manipulation and lie. Before mass culture held out the
promise of our participatory power, inviting everyone in to
join the party and in the process making revolution through
culture just another stylistic trope, the underground thrived
on the idea that you could strip away the inner workings of
culture and reveal the deliberate machinations within. In
other words, when culture was a direct instrument of propaganda and class stratification, there arose from within an
opposition—an underground, a resistance. We worship the

Dadaists, the situationists, the surrealists, the early modern-
ists, the Beat writers, the punks—just some of the figures who
fought for the right of the non-expert, the everyperson artist,
to break down the conventions of art, install a urinal at a
gallery show and call it *Fountain* (as pioneering Dadaist Marcel
Duchamp did in the early twentieth century), and generally
show up the false precepts of an ossified culture specifically
designed to exclude those without the proper pedigree. Until
the onset of art-as-entertainment mass culture, the strategy of
the cultural gatekeepers was not to embrace and encourage
every shocking possibility, every scandalous reappraisal of
value and worth, every stupidity, but, instead, to repress and
deny it—refuse to give it the sanction of commodity our society now extends to all but the most extreme acts.

In response to this repressive approach (which still
lingers today), it made sense to develop methods to challenge the power structure that conferred authority on cultural doings. One of the most popular ideas of the 1960s and
beyond was to drop out of society, found radical parallel
structures and economies of meaning in which it was possible to reinvent culture. You and your friends can't show
your urinals? Start your own gallery. You'll teach them! This
is (was?) certainly the ethos of DIY punk culture. "I think the
most radical thing punk has done is set up an independent
network, completely outside of corporate or government
control," Tim Yohannon, the late publisher of the famed,
resolutely indie punk zine *Maximum Rock'n'Roll*, told *This
Magazine* in 1994.

There is no denying the urgency of the belief that it is still possible to drop out, to establish independent networks, to live free of the trappings of commercial society. But as the many zines, punk songs, and indie works that focus on pop culture suggest, the entertainment universe is one that has colonized us completely. To "drop out" is to negate who we are. When we write in our zines about boring jobs, or our obsessions with certain bands, movies, and "stars," or our night out drinking too much and throwing up outside of Burger King, we are writing about the way we as individuals are forced to confront a hostile, unfriendly world that reduces us to pieces in the marketing puzzle, quotas to be filled, profits to be made. We can pretend that the CNNs and Time Warners of the world no longer affect our lives because we have decided to ignore them, but our obsession with mass culture and its trappings conjures up its own truth. When mass culture became all-consuming, all-accepting, all-entertaining, the underground disappeared—leaving us to deal with our need to assert ourselves as individuals without necessarily burning down the KFC or blowing up the Cineplex or founding our own alternatives, but without whole-heartedly buying into the entertainment complex that invites us to eat rubber chicken while we "Defeat the Dark Side and Win!"

Today, the Museum of Bad Art has a package of press clippings that would make the National Gallery of Canada drool. Taking note, even established institutions are searching for ways to connect high art to the purported lowness of our day-to-day. "When museums poll visitors on what they want, the answer is to feel connection between art and everyday life," reports an article on the struggle of well-known museums to adapt their heretofore exclusionary strategies to this new anything-goes environment.

The moment that the guardians of high culture stepped aside, inviting the pop hordes to rush in and fill the vacuum, the underground ceased to be. So where did it go, this underground, a subterranean culture that existed to liberate us from the sanctimonious, self-serving moral trappings of so-called mainstream society? The California rock critic Greil Marcus drew a line in the sand when he argued that the day in 1976 when the proto-punk band Sex Pistols shocked Britain by uttering the word "fuck" on TV might very well have been "a major event in history." His argument is that the underground as we understand it today began with the Dadaists and surrealists and situationists and ended when punk rock made it to TV—at which point there was no status quo left to challenge. For Marcus and many other cultural critics, from the moment the underground surfaced on television, nothing would ever be the same again.

But Marcus leaves it at that, and doesn't ask an important question: if the underground died in 1977, why is it that we generally understand it to be the other way around? We consider punk rock to be just the beginning, the impetus for a whole host of other provocative spectacles, unholy underground perversities, barbaric bizarreries that sicken the young and infect the weak.

It would seem that, ironically, the bonfire spectacle of punk (fuelled by the media's attendant frenzy) caused the average bystander watching it all on TV to believe that the underground was not just alive and well, but threatening the safety of the mainstream. The truth, of course, was the opposite: it would be the mainstream that would threaten and destroy the underground, leaving would-be cultural radicals—the kids of AR and so many more of us—with no place to go to enact our rebellion.

■   ■   ■

We each have this romantic idea of an underground culture in our mind—a loose community of bold nonconformists who reject the bogus mores of tradition in favour of a bohemian devotion to the moment that not only produces memorable works of art but also implicitly challenges the pedestrian workings of the "system." It is this idea, this mythology of underground culture, that inspires our lifestyle culture desires and leaves us longing for more than we even realize. We long for this mythical underground world, and in the process we devalue our lives. "Thirty years ago," writes one essayist ruminating on the nature of Woodstock '99, "something vital and lasting . . . broke apart, and now, thirty years later, that sense of connection, of some overarching narrative frame for our lives, still hasn't been repaired or replaced."

Instead, we have a society of instant moments and perpetual excitements. It's a world that effectively undermines our "underground" ambitions by offering them up to us on a Styrofoam plate. I'm often asked, in a variety of ways, "What exactly is underground culture?" But I rarely offer up a straight answer. You might as well ask me what, exactly, mainstream culture is. Certainly, I'd use the same adjectives: weird, compelling, disjointed, dysfunctional, upsetting. What's more upsetting than the local mall? More compelling than the panorama of every highway exit in North America dotted with the same cluster of McDonald's and Pizza Huts and IHOPs? What's weirder than Spice Girl dolls and violent Beanie Baby collectors? Mainstream culture has become what underground culture used to be: instant provocation and meaningless violence posing as a challenge to the status quo through the constant pushing of boundaries. These are the tricks of mass culture, and we see them every day on TV, on billboards, in our newspapers, in the toys we buy our children. A mainstream newspaper reviews "OZ," a prison drama that regularly features nudity, rape, grotesque violence, ethnic slurs, and extreme profanity. The paper isn't appealing for calm, a return to order, an immediate ban on this kind of programming. Rather, the opposite: the paper is calling for more shows of this kind. What could our underground artists possibly do to trump lushly filmed scenes of anarchistic violence in which the state and its machinations are mercilessly mocked at prime time on popular cable stations serving millions across North America? (I never miss an episode!)

Since the 1950s, politicians have chosen to attack popular culture as a manifestation of an evil, amoral, underground youth culture. In 1998, Ontario premier Mike Harris even took to railing about our fave duo Beavis and Butthead as a way to buttress support for his province-wide school "code of conduct" plan. Thus the cliché is sustained: underground (or the *faux* underground that "Beavis and Butthead" and Much-Music/MTV represent) is portrayed as foul and dangerous and corrupting. In its stead, our youth should have mainstream culture. But what is that? Devastating reductions to the funding of the Ontario Arts Council by the Harris government make it clear that the premier was certainly not advocating a move away from pop culture toward the traditional arts, such as painting, sculpture, writing, music composition. So what, for Mike Harris and his ilk, is the alternative to "Beavis and Butthead"? What does a positive, mainstream culture look like, other than school uniforms? Mainstream mass culture and underground culture have essentially fused, leaving our politicians flailing.

The collapse of the mainstream into the underground (or vice versa, depending on what you miss most) has been instrumental in strengthening the pull of lifestyle culture on the TV generations. Our devotion to the brief radicalism of the late 1960s and the momentary extremism of the punk rock '70s is evident in the exponentially growing number of plots that deal with these time periods—and just when interest in regurgitating these eras in hackneyed plots seems about to expire, new rebellious periods are postulated, such as glam, gangsta rap, and rave. And yet we are somehow never there, always missing the fulcrum of artistic and cultural and social change. We didn't get to see the Sex Pistols, or Bob Dylan, or even bp Nichol with the Four Horsemen, first-hand, and so we are left searching for the kind of sustaining iconic experiences that can validate the place pop culture has in our lives; we seek the kind of seminal spontaneous pop moments our baby boomer critics blithely claim as their own. We've seen the Woodstock "rockumentary," we've read the integral punk texts, and we bought it all reissued and digitally remastered. If only we could hold the magic as easily as we can buy a boxed set with accompanying DVD footage. In his time, Greil Marcus saw The Clash live. In mine, I saw former Clash singer Joe Strummer fronting the now defunct Pogues. Joe was doing his best Shane MacGowan imitation; we were jumping up and down, crowded in like animals in a tent at Toronto's CNE fairground. Someone threw firecrackers at the stage and the bouncers dragged him out. We were drunk, we applauded, we were glad, worshipping, for a night, this pathetic panorama of pseudo-punk rebellion as if we had just experienced the real thing. As if there ever was a real thing.

Today, it seems as though anyone born in the 1970s and beyond must always experience certain aspects of their immediate cultural legacy in a second-hand way. The forces of retro and repackaging rely on a myth-making that succeeds in getting us to buy product but doesn't satisfy the ever more powerful urge to experience first-hand the caustic confrontations at the heart of all those infamous cultural shifts we sat out. This, I think, is not so much a generational argument as it is an argument about the way mass culture is packaged and repackaged and presented as a moment in time that most people missed—bygone eras whose "underground" mystique can be made at least partially accessible for a low, low price. In that way, our newly merged mainstream/underground pop culture keeps us clamouring for more product, ever unhappy with what we couldn't get to, or didn't know about. Whether it happened two weeks or two decades ago, you missed it. You weren't there.

■ ■ ■

The notion of a mainstream culture and a culture in opposition to that culture (a counterculture) makes some kind of sense as an economic model: sort of independent business Davids versus giant multinational Goliaths. It's comforting for people to feel that they have the illusion of choice in the cultural marketplace, even if they themselves aren't sure what those choices are or how they might access them. Oh sure, we like the idea that there is an underground. We perpetuate the pervasive myth of an underground that "infects" the mainstream, mainly because it comforts us to imagine those brave underground warriors agitating against the conformity and commercialism we have to put up with.

So we like this sexy idea of Rushkoff's—the dangerous, viral underground that we handle only when wearing masks and gloves and goggles. But we don't want to be confronted with the choices and implications alternative culture presents on an everyday basis. We don't, for instance, want to hear

Braino on the radio as we make our way to work in the morning. That tinge of guilt we feel each time we pass the organic vegetable section of our grocery store or decline the ethical mutual funds in favour of higher-earning planet-wrecker funds represents our conflicted interest in both accessing the "alternative" and maintaining the comfortable status quo.

Our confused relationship to underground culture is crystallized when large chain stores try to put an "alternative" spin on their products. Tower Records was one of the first massive chains to aggressively market exactly the kind of pseudo-underground ethos that many of us feel most comfortable with (and are most likely to buy). In the books section of your average Tower Records is a large selection of what they call "Outpost Literature." This will include the requisite Beat writers, and a small bandwidth of other acceptably socialized "outpost" writers like Irvine Welsh and Charles Bukowski. Next to this shelf of books you might find something like R. Crumb's Devil Choco-Bar. This is a fascinating object, perfect for the Tower Records business plan, which is to allude to but not actually represent counter-culture precepts. The R. Crumb Choco-Bar features noted 1960s comic artist Robert Crumb's signature well-endowed babe on the wrapper. She's winking, smiling devilishly, and saying: "Eat Me!" Here, then, is the epitome of proxy underground culture: it's a candy bar! You don't even have to deal with the cost of owning a book you'll never read! But then, when I turn the damn thing over, lo and behold, it's also an ad for famed Massachusetts indie comic-book publisher and

distributor Kitchen Sink Press. Half of the back label provides the Kitchen Sink address, 1-800 number, and an exhortation to "write or call for a free catalog."

This isn't just smart marketing, it's also a total subversion of the distinctions we're always trying to make—that one thing is underground and another thing is aboveground. What you get with R. Crumb's Choco-Bar is the pseudo-hip borrowing of 1960s hippie culture in a cookie-cutter chain outlet whose corporate game plan includes Outpost Literature and Mariah Carey. What you also get is this chain's focus-grouped appeal to suburbanites craving the pseudo-underground being manipulated by a real, honest-to-god independent publisher whose comics and books are too outpost for the Outpost Literature section—but whose candy bar fits right in.

At this point in time, should I desire an underground

book or zine or CD not available in my local managed-by-satellite, giant-size emporium, I simply access any number of online catalogues, make my choices, and pay by credit card or cheque (I can also call 1-800 numbers or write in for, as the multitude of ads go, "my free mail order catalogue"). Like everything else, underground culture is for sale twenty-four hours a day.

Of course it's worth remembering that even in the caustic punk era the integration of alternative culture into the overall narrative of a very weird, very mainstream lifestyle culture was already well underway. The level of accessibility one finds today might well be novel, but the notion of an underground movement, like punk, attempting to establish its own ideology and "style"—even as it is consumed by the "mainstream" conservative marketplace appetite for order and dogma available for a price via mail order—goes way back. Dick Hebdige makes this observation in his seminal 1979 cultural study *Subculture, the Meaning of Style*:

> Punk clothing and insignia could be bought by mail order by the summer of 1977, and in September of that year *Cosmopolitan* ran a review of Zandra Rhodes's latest collection of couture follies which consisted entirely of variations on the punk theme . . . the article ended with the aphorism—"To shock is chic"—which presaged the subculture's imminent demise.

Similarly, the widely archetyped but little-read William

Burroughs wrote as early as 1971 in his novel *The Wild Boys*:

> April 3, 1989, Marrakesh. . . . The chic thing is to dress in expensive tailor-made rags. . . . There are Bowery suits that appear to be stained with urine and vomit which on closer inspection turn out to be intricate embroideries of fine gold thread.

And so, even at the height of so-called rebellion, the myth of rock and roll and the myth of underground culture fuse together into the more culturally accessible archetype of style. Style that everyone can buy, style that television shows can emulate, style that can be adopted without actually having to, say, live in the gutter or do a lot of heroin or otherwise opt out of the prevailing values of the mainstream structure. Style, of course, is the second half of the word lifestyle, and that's no accident.

The Active Resisters didn't organize a press conference to announce their plans to smash the state; they organized an anti-press conference to lecture the media on how they aren't going to tell them anything, because the media will just lie about it anyway. They use the readily accessible precepts of radical and underground as the media perpetuates them to try to inform us, through the media, that there are other options. The theory here is that by controlling the amount of information the media is given, AR will be able to shape the context of the story, focusing reports on its agenda—not on their ripped jeans and all-around-dangerous

underground nature. In the same way that Kitchen Sink uses
Tower to sell the R. Crumb chocolate bar, AR attempts to
manipulate mass culture to represent ideas and "products"
that would otherwise be distorted or rendered invisible. The
result is a challenge to our cherished myth of the underground—a myth no longer sustainable in a world where if
it hasn't happened on TV, if you can't find it in the shelves of
the alternative section of your giant chain record store, it
doesn't exist. Today it's not Tower versus Kitchen Sink but
Tower *and* Kitchen Sink. It's not AR versus the tabloid *Toronto
Sun*, it's AR *and* the *Sun*.

■　　■　　■

"**D**on't just say your town sucks," advises Oakville punk
Giz. "Make it not suck!" Giz and her co-conspirator,
Cory, sport multicoloured hair and big black boots and are
the antithesis of what you would expect smart, motivated
young people to look like. When I come across them, they
are conducting a "freeskool workshop" (one of a staggering
twenty-odd caucuses and group discussions that took place
every day around the city as part of AR). About thirty people
look right at home crammed into the decrepit upstairs pool
room of the Queen Street club The Big Bop—renamed the
Bakunin Bop, after the Russian anarchist, for the week. This
discussion is entitled "How to develop an active scene in the
boonies," and Cory and Giz have a lot to say. At the time of
the conference, they are publishing a zine (*Punk Fiction*),

putting on regular punk shows and benefits, and running the
Oakville, Ontario, group Youth Against Hate (YAH!). Led by
this dynamic duo, the consensus in the room is that if you
want to start something up in a small town or a suburb, you
have to be more creative than in the big urban centres. In
other words, you have to use music and other "fun" events to
attract kids into a larger activist scene. The most important
thing, Cory and Giz advise, is to not give up, to keep organizing and putting on shows and networking. "You're creating
a creative space," they say. "And then people will just pop up
out of nowhere. Don't get discouraged. There's lots of
common ground that alienated kids in the 'burbs have that
you can tap into."

Back at the Art and Revolution Core, alienated kids from
the 'burbs are hard at work shaping cardboard and papier-
mâché into huge puppets. There's concern that planned
images like an eight-armed "octocop" and an enormous
squeegee kid on a crucifix will come across as too negative.
Blueprints are drafted for manufacturing the hundreds of
squeegees that will be handed out to those in solidarity with
besieged street youth. Though the atmosphere is tense, and
the emphasis has shifted from discussion to production,
everyone listens patiently to suggestions on ways the puppets can interact to create a positive message.

"It's important to foster a sense of creativity in the community as a whole," says Dave Fingrut, "so the blandness of
left-wing political ideology doesn't turn people away. Art is a
really good medium for getting across political messages."

But, of course, it's not quite as simple as that. You can't just slap a tune over your rhetoric and expect to change the world, any more than a pop star who sings about the homeless can expect that her song will bring about shelters and affordable housing. Remember "We Are the World"? As much as lifestyle culture represents a collapse of the distinction between mainstream and underground, it also represents the difficulty of cogent political activism in an age where everybody wants to be their own personal cause, their own underground myth, subject of their own fan club.

For the Active Resisters, then, the struggle becomes not just to articulate one's need to be a participant in the product universe, but also to articulate one's particular ideological perspective on that universe in such a way that people are attracted and motivated to be part of something more than just the manufactured imagery of cultural rebellion. The problem the Active Resisters face is the problem at the heart of lifestyle culture: how do we speak of and through mass culture without losing our identity, without being subsumed by generic myth? For the Active Resisters to achieve their goal of a reinvented, liberated, creative free space—an anarcho-aesthetic culture—they need to find a way to appeal to the mainstream, to be popular while maintaining the substance that is lost when a political/aesthetic idea becomes mall iconography.

This struggle is what emerges from the collapse of the underground. It is the struggle for identity central to the possibility of authentic individual creation in our prefab world.

New York digital painter and expatriate Winnipegger Kevin Mutch describes this struggle in terms of the conflict between idiotic, sugary pop and an intelligent yet accessible creativity. As he told me via e-mail: "I consider 'unpopular' culture to be work that is about pop culture and uses some of its styles but is not popular itself."

Mutch, speaking from his 2,000-square-foot storefront in Soho, personifies the opportunistic new art world of lifestyle culture. His is an "endlessly producible" art (you can order "prints" right off the web) that stands as a critique of, and an offering to, the commodity world. Slick and colourful as a postcard, as safe as an image on your TV screen, Mutch's work comments on the way art history and pop culture have, essentially, fused into generic visuals, affording his art—Barbie-like figurines with the faces of real women, giant apes holding boots—an appeal through instant recognizability. When we're great-grandpeople living in Florida, we'll have his G.I. Joe reining in a plastic horse with a background of Astroturf stretching toward puce sky hanging on the living-room wall of our condo. Mutch's work represents our cele-bration of the unpopular—the pseudo-underground of cool in which some vital understanding of who we are can be expressed only via the paradox of on-sale, endlessly repro-duced originals portraying the perverted essence of shared pop memories.

Something clicked in my mind when Mutch explained his concept of unpopular pop. Yes, I thought, this is what the AR lifestyle-culturites—what we all—strive for: intelligent,

Outdoor
Life
*by Kevin
Mutch*

meaningful creative actions that nevertheless acknowledge the primacy of pop culture.

There are those who wonder how "unpopular pop" can supplant a money-hungry culture industry that couldn't care less what message its "product" puts forward as long as it sells. (The popular "OZ," for instance, conveys a message of nihilism and corruption juxtaposed with the usual ads for cars and beer.) A new wave of cultural critics is quick to dismiss unpopular pop, the cultural machinations of Art and Revolution, as being just another example of our search for a pseudo-rebellion that doesn't exist, a rebellion that has infected our view of the world by giving us licence to sit slumped in our easy chairs, remotes at the ready, all the while laying claim to dissent. What is cultural revolution in an age when every rebellion seems like just another marketing opportunity? Foremost among these critics is Thomas Frank, editor of the acerbic journal *The Baffler* and author of *The Conquest of Cool.* "Our problem," he writes,

> is that we have a fixed idea of what power is, of how power works, and of how power is to be resisted. It's an idea called "hip" and it holds that the problem with capitalism is that it oppresses us through puritanism, homogeneity and conformity and that we resist by being our selves, by having fun, by pushing the envelope of uninhibition, by breaking all the rules in pursuit of the most apocalyptic orgasm of them all. It's an idea that hasn't changed at all in 40 years, even as capitalism has undergone revolution after revolution. And it's an idea that is now obsolete as a mode of dissent.

Frank's angry, swift condemnation of style as rebellion is perfectly evoked, and yet it offers little solace to the Guerrilla Media/Active Resisters and the rest of us lifestyle-culturites. We are the ones who have to continue to find ways to make our popular culture into something more than just a glittering heap of disposable trinkets we spend X hours a day unwrapping. Surely we prefer to see our stylistic/artistic machinations—the things we collect, the zines we produce, the dreams of celebrity we harbour—not as petty, symbolic, useless affirmations of the pseudo-rebellion of pop, but rather as a form of noncompliant compliance, of unpopular pop.

Our world-view implicitly acknowledges that culture today is as much about the style of the substance as it is about the substance itself. Given our general obsession with cultural creations, with proliferating narratives, with the telling and retelling of the few stories that there have ever been to tell, it's hardly surprising that the Active Resisters— and many of us who seek to "rebel" without burning down fried chicken emporiums—should choose the path of redemption through a reclaimed culture. So what can we say to Frank, who accuses both the latter-day cultural activist and us passive resisters of doing nothing more than perpetuating a kind of corporate hedonism aspiring to commercialize "cool" and "style" and "hip"? What, then, is the alternative to alternative in an age when the Woodstock '99 art director can tell reporters that "If there's not the same yearning for peace and harmony among today's Woodstock kids, it's because there is peace and harmony now" with a straight face? (In case you've forgotten, Woodstock '99 ended in a mini-riot complete with fires, looting, and the mysterious disappearance of all the cash machines on the site.) I'm asking the questions, but I don't really have an answer. Perhaps this is because Cory and Giz and Thomas Frank are all correct. If we are to make any kind of cohesive challenge to the way our mass culture/society works, it isn't going to be by holding wild parties, ingesting rebellious quantities of quasi-illegal soft drugs, and buying "phat" outfits. At the same time, our desire to assert a new kind of relationship between us and the commercial world can't just be about throwing off the fetters of pop that make us who we are. Without the pit of the underground to fall back into, the search for a new kind of mental environment, a new kind of unpopular pop, continues.

■ ■ ■

In a society that celebrates the riot as a kind of cathartic admission of what we all know but won't say, violence becomes the last bastion of uncommercialized rebellion. Indeed, there are some whose urgent need for the authenticity of a genuine underground leads them to celebrate riot, murder, terror, and other forms of extreme violence. These are subjects of increasing fascination—destruction as the only true underground act now possible. Just as the moment of the underground's collapse was the moment that instilled in many of us the longing for a seedy counterculture, we continue to search for pop's promise of authenticity and rebellion, our search taking us farther and farther afield. Led on by the magazine named, paradoxically, *Pure*—dedicated to shocking acts of perversity and violence—a plethora of zines, magazines, videos, and websites suggest that there is an equation between acts of destruction so heinous they can never be bought or sold and the desperate search for authenticity that is the legacy of an "underground" that doesn't exist. As one scholar notes: "Zines such as *Murder Can be Fun, Answer Me* and *Dead Star: for John Wayne Gacy,* celebrate mass murderers as the ultimate un-cooptables, positing pure evils as the only purity left." These publications continue to proliferate, with magazines like *Eye* and *Panik* reaching a wide audience and sporting a healthy number of ads. A November 1999 issue of *Panik* featured an interview with a guy fascinated by 1970s German terrorists Baader-Meinhof and a glowing article on an industrial band. That article gushingly begins: "Pictures of dead bodies, spilled entrails, and almost pornographic portrayals of young children are the sort of images adorning the pack-

aging of a Brighter Death Now release." Do a search for serial killers on the web and you'll be staggered by the results, not just in terms of the number of sites but in terms of the creative energy many of us seem to employ in our celebration of the celebrity murderer. The irony of the *Pure* movement is that mass corporate culture has already, indirectly and directly, celebrated everything from kiddie porn (Calvin Klein billboards of underwear-clad strung-out twelve-year-olds) to terrorism to serial killers. In an age when you can buy the Charles Manson font for your word pro-cessor, the suggestion that celebrating acts of violence and perversity is a kind of reli-gious experience above the pop fray becomes about as relevant as the latest

This is what the Charles Manson font looks like.

government promise. Which leaves us to wonder: is this what the "underground" has come to? Is this the legacy of our quest for authentic underground experiences? Is it at this perverse dead end that we hit the brick wall of unpop-ular pop?

Our creepy obsession with violence and celebrity and, particularly, the space in mass culture where they connect, is not just about pathetic lifestyle-culturites asserting the depth of their confusion by setting up serial-killer websites. You might remember a 1980s figure known as the Rainbow Man. His gig was to show up at major sporting events across the United States and dance wildly until his mangy rainbow wig was shown—for a few seconds—on national TV. He was addicted to it, and at the height of his fame he made appearances on several talk shows. Eventually, the media lost interest. Unable to get back on TV, ignored even at minor sporting events, he ended up taking hostages, demanding to be put on the networks, and, eventually, languishing in jail. The Rainbow Man showed how, at the extremes of lifestyle, we lose everything but our driving need for validation through mass culture. Of course it took his incarceration to make him a genuine cult figure, whose story has now been told in several zines and indie documentaries. And so the Rainbow Man demonstrates what can happen when the underground and the mainstream fuse. Here is a figure who was at once a recognizable pop icon, a bizarre performance artist (in the spirit, perhaps, of what we now call Outsider Art), and, finally, an "underground" hero. If the Rainbow Man had found a way to express his desire to be part of cultural discourse in some other way (the anti-press conference?), it might all have turned out differently; his final attention-getting scheme—a descent into pointless, violent crime, the ultimate in solipsistic self-expression—might well have been avoided.

But the myth of the underground—linked as it is to the myth of the noble bohemian, the crazed genius, and the dangerous destitute—is too valuable a marketing tool to be jettisoned simply because it is causing people to lose their minds and perpetuate, if not perpetrate, horrible acts. "Newspapers are content to cover the easy things. Their sudden bulletins on the odd, the deviant, the discontinuous and the novel aim to produce not understanding, but astonishment," writes one journalist turned media critic. The media will always latch on to sensationalist representations of the underground and treat such phenomena the way they treat an entire underclass of disenfranchised individuals. The poor, the young, the political, the stupid, the radical, are all spectacle, they are the Rainbow Man in all his bewigged, wigged-out glory; they are the raw material for our idea of an underground that doesn't exist, an idea that keeps us in check and at bay, combing through the perverse (yet somehow sanitized) anything-goes world of mass culture in search of that next genuine "thing" we can be a part of.

■　■　■

The next wave of would-be revolutionaries do not want to end up as stylistic tropes or viral memes. "Once and for all," writes artist and explorer Scott Treleaven in his punk/pagan/Goth/gay zine *Salivation Army*, "There is No Scene." Scott longs for an uncorrupted network that cannot be colonized by marketing forces or feel-good youth magazines. To understand the urgency of his vision is to confront the urgency with which everyone, from giant corporations to burgeoning entrepreneurs to well-intentioned branches of government, seeks to replace these last vestiges of angry, ugly possibility with ersatz mags dedicated to the predetermined positivism of convention and commerce. And yet, Scott is not a nihilist; he, too, lives in the lifestyle culture universe and wants to be able to promise a lasting legacy of cultural participation. He ends his manifesto with words of encouragement for all those who share his hope for the survival of the anonymous, desperate loser who, nonetheless, belongs: "We are the new circus," he insists. "We are the envy of the fucking world."

Hope springs eternal, though many questions go, as yet, unanswered. Long after the kids have thumbed their way back home, and the puppets have moulted into the paper and glue they came from, the large-scale theatrics of Active Resistance '98 will, no doubt, be played out on small stages in boonies and suburbs and downtowns across North America. Thomas Frank is right to be sceptical, but perhaps he is overly dismissive of the possibilities. Can the collapse of the underground lead to a cultural reclamation of public space for the people?

A new relationship between our pop iconography and our lives demands a new language. And it is in the quest to utilize and make sense of this new language that the contradictions and optimisms of a reinvented activism merge with our mass culture predilections. Here, in the strange world of unpopular pop, we will find the mythical underground's true legacy.

TRY AND FIND ME: LIVING THE LIFESTYLE

PART TWO

MUTATIONS: THE NEW LANGUAGE OF PLUNDER

CHAPTER THREE

I got a funny feeling they've got plastic in the afterlife.

— Beck, "Cyanide Breath Mint," *One Foot in the Grave*

erritt, British Columbia, population 7,000. An unassuming small town in the interior of B.C. Hardly the sort of place you would expect to find a thriving zine scene complete with its very own pirate radio station. And yet, propelled by a moribund indie rock enthusiast in his thirties who goes by the moniker Bleek, Merritt has been a bastion of zine culture since the mid-1990s. Bleek is a dour, soft-spoken, uncertain fellow. Like the town of Merritt itself, he's an unlikely emissary for the new language of unpopular pop that is the legacy of our ongoing search for authenticity. At the same time, Bleek and his homebase of Merritt strike me as the consummate ambassadors to usher us into the elusive world of a new language—a kind of social operating system—that I like to think of as "plunder."

Plunder is a way of writing and speaking and making

music and art and film and video that represents the way we now live our lives through the filter of pop. Plunder is lifestyle culture's alphabet. Why wouldn't we find it in Merritt? Plunder is everywhere, it flows into every disconnection, joining us together, opening up new possibilities in the arts, in business, in communication, while at the same time reducing North America to one huge suburb of interconnected generic mass culture references. Mass culture is changing everything—particularly our sense of who we are and what we deserve. And yet, we have had no language to speak to the mass culture that has shaped and dominated and changed us. So we're in the process of inventing new words, new grammars, new rules to remind us that in the warp zone of lifestyle culture we are in charge. Everything fake is real again. Everything old is new again.

Imagine plunder as a kind of superimposed pop mélange that connects a far-flung diaspora of creators and consumers. So pervasive are the archetypes of mass culture that we have begun to use certain images, phrases, pop culture moments, snippets of songs and jingles, as a language. As a result of growing up with a mass culture that, like a benevolent parent, was with us every step of our development, the TV generations have begun to speak in the language of pop.

Just look at "Beavis and Butthead," pop's most self-referential show. Here is plunder in action. The show is not funny unless you are part of the pop culture world. The TV generations instantly recognize the videos the duo spend most of the show mocking; we instantly comprehend the bland dynamic of Quickie Mart, suburban living room, generic high school that holds the boys in sway. We speak their language. No wonder earlier generations find the show stupid and offensive. They miss most of the subtle jokes directed at an audience of culturally obsessed fast-food kids who know exactly what "Beavis and Butthead" is a satire of— not the world of suburbs, uptight principals, and demanding parents, but the world of meaningless pop promises we all live in; not the world outside us, but the world inside us.

The show works because of the language of plunder it employs. Videos from the last three decades appear and disappear in tantalizingly familiar rhythms—recognition, mockery (we liked that once?). Plunder is this process of recognizing the instant stereotypes we store in our brains, prefab video moments we have constant access to. What does plunder look, sound, feel like? A hundred years of mass media stuck in the blender, poured out as a shake of stolen song snippets, abbreviated fictions intermixed with collaged moments, self-referential vignettes that evoke everything from film noir to country and western to manga. So plunder: a natural part of the lifestyle culture evolution, the language of mass culture we have developed as part of our attempt to validate and reclaim the pop world that so dominates and demeans us. It is through plunder that we extricate ourselves from the pop culture morass our brains seem stuck in. "We have learned a visual language made up of images and movements instead of words and syllables," explains James Gleick in his book *Faster: The Acceleration of Just About Everything.*

"It has its own grammar, abbreviations, clichés, lies, puns and famous quotations." The result is a perpetually plundered Beavis and Butthead world in which we speak to each other via our shared assumptions about the pop culture universe: "The audience has gotten more sophisticated," comments a president of MTV animation. "You can take certain leaps without people scratching their heads."

But plunder, as Bleek and his many cohorts will show us, is not just a way of accessing lifestyle culture, a manner of communication that allows us to follow along as Beavis and Butthead and Braino borrow and reinvent bits and pieces of the pop zeitgeist. Plunder, at its most evolved, is an aesthetic that insists on our right to a participatory culture; it's a way to evoke a mass culture world that beckons us forward but always seems to leave us on the outside looking in.

■　■　■

Originally from Seattle, Bleek has lived in Merritt since 1994. In 1995, he introduced zines into the area with the publication of various ongoing projects, including his current zine, *Speck*. In 1998, he followed this up with the introduction of Merritt's first and only pirate radio station, Merritt Free Cast Radio (MFCR for short).

Bleek's MFCR microcast radio transmissions were nothing spectacular. For roughly a year, he played aberrant college-rock tunage. Interspersed between these relatively commonplace songs, Bleek broadcast overtly weird music coming out of a pastiche spoken-word/sampling format. So, in between tracks by better-known groups like Everclear, Yo La Tengo, and The Chemical Brothers, listeners to MFCR were treated to the social commentary of Landscape Body Machine's "No Cable," or the Dead Kennedys' "Kinky Sex Makes the World Go 'Round." Classics of avant-rock radical chic, these songs generally parody consumer passivity with a healthy mixture of political theory and punk attitude. While the region's two or three sanctioned radio stations offered up their usual mix of local news, soporific oldies, and new country, Bleek spun California plunder supergroup Negativland's outlawed "U2," a song that features hitmeister Casey Kasem repeating the glib phrase "That's the letter U and the numeral 2" while a muted chorus hums the tune to Bono's well-known dirge "I Still Haven't Found What I'm Looking For." Heady stuff for the rural backwater of Merritt.

Pirate radio's recent roots can be traced to the ground-breaking activism of WTRA, founded to serve the ghetto of Springfield, Illinois, in 1986. The activist spirit of what became known as Black Liberation Radio spread around the United States and eventually found a home in the foothills near San Francisco with the foundation of Stephen Dunifer's Free Radio Berkeley movement and his attempts to legitimize independent radio in America and around the world. The fact that Bleek found the wherewithal to create his own vaguely pathetic version of pirate radio speaks to the power of lifestyle culture's grassroots ethos. The airwaves, like the Internet, are one of the few access points into mass culture available to the individual. As a result, pirate radio stations, like websites, continue to proliferate. But while all pirate radio efforts represent the movement toward cultural redemption embodied in lifestyle culture, the solitary efforts of Bleek were a response to a need considerably different from the ones that inspired WTRA and Free Radio Berkeley. The TV generations have picked up on pirate radio not as a way to give voice to an under-represented, aggrieved community, nor as an attempt to radicalize and organize, but as yet another way to answer the siren call of pop culture. Bleek turned to pirate radio and the lingua franca of plunder as a way to articulate his desire to fashion an individual identity out of mass culture—despite the fact that his white, male, middle-class, thirty-something self is well served, being the biggest target market in the world.

What is missing for Bleek in the vast array of diversions that claim to speak for him? One might argue that within the structures of the mass media, no matter how many Speaker's Corner segments and e-mails and letters are aired, it all comes down to the fact that a relative few are in control of what gets said, purportedly on our behalf. The language of plunder is a radical recognition of the inherent difficulty of conveying individual and personal truths via mass culture. No matter how inclusive and supportive mass culture tries to be, there will always be people who feel shut out, voiceless, powerless. The nature of any medium of mass communication is to equalize. We are all equal under the watchful gaze of television. And yet we are also somehow reduced. We are represented, true, but in such a way that, even as we are being entertained or informed, we feel we are also being grouped together, penned in, fattened up for the slaughter. The Italian semiotician Umberto Eco puts it this way:

> Faced by the prospect of a communication network that expands to embrace the universe, every citizen of the world becomes a member of a new proletariat. But no revolutionary manifesto could rally this proletariat. . . . Even if the communications media, as a means of production, were to change masters, the situation of subjection would not change. We can legitimately suspect that the communications media would be alienating even if they belonged to the community.

Mass media is inherently alienating. There is a significant gap between our lives lived in the cesspool of pop and the luxurious days beside the pristinely chlorinated pool that pop promises. So how do we attempt to confront the alienation and disaffection and solitude we perceive in that gap? The answer, for me, is found in ideas associated with plunder—ideas that can be located in the kind of somnambulistic pirate radio that Bleek undertook in Merritt.

Like the boys of Braino, like the Evel Knievel obsessive, like the participants of Active Resistance and the majority of less overtly militant creatives who want to bite into the pie but not necessarily bake a whole new one, Bleek is motivated by something much harder to express in words and deeds than, for example, economic hardship. Bleek's plunder-inspired antics are a lifestyle, not a way of life. They are what McLuhan describes as a "total involvement in all-inclusive nowness that occurs in young lives via TV's mosaic image." This distinction between lifestyle and life becomes ever more important when we realize that, while relatively few people put it all on the line making illegal music in the style of Negativland or the hardcore dance pirate DJs of London, England, who face threats to their livelihood and their liberty for their endeavours, these activities create a ripple effect: the confrontational, highly charged satire of Negativland played on the well-mannered, quasi-illegal, too-small-even-to-bother-with MFCR.

"I just thought I would do it until I got some kind of reaction. I'm not really sure what kind," Bleek tells me after my phone call wakes him from a day nap. (Like many of our lifestyle culture entrepreneurs, Bleek doesn't have a regular job. When I talked to him in spring 1999, he was driving a disabled child to and from Vancouver once a week, and had a part-time thing painting little desk clocks for a local craft operation. He was also spending quite a lot of time working on *Speck* and its website.) "I got quite a bit of good feedback from people. Unfortunately nobody lived close enough to be able to hear it. It went for two to three blocks or so."

Every night for almost a year, Bleek was broadcasting an illegal radio show that barely extended past his own driveway. All that energy expended, and for what? Why even bother? But Bleek sees it a different way: "My idea of proper radio is everyone would be doing this, transmitting, then we'd have a real choice . . . things that wouldn't occur to you that you were going to hear. I think that's where radio ought to be. It should be always changing."

Bleek didn't proselytize or reveal himself when doing the show. He rarely spoke on MFCR, only occasionally piping up to identify the songs we just heard and make oblique statements like "You're listening to Merritt Free Cast Radio . . . a station owned and operated entirely by . . . me." Part of this, no doubt, has to do with the fact that for Bleek, as for the stunt-jumper enthusiast, his endeavours constitute personal challenges that seem meaningless outside of the context of his life and needs. Operating without a constituency and with an artist's passion, Bleek was all alone out there, a solitary voice happy to be lost between the points on the dial.

At the best of times, Bleek's microtransmitter couldn't have broadcast more than a couple of miles. His largest listenership on any given evening was probably something like twenty people. On some nights, probably nobody was listening at all. If Bleek were in an urban centre, his simple broadcast would have had the potential to reach hundreds, even thousands. Which is beside the point. Reaching people was somehow secondary to MFCR. Bleek spoke of his desire for some kind of response from the outside world. In the end he got it, but it seemed as much a reason to give up on the project as anything else. I'll let him tell the story:

I was in Kamloops one day picking up a group of students that had gone on a retreat and we just happened to be walking around and we saw [MuchMusic VJ] Sook-Yin Lee doing an interview with a transsexual having a garage sale. So we went up and met them and she asked a bunch of questions and we said you gotta come out to Merritt, we've got zines, we've even got a pirate radio station. . . . Eventually MuchMusic came to my house and took pictures of the system and everything. It was ridiculous, completely ridiculous. It was silly. You know, when you're being interviewed on TV you miss some things, things you wish you would have thought of—like, I think video music stinks, it's a terrible way of exposing and presenting music, it's selling fashion, it's not selling anything original. But I thought I'd do it, I thought it would be fun. I was kinda hyped about it. But then there were a bunch of teenagers and zinesters in my house waiting to meet these people—and I thought, this is silly—is what I'm doing here on this grand a scale? It's not, it's really not. I should have been more low-key about things. A couple of positive things that might have come out of it is that somebody may have seen it and been inspired to do something like that. I sort of felt, isn't this funny how I duped MuchMusic?—but I don't know if I did.

Bleek is never quite sure why he bothered in the first place. He wants to be recognized, he wants to think he put one over on "the man," but, in the end, he senses that in some fundamental way our capacity for overt rebellion through the structures of the mass media are severely limited. For Bleek, sending out pirate radio to no one was a subtle form of cultural plunder, of speaking a language that is rebellious when whispered but ridiculous when said out loud. Despite the fact that he was working in a format that, theoretically, could allow him to broadcast to thousands, he was actually embarrassed when he got his chance to do just that via MuchMusic. It was as if seeing himself on TV made him realize that MFCR was an assertion of a private, personal act of dissent—not the public affirmation of our pop love affair that it was being made out to be. Like most of us, Bleek wants to have a voice, wants to see and hear himself, is tired of feeling alienated and reduced. And yet, he intuitively knows that the answer is not just to become what he disdains. In a way, his confusion is emblematic of what it means to plunder, what it means to whisper the language of pop to ourselves. Though it might accomplish little in terms of actually creating lasting works of art or new methods of communication, the very act of *doing* has a significance. What matters is that somewhere, somehow, the new language of mass culture is being spoken—plundered.

This fluctuating, ever-present underground desire is the heart of plunder. It's the heart of pirate radio, the heart of our search for forms of music, writing, and image that can encompass our mass culture without validating its capacity to alienate us. Plunder is the connective tissue of lifestyle culture. It's also a noble sentiment that infuses everything it touches with the kind of contradictory possibilities that lifestyle culture suggests. "I did it because I love the music and was hoping that it would inspire somebody to try it, to go out there and do it," Bleek says, echoing one of the founders of Springfield's WTRA who, when asked how people could support their quest not to be shut down by the U.S. government, responded: "Go on the air! Just go on the air!"

■ ■ ■

In the world of pop music, we can trace the origins of plunder back to the early 1980s, when synthesizer music, sampling, and the auteur record producer, who could remix and re-imagine the work of "the artist" to produce something note-perfect and radio-ready, were taking hold. From the Art of Noise to Herbie Hancock, something different and vaguely repellent was happening to pop music at that time—it was the Muzaking of rock, the soundtrack for a vapid new age. At the same time, this proliferating use of keyboards and drum machines, combined with the motif of recognizable quotations lifted from old songs, was laying the groundwork for new possibilities. "Prior to rap," writes music scholar Tricia Rose, "the most desirable use of a sample was to mask the sample and its origin; to bury its identity. Rap producers have inverted this logic, using samples as a point of reference, as a means by which the process of repetition and recontextualization can be highlighted and privileged."

As rap and hip-hop and dance techniques proliferated and became popular, lawsuits mushroomed, and it became obvious that mass culture's ability to borrow from itself was a challenge to the old standards of copyright and ownership. It was corporate mass culture's relentless marketing and hit-making that created situations in which the relationship between artist and audience became one of almost equal ownership: songs were marketed as symbols of rebellion, of freedom, signifiers that were intended not only to entertain but to connect to the primal stuff of our lives. Stadium rock sold not a song but a personality, a way of acting, an overall experience, an event that represented something much bigger than a star belting out a hit to twenty thousand people. "The majority of fans don't go to see the artist," said the late famed California concert promoter Bill Graham, "but to be in the presence of the artist, to share space with the artist."

Just as the principle of lifestyle culture involves the way we take the miscellany of pop and use it not as entertainment but as a fundamental aspect of our lives, so too must plunder rely on the belief that somehow, somewhere, this stuff matters. In pop, the song, divorced from its creator's intentions, takes on a life of its own. Archetypal stadium hitmeister Bruce Springsteen put it this way in 1984: "The song 'Born to Run' means a lot more to me now than it did [in 1974]. I can sing it tonight and feel like it breathes in all those extra years. It's one of the most emotional moments of the night. I can see all those people and that song to them is like—that's their song, man. It's almost as much the audience's as it is mine."

The rise of sampling, then, must be seen in its larger context as the natural evolution of pop from singular event to broader life experience. As a grassroots phenomenon, sampling was something that record companies could neither ignore nor prevent, largely because it was preceded by several decades in which audiences willingly believed that they owned the music, that the songs of their pop stars were, in some sense, their songs. At the same time, music was becoming artificial, generic, lacking the wounded grandiosity of old-style stars like Springsteen.

Today, the idea of a direct connection between us and our pop artists remains, though the questions of ownership and artistic integrity and corporate profit-mongering force us to constantly reevaluate the artist's allegiance to us, the fans. And so we respond to that instant parody, the pop song, by turning it into something else—either materially, by sampling its core, or spiritually, by evoking it in our lives in ways that are counter to the spirit(less) world in which the capitalist mantra is applied to art.

The pop music industry opened the doors, made it possible to question the authenticity of every piano chord and high-pitched wail and riff. Is it really that surprising that the contents of this Pandora's box of electronic subjectivity would spread, take hold, develop in ways that were as unimaginable then as they are unimpressive now, some twenty years later? Today, we fall on pop like the hungry cannibals we are, willing and able to taste our own flesh, unsure of what we could possibly be made of. Just as sampling has stolen ideas from collage and pastiche, plunder has built a foundation on sampling and extended the search for a new mass culture language that encompasses our ongoing quest to authenticate our lifestyle culture lives.

■ ■ ■

A crucial moment in the evolution (revolution?) came in 1989, the year I started my studies as an undergraduate at the University of Toronto. While I was swilling beer and tormenting my roommate by repeatedly blasting the Jane's Addiction tune "Been Caught Stealing Once" into the wee hours of the night, elsewhere in Toronto one of the pioneers of plunder, John Oswald, was crossing more serious boundaries. That year, Oswald, musician and music theorist, put out his radical restatement of rock 'n' roll in the form of the now legendary *Plunderphonics* CD. Now, before I go on, I should say that "plunderphonics" has also become a recognizable term "coined to cover the counter culture world of converted sound and retrofitted music." A "plunderphonic," according to Andrew Jones, former music editor of Montreal's alternative weekly newspaper *The Mirror* and author of a book about experimental music, "is an unofficial but recognizable musical quote." Oswald himself describes this process as one in which "collective melodic memories of the familiar are mined and rehabilitated to a new life."

The CD *Plunderphonics* was the natural evolution of Oswald's developing philosophy, which he has been diligently exploring since the foundation, in the early 1980s, of his unassumingly named Mystery Tape Laboratory. The CD consists of a series of songs employing recognizable—though radically remixed—snippets from the oeuvres of pop stars such as Michael Jackson and Dolly Parton. *Plunderphonics* was a startling repudiation of the pop ethos, a deliberate, daring effort to re-imagine mass culture. The cover featured Michael himself, appearing as a naked woman from the neck down. To make a long story short, Jackson's CBS Records was aggrieved. They launched an action against Oswald and promptly forced him to destroy the roughly three hundred remaining copies of the CD. (Hundreds, however, had already been sent out to colleagues, college radio stations, and stores.) It was a grim, bleak response to Oswald's argument expressed in a 1988 article in *Keyboard* magazine: "Music is information and, as such, is a renewable resource. Intellectual real estate is infinitely divisible. The big difference between the taking of physical property and the taking of intellectual property is that in the latter case the original owner doesn't lose the property. They still have it. Theft only occurs when the owner is deprived of credit."

Well, not according to CBS Records, and, a few years later, Island Records, who sued the aforementioned Negativland in 1991 at the behest of Irish supergroup U2 (The results were the same: destruction of the CDs and the master tapes, though both recordings are available if you search around a bit.) Now Oswald's argument might be moot as far as the record industry and the courts are concerned, but in the world of independent culture, his point was well taken. Plunderphonics—the concept, the technique, the aesthetic—began to proliferate.

"These are symbols in our unconscious," explains John Magyar, one of the organizers of a 1998 Toronto plunder music festival. "They are our emotions—they are like a language—like the English language. It's natural, it's the obvious thing to do. We're all artists playing with the tools given to us. We recover, reassemble, send it out again." The industry's reluctant acknowledgment that sanctioned plunder was inevitable made us wonder to what extent cultural products could be said to be owned in the traditional sense. Who owns what portion of the mental environment? This is the question that plunder asks. It's a question central to our lifestyle culture desire to assert ownership over our own lives. It's a question that challenges not just the right of corporations and pop stars to own their own songs, but the right, for instance, of governments to claim ownership over the airwaves (which are then doled out to the highest bidder). "The most significant result of the recent innovations in pop production lies in the progressive removal of any immanent criteria for distinguishing between human and automated performance," warns pop critic Andrew Goodwin. "Associated with this there is, of course, a crisis of authorship."

As the idea of approximating familiar riffs and beats, or amalgamating several different songs into one new song, took hold first in clubs, then on rap records and dance records, and finally in every conceivable form of popular music, arguments over who owned what became extremely difficult to articulate. "A crisis of authorship" became imminent. With Oswald and Negativland, the matter was pushed farther down the path of cultural reclamation, resolved to the satisfaction of the corporate bean-counters and roving bands of lawyers, but not to the satisfaction of new generations of creators who find, in the legacy of John Oswald, a resurgent, revelatory struggle to assert individuality over conformity.

Negativland and the band's main protagonist, Mark Hosler, have continued to rail against the establishment. After five plants refused to press their 1998 CD release *Over the Edge, Volume 3: The Weatherman's Dumb Stupid Come Out Line*, Hosler raged to *The Washington Post*: "The idea that there's a gray area, that there's some instance where somebody should not be profiting from someone else's transformative reuse of their work is anathema to them. . . . If you have a world where your culture is privately owned by those gigantic transnational corporations, that's a bad thing for art, for science, for creativity."

As the angry elder statesman of plunder, no one could have expressed more cogently why plunderphonics continues to lure devotees. Our universal urge toward lifestyle culture is one that has less to do with recognizing our manipulation than it does with revelling in and appreciating and accepting and validating those who allow themselves to be manipulated, entertained, appealed to. That's why it seems to me that the most successful acts of plunder occur just below the surface—an idea spreading almost by accident that, nonetheless, contains within it a sense of purpose. Bleek's pirate radio station, Oswald's *Plunderphonics*—these were as much acts of celebration as they were acts of larceny. Plunderphonics as a musical device, pirate radio as a legitimate, zine-like way to put forth your ideas—these ideas found their way into pop culture not because of political agitation, not because someone told us they were good for us, but because they were, first and foremost, something to do. Something fun to do that became, unconsciously—the way a baby learns to speak—a way to talk about the world around us.

"I am one of those," states pioneering musical experimenter Chris Cutler, "who is convinced that a music for our own times, a music that might have a chance to find hope, give pleasure, bring meaning to consciousness of the present, must be made from new means and through new relations that make the present what it is."

"The absolute fake is offspring of the unhappy awareness of a present without depth," warns Umberto Eco.

"It excites me that there is actually music that is illegal," says plunderer Marc Gunderson. "It's stunning and exciting and kind of motivational as well." Gunderson, like Bleek, is a quiet fellow. He lives in Columbus, Ohio, and though he's obsessed with plunder music and spends most of his free time pursuing his project, the Evolution Control Committee (ECC), he limits his activities: he has a day job and releases

WE WANT SOME TOO

tapes and CDs in a low-key, semi-clandestine manner that he hopes will keep him safe from litigation. Gunderson marries the high-drama political terrorism of Negativland with the sonic whimsy of Oswald to create funny, fused songs that don't shy away from the recognizable: "14 'original' violations of copyright for your manipulated enjoyment" is how he describes his *Gunderphonics* tape, which arrives jammed into an old eight-track cassette case. Highlights of the tape include an ingenious wedding of Public Enemy's "Rebel Without A Pause" with the sappy samba of Herb Alpert and the Tijuana Brass. He also savages George Bush, Led Zeppelin, and, of course, the perennial plunder target, U2. The result is an entertaining, biting tape put together on a $150 Teac W-450R dual-cassette deck. And what motivates him to spend his time making tapes that blatantly mock copyright while paying homage to the pioneers of plunder? In defence of plunder, he argues that "corporate culture is leading us away from common sense." The more corporations try to limit our creativity, he argues, the more they are failing to see that they cannot copyright the ephemera that makes up our day-to-day lives. "It's common sense for us to do this. Kids making a collage with pictures from a magazine are making illegal art. . . . We're surrounded by cultural detritus no matter where we look. . . .We want to fight back, turn the tables— we don't have to be the unwitting consumers of this, we can reflect it back."

Marc Gunderson is a relatively normal guy. It's not like he's out on the street passing out tracts, looking for converts to the Church of Plunder. These are not people who spend their time biting the heads off chickens or plotting armed revolution. In another time, in another place, they would never have become plunderers, foot-soldiers on the long march to cultural redemption. But in our world of exclusivity and alienation they have sought and found ways to express themselves, ways that are at once harmless and dangerous, subversive and silly. They have looked for a language to express their alienation, affirm their individuality, and found that the best way to say what they have to say is by manipulating the past tense into the immediacy of plunderphonics.

Caught in the struggle to "make the present what it is," our plunderers lurch from one project to the next, launching attacks on a friendly, unsuspecting populace made up of friends, neighbours, progressive rock stars of the 1980s, presidents of the United States. In plunder, no one is safe, no one is martyred, only the truth is dogged, footnoted, harassed, and encumbered with the search for a new language of absolute fakes and instant memories.

■   ■   ■

As I was working on writing something intelligible about plunderphonics, I received a CD in the mail from Essential Media, a Los Angeles–based catalogue/website of "counterculture" (yes, they take credit cards). The disc in question was called *Deconstructing Beck*, and it was devoted to, as promised, plundering the songs of the depressed California slacker best known for the tune "I'm a loser baby . . . so why don'tcha kill me?" Featuring thirteen different contributors including our pal Marc Gunderson's ECC, it's also a horrendous hour of noise. If I had to describe it politely, I would call it "interesting." The CD represents a project taken to its inevitable conclusion: it's a dead end of ambient noise shrieks and stolen Beck clips that shows what happens when lifestyle culture moves from being an individual, largely unorganized event to being a deliberately political assault. The fact is, plunder as a concept continues to evolve, leaving the overt, often deliberately unmusical world of plunderphonics well behind.

Ironically, the music of Beck is one of the best examples of the way the aesthetic of plunder, but not its painful pastiche technique, is asserting itself in the creative acts of the TV generations. The place where plunder evolves/disappears into the mainstream of mass culture is not in the *Deconstructing Beck* CD, but in the work of Beck himself. In pop music today it is not plunderphonics that takes up the mantle of plunder but the still-developing genre of music that has been named "post-rock."

Since at least 1994, reinvented electro-slacker cum folk star Beck has waxed nostalgic, making music that embraces everything from the electric acoustics of Bob Dylan to the spacey grooves of The Stone Roses. These are cunning albums that allude to the possibilities of plunder without boring us to death with them. The songs fuse into one elegiac whole that reminds us of something we can't quite articulate. And yet, the albums refuse to give in to nostalgia, to the idea of the instant pop past as somewhere better than where we are now. When Beck sings "the world is a holiday/smoking in an old ash tray/they just blow it out their nose and say okay/so let's try and make it last/the past is still the past/and tomorrow is just another crazy scam," he is peeling back the layers of the past until he reaches the thin fake skin of future. We're all dead, dying, doomed to a life of indulgence and meaningless indolence. Go on holiday. Smoke another cigarette. Nothing matters, because nothing is real. In pop, the search for what matters has no beginning and no end. Authenticity is just another bad joke we're all in on. "You can't write a pure country song anymore," he told *The New York Times*, discussing his 1998 album *Mutations*. "You can't write a pure Appalachian ballad. Because we live in a world where we've all heard speed metal, we've all heard drum-and-bass, we've all heard old-school hip-hop. Even if you're not influenced by it or you're not using elements of it, they're in your mind. That's why I called the album *Mutations*, because it's trying to embrace the evolution, embrace the impurity of the music."

We can link Beck's aesthetic of impurity to an ever-expanding ethos influenced by the language of plunder. Musical genres like post-rock, alt-country, Braino's jazz-punk, and hip-hop/dance/electronica continue to explore plunder, as do new forms of writing, visual art, and film. Profound, subversive, and personal, the grammar of plunder is apparent in much of this work, though not always plunder's abrasive vocabulary.

■　　■　　■

Alternative country (alt-country) is a kind of nihilistic merging of punk and pop with country and folk. It is a subgenre of post-rock, notable as one of the best spaces to explore the way the language of plunder continues to evolve and fuel our quest for what can be said to be authentic in the pop world. Alt-country takes the gritty honesty of country music at its best and merges it with the reflexive irony and soundscape moodiness of the late-twentieth-century urban experience. Here, authenticity is a sound, not an accent or a place of birth. Think of these acts as doing for the classic country of Hank Williams and Johnny Cash (who got into the alt-country phenomenon with his deadpan cover of Soundgarden's hit "Rusty Cage") what Shane MacGowan and The Pogues did for traditional Irish music. In the same way that The Pogues' violent, raucous sound both harkened back to an illusory past and promised an apocalyptic future, alt-country bands like Toronto's Sadies manipulate sly references to steel guitar, good old boys, and "Little Miss Sadie" so that they seem not retrograde but cathartic, a way of reclaiming the pompous pop of the past and restating it.

What's exciting about alt-country, besides the fact that many of the great new musicians and songwriters are stray-ing into this territory, is the way the genre (or the anti-genre) communicates so much information through the simple form of the pop song. This is not Jimmie Rodgers hopping freight trains with a free-spirited yodel. This is suave, jaded, post-everything rock 'n' roll that captures a moody abandon-ment—a few strums of the guitar and crooning vocals and you cannot help but be drawn into this hazy world where everything new is flaked with a coat of rust. Along with Beck, college rock faves like Iowa's Will Oldham and his ever-fluctuating Palace project are quintessential examples of alt-country's longing for a simpler pop past that never existed. Palace features cryptic but somehow instantly evocative vocals delivered in a warbling monotone and backed by reluc-tantly amplified guitar, bass, drums. The result is a restatement of what we know, a backwards march forward, a random actualizing of the slacker sensibility. "It is longing that I feel to be missed or to be real," croons Oldham on the *Palace Brothers* album as we nod into a defeated slump, high on the musical equivalent of a post-modern suicide.

For a bigger, less precious, more expansive sound that utilizes the language of plunder, we can turn to jazz-punk—an expansive, cinematic music that quotes film and television and pop music genres, creating, in the process, whole new dizzying worlds. Along with Braino, Montreal's acclaimed godspeed you black emperor! is a good example. It is a band featuring upwards of fifteen members with a line-up includ-ing classical string instruments like cello and violin—plus the traditional electric guitar, bass, and drums. Their first and best album (titled $\int a \infty$) was noticed across the western world, singled out for its moody, creeping sound. The album builds slowly, a brusque voice informing us that "The government is corrupt and we're all so many drunks with the radio on and the curtains drawn./We are trapped in the belly of this horrible machine/and the machine is bleeding to death. . . ." Then the band kicks in, pushing a rhythmic, potent, instrumental chorus over the top like earth on a coffin. David Bryant of godspeed describes the first album as "a movie without pictures."

■　　■　　■

The 1960s and '70s gave us collaged films that juxtaposed jarring images with the intent of shocking us and turning us away from the spectacle of mass culture and consumer society. Thus the title of French situationist Guy Debord's 1973 film *Society of the Spectacle*. ("Returns by request!" an e-mail press release from Vancouver art-house Blinding Light informs me in 1999.) The film uses a barrage of clips from movies, porn, TV ads, and new footage that would make any music video director jealous. Similarly, Canada's great, pioneering experimental filmmaker Arthur Lipsett made films like 21-87 and *Very Nice, Very Nice* in the early 1960s before he left the National Film Board. Lipsett's critique of consumerism, his visceral fear of what we have become, would have been much better understood at the end of the century. As it is, he died an unknown, leaving us a handful of haunting, collaged films that move effortlessly from a woman masked in her own make-up, to a crowded street, to monkeys in a cage, to the filmmaker and his bearded buddies pretend-shooting each other. Lipsett's and Debord's films are the ahead-of-their-time equivalents to a plunderphonics technique in which we are repeatedly slapped with our own complicity. The films are acts of violence that leave us, strangely enough, still standing to leave when the lights go up. Films from a time when the electronic age was just taking hold, they are not speaking to us in a new communal babel, but, instead, employing a foreign tongue to show us how strange we've become.

Nevertheless, these films, and many others like them, have allowed plunder as a visual strategy to proliferate. We see plunder daily in our frenetic music videos, on "The Simpsons" ("Itchy and Scratchy" and the beefed-up, verbally challenged tough guy McBain), or in "South Park" (the flatulent cartoon within a cartoon featuring the "Canadians" Terence and Philip). Plunder is also evident in post-modern shows like "Seinfeld" that disrupt the conventions of the sitcom (one episode starts with the credits and ends with the opening) and employ a non-stop barrage of pop culture references with the effect of refreshing the trite conventions of mass culture that, ironically, make plunder (and lifestyle culture) so prevalent and possible.

Not surprisingly, though, the most relevant and heart-rending use of the plunder aesthetic in film and video occurs on the edge of narrative, where experimental film meets the details of our daily lives. Sadie Benning (dubbed the Pixelvision Priestess for her use of the infamous Fisher-Price movie camera) locates her adolescent antiheroine at the heart of a vapid pop culture nexus in her accomplished 1998 independent release *Flat Is Beautiful*. While Mom screws her beefy, shallow boyfriend and absent art-scenester Dad calls from overseas, eleven-year-old Taylor plays endless rounds of some low-tech video game, watches Michael Jackson on MTV, and consumes junk food. It's the 1980s in Benning's hometown of Milwaukee, and the film is a strangled, whispered search for what was real in a despairing childhood as preprocessed as a Twinkie. Shot in grainy black-and-white Super-8 film and colour video, the details of Taylor's pastimes slowly take on the cadence of confinement—her house is a prison, the TV is a lie, the video games give her nightmares of alien invasions. Throughout the film, the characters wear flat masks, painted-on faces displaying blank smiles. The film bombards us with apparently tangential visual information, forcing us to realize how easily the specificity of our lives can be evoked and then discarded. Plunder at its most poignant, its most fearsome.

■   ■   ■

While film affords the luxury of instant access to our visual culture, writing has the advantages of suggestion and distance. In the new forms of plundered writing, a single paragraph can rip through fifty years of pop culture history, evoking sitcoms and Disneyland and Kerouac and a death in the family with a pathos and oblique imprecision that most closely approximates the flow of images as they speed past our

cosmetic contact lenses and into our dizzy minds. It's no accident that writing in zines is moving toward a kind of meta-
referential language that circumvents traditional narrative in
favour of the possibilities of plunder (remember Jeffrey
Mackie's frenetic Jaclyn Smith poem from *Junkfood Architecture?*). Of course, there will always be critics, like the retrograde Neil Postman, who see the written word as the last
bastion of civilized, logical thought. Writes our surly authority:

> On the one hand, there is the world of the printed
> word with its emphasis on logic, sequence, history,
> exposition, objectivity, detachment and discipline.
> On the other, there is the world of television with its
> emphasis on imagery, narrative, presentness, simul-
> taneity, intimacy, immediate gratification and quick
> emotional response.

But new—and even not so new—generations of writers
are responding to the challenge of the televised by finding
ways to articulate the visual immediacy of our mental environment. In this writing you won't find an emphasis on se-
quence and history and logic. Instead, our need to connect, to
assert the truth of lifestyle culture, is brought to the forefront.
In the same way that Sadie Benning depicts a childhood lost
in a whirl of video games, cheesie poofs, and sodas, so too do
a new generation of writers evoke a sensibility with no locus,
fusing childhood memories with mass culture addictions. The
stories coming out of the writers of the TV generations call

upon the bank of visual images already deposited in our minds, that giant video store of prefab moments that need only be mentioned to be instantly recalled. Thus Governor General's Award nominee Elyse Gasco can begin a story:

> It's a different time and it's one of those homes for girls, a place for pregnant girls to go away to and have their babies quietly, a convent type thing where it is hoped that all the hushed holiness will keep the girls from heaving and grunting too loudly. One of those places. You know. You've seen the same movies I have.

Or, from the critically acclaimed, younger, and more adventurous Golda Fried:

> Three goth guys are at a table with their over-stuffed knapsacks and strapped up mouths. There's three of them. They're probably in the same band. So are you in a band?
>
> I don't care that they're too beautiful for me. Or that they probably want blowjobs. Or that there's a really boring spoken word artist on stage who we're supposed to be listening to.
>
> I dream I am a butterfly landing on three white statues of Greek gods in a New Orleans cemetery.

Before the TV era, both of the above passages would have been difficult to comprehend. But now, even something as fragmented as the Fried excerpt is an affable invitation to enter a world where the little things are always at stake, where every encounter is a semiotic plunge into the heart of pop culture. We move from Greek gods, to New Orleans, to three Goth guys, to the dull spoken-word artist with ease because each of us holds in our minds a preconception of what Greek gods and New Orleans cemeteries and Goth kids look like. No need for further description here. And yet, there is a gruesome disaffection in this passage, a not so nice evocation of what it's like to be always out of kilter, to be always keeling toward some miscellaneous mass image. In this tender book of stories, the characters are always looking for their lives, their friends, their guitars. What they find, instead, is the temporary uncertainty that drives plunder forward.

Fried, by the way, was a Montreal zinester before she was a book author. Similarly, Sonja Ahlers of Victoria, B.C., put out a profusion of intricate little chapbooks before having her work collected and published by upstart indie publisher Insomniac Press in a book called *Temper, Temper*. Words appear only in fragments in Ahler's project. She works with a mass of symbolic pop culture hieroglyphs, fusing drawings, handwritten and typewritten bits of prose, snippets from magazines, and instantly recognizable headlines like "no hard feelings." The wing of a dragonfly. A bodiless self-portrait. The scribbled lines: "I can't kill myself tonite 'cause I have to work tomorrow." This is the new literature, our lives as plundered by-products, more evocative than many a thousand-page novel adorned with lavish descriptions of places we've already been, people we already recognize, plots we're already bored with. "It's a generational thing," Ahlers says of her work's unconventional method of storytelling. "I'm trying to tell the story, but the idea of plot is elusive."

*Frenetic collage and whimsical poetry
meet in the work of Sonja Ahlers.*

Incorporating graphics and text into new ways of communicating isn't all so despairing, though. There's a lot of hilarity in these books, and in many of the other printed projects that swirl around the nexus of mass culture. One of my favourites is a zine tribute to Mr. T put out by the good people of Vancouver's Rubber Popsicle Factory. Entitled *Pity the Fool*, each page is a reinvention of that angry 1980s icon best known for his role on "The A-Team" ("I ain't getting on no plane, Hannibal!"). Another one of my favourites is a zine

Some of the many zines that plunder our collective pop consciousness and have a good time in the process.

that consists of images and found moments from the "Bionic Woman" oeuvre, including the board game, the novel, and Lindsay Wagner's appearances on talk shows. There are hundreds, even thousands, of these offhand projects kicking around living rooms and basements across North America. I've seen similar tributes to the fast-food cherub Big Boy, to various superheroes, and to other marginal and not so marginal cultural icons. Fusing the whimsy of pop culture iconography and the desire to somehow humanize and reassess the icons stuck in our minds like bad jingles, these projects represent the way we are inventing "a written language that approximates the oral and offends the literate."

■   ■   ■

I n all these projects, there is the attempt to find a language, a way of speaking, that can convey what is authentic and true about mass culture as it appears in our memories and everyday lives. There is the sense that somewhere in the far reaches of falsity there must be an authenticity. Just as people now locate a truth in the artifice of, say, Jap-pop culture—collecting Hello Kitty lunchboxes and Sailor Moon colouring books and Pokémon cards/characters, all imbued with an edgy plastic anti-nostalgia, a sense of instant history—so too does the lifestyle culture movement merge with the possibilities of remixology to speak through plunder to the undiscovered country of complete and total artifice.

This is easily demonstrated when we look at what the visual/performance artists of the TV generations are up to. Brash youngsters Art Club 2000 make the scene in a New York gallery, displaying their Gap concept art exhibit, a satiric in-joke that includes making the gallery look like a Gap store, pseudo-fashion-shoot glossies of the gang dressed up in Gap outfits, and an analysis of the garbage ("garbology") of your average Gap outlet. Swiss-based Jerelyn Hanrahan tours the world with her Gesture as Value bank machine, a money dispenser adjusted to accept and spit out "gestures"—artist-fashioned "bills" that aren't worth much at the local liquor store. Ottawa's Germaine Koh finds snapshots in the garbage, converts them to postcards that evoke the generic (sub)urban life we all share with each other, and then sells them back to us. Juniper Tedhams of Austin, Texas, converts Chicago's

"One of the 33 photographs found June 1993, north-east corner of 11 Street and Avenue B, New York," Germaine Koh

"One of the 38 photographs found December 1995, east side of King Edward Avenue between York and Clarence Streets, Ottawa," Germaine Koh

Randolph Street Gallery into a *faux* mall display for her forty-eight projects—the "good things" that lifestyle magazine *Martha Stewart Living* recommends bored women produce for their own edification (including the fan trellis and valentine lollipops). New Zealand's Fiona Jack puts up billboards selling Nothing™, and over one-third of Auckland's population sees her advertisements. Art students at Leeds University "perform" a holiday to Costa del Sol, Spain, inviting their faculty to the "opening" at the

Leeds Airport; guests arrive just in time to observe the students, decked out in gaudy tourist gear and sporting simulated tans and fake snapshots, emerging through a customs gate. Russian expatriates Komar and Melamid poll the citizens of various countries on their art preferences, and paint the results of each country's most- and least-preferred canvas; they release a CD and book to support their art-for-the-people inclinations. In Sackville, New Brunswick, Fredette Frame hires a plane to fly over town pulling a banner that asks: "Oh my god am I here all alone?"

At the turn of the century, portraying the world of stuff is not just a priority but an international series of incidents. These happenings in the art world reveal to what lengths creative action has become an attempt to use the language of plunder as a way to give voice to that entity that has grown up between our lives and our stuff. "I'm interested," says Juniper Tedhams, whose exhibit of Martha Stewart crafts garnered her plenty of press, "in authoring desire equivalent to the desire I see created in magazines." Tedhams wants to do something other than satirize the unfulfilled desire at the heart of lifestyle culture; she wants to pay homage to it by reconstructing it. We pay homage to the gods of style; we collect and arrange and rearrange and hope that what we are doing makes some kind of sense. The Museum of Bad Art, the artists discussed here, the zinester, the fanatic PEZ-dispenser collector, all challenge the dissemination of product as product. But they also challenge our traditional conception of art as something more than product. Was

Warhol's soup can a visionary restatement, the first verb of a plunder language more and more of us are turning to in order to convey an understanding of our store-bought lives? To put ourselves in the hands of our product revisionists is to take another look at the stuff around us. It is to admit that we must find some way to reconcile ourselves to our ugly world of stuff, a world where only we can confer authority on our lives, on the things that make up our lives. "Beauty is boring," proclaims the Toronto artist/activist Sally McKay, whose solo exhibit at the Art Gallery of Ontario consisted of a mock collection of Fisher-Price kiddie phones and heaps of Ernie and Bert dolls. "Art on its own isn't that interesting."

Heaps of Ernie and Bert dolls from artist Sally McKay's show in the Art Gallery of Ontario.

∎ ∎ ∎

Once, Bob Dylan "embodied a yearning for peace and home in the midst of noise and upheaval." Now, Beck and our other plunder pioneers embody the possibility of authentic noise and upheaval in the face of a pacified, commodified, "peaceful" collective homogenization that leaves us placeless, faceless, rootless. Picking up on the retrograde critic's longing for "the old ways," plunder exposes this longing as far more primal and desperate, forcing us to realize that we can no longer "share space with the artist" because we are all the artist. "The artist" no longer exists.

Even our celebrities are starting to recognize the difficulty of maintaining their personas in the world of an instant lifestyle culture. Minneapolis's resident pop star abandoned the moniker Prince in favour of a series of symbols defined in the press as "the artist formerly known as Prince," then settled into his current incarnation known simply as The Artist. The name changes mirror his transition from a corporate pop star to an obscure indie music innovator with his own record label selling songs off the web in MP3 format.

Prince, I suspect, didn't come to MP3 randomly. MP3 is, in fact, another concrete aspect of our plunder ethos. Essentially a digital format that allows one to download songs from the Internet with the exact quality one gets from a store-bought CD, it represents a new wave of technologies that attempt to capitalize on, and at the same time placate, our growing need for self-determination. MP3 is part of our ongoing dialogue with those who preside over pop culture. On the one hand, we want to move toward technology that enhances our ability to assert "consumer choice." MP3, dial-up movies via cyber-optic cable, the 500-channel universe, and the Internet are all examples one can point to, arguing that it is with the development of these technological innovations that plunder's legacy is bearing fruit. But if it's true, it's a bitter fruit we're growing. Though glossy magazines of web culture idiotically promise that the MP3 "is doing to record labels what the TV zapper did to television networks—shifting power to the consumer," plunder's rootless anger makes it apparent that consumers already have too many "choices," too much power to reduce their lives to a series of cultural on and off ramps. "They approach the airwaves as a vast smorgasbord," social psychologist Robert Levine tells James Gleick, "all of which must be sampled, no matter how meagre the helpings." In the world of more and more, we starve. MP3 and other impending technologies might well have the effect of bringing us to an even closer relationship with pop culture than we had before. This, however, is not plunder; it is the situation that makes the language of plunder necessary to ensure that we find something to eat at the buffet table—even if we have to cook it ourselves.

What is art, what is authentic, what is original, and what is a copy? More channels, more choices—you have ten restaurants on your block, but they're all serving the Big Mac. Coming out of our search for an authentic underground rebellion, plunder instils in us not just a crisis of ownership but a crisis of authenticity, a crisis of the "real" choice. The resolution to our unease is not more access to more of the same but the recognition that it *is* all the same, all one thing, available and possible for all of us. What changes with plunder is the perception of the possibilities. The first time Bleek heard pirate radio, he heard a truth that he had always known but could never express. The first time a song that comprised primarily other songs was played on the radio, our collective understanding of pop as a thing of singular ownership bestowed upon the people changed irrevocably. As the mental environment shifts, we have unconsciously begun to assert our new language, a way to possess without actually owning.

The search for a valid way to speak in the dialect of unpopular pop is—has to be—both personal and collective. Each of us comes to it in our own way, but we all inevitably arrive at a shared conclusion that allows us to talk to each other about our pop heritage, knowing that we are at once speaking ironically and completely seriously. In the fall of 1999 a small Toronto publisher put out a novel I wrote called *Lurvy*, a dark, jokey retelling of E. B. White's children's classic *Charlotte's Web*. (In my version, the pig dies.) *Lurvy* was a book I had started a few years earlier, in graduate school, inspired in part by a fellow I met there who was working on a novelistic adaptation of Orson Welles's film noir classic *Touch of Evil*. Like Bleek, I still don't really know what started me down the path of plunder. People have asked me what I was thinking when I decided to retell *Charlotte's Web*, but for the longest time I wasn't quite sure how to respond. Then it hit me: what I had been doing was attempting to explore the strange space between identity and mass culture. I grew up with visions of friendly barnyard animals and benevolent farm folk implanted in my mind, first via a copy of the book I received on my third birthday, and then through repeated viewings of the movie, itself a pale copy of the original. *Lurvy* was my sarcastic, in-joke attempt to make sense of that shadowy world—for myself, and for others who share my unease with our mass culture lives of manufactured memories.

One of the many fabricated pop culture moments that make up Lurvy, a dark, tongue-in-cheek retelling of Charlotte's Web.

Why shouldn't we retell our stories to ourselves, take to the airwaves, quote pop songs in our pop songs? Like all languages, like my *Lurvy* project, plunder emerges out of necessity. Frame by frame, track by track, pirate radio station by pirate radio station, we use plunder to find a way to speak to something that escapes the critic's futile whine, the buy-and-sell of industry. We create a new language of loneliness and desperation that, ironically, in highlighting just how collective our existence is, takes place in a never-never land which each of us recognizes from our solitary dreams. Plunder becomes a device by which we affirm the fakery of pop culture, the longing we feel as a result of our futile search for a nonexistent underground. With plunder, we give voice to what plagues us—our complete and total lack of conviction in the present of our own lives. The circle closes and we are inside, doing a hula-hoop square dance. In some hypothetical future all our own, the wolves howl and the boxcars roll. The land is open, unadorned; no one exists but you. At the foot of Bleek's driveway, a lonely voice on the far reaches of the dial reminds us that the process of reclaiming our identity begins one person at a time.

THE REAL

CHAPTER FOUR

*Saying it was only a TV show
is like saying it was only a friend,
only my brother, only my father.*

— David McGimpsey from "In Memoriam: A.H. Jr."

I'm in the cluttered office of Steve Mann, boyish professor of Electrical and Computer Engineering at the University of Toronto. There are bits of computers everywhere. He moves aside boards and wires so I can sit down. Mann's hair is tousled and shows a bit too much sweaty forehead. He wears a tweed jacket over a sweater—somewhere under all that there's a shirt and tie. Clearly, Mann's obsessions do not extend to fashion. "He walks stiffly, stares intently," wrote one journalist, "his social skills are nonexistent." Mann is one of those stereotyped brilliant tinkerers whose intent interest in the world in front of him is remarkable for the fact that what he sees in that world is nothing like what we see.

So what does Steve Mann see in our world? Well, for starters, he sees an inevitable profusion of realities. Faced

*Steve Mann evolves
(from early 1990s to late 1990s).*

with the prospect of being constantly filmed, constantly documented, constantly under surveillance—as we already are on stretches of highway, in malls, in banks, in stores, in parks, in apartment building lobbies, in high-rise office tower elevators—Mann wants us to reflect all this observational energy right back in the face of our government and corporate oppressors. We will do this by utilizing Mann's triumvirate of creations: WearComp, WearCam, and WearTell. In case you haven't figured it out yet, Mann is an inventor. Since his tenure as high school goof in hometown Hamilton,

Ontario, he's been fiddling around with wearable computers, trying to find technological innovations to accommodate his futuristic, libertarian, sci-fi-paperback vision of the future. "People can't survive without clothing," he says. "We're acclimatized to it, we can't even go out without shoes. So it's an evolutionary stage. We'll evolve towards WearComp as an evolution and at some point in time we will feel naked without it. That'll happen."

In other words, Mann is jubilantly looking forward to a time when we are plugged in, twenty-four hours a day, seven days a week. Current incarnations of WearComp and its spin-offs include a pair of sunglasses that double as a monitor, a mainframe in your pocket, and wiring under your blazer. Without getting into details, it's safe to say that Mann's inventions perform all the usual functions of the home computer with the additional bonus of cellular phone, vid-phone, options for visual and audio recordings, and, of course, portability. But I'm not going to belabour the technical details of Mann's inventions—partly because I don't understand them, and partly because I'm much more interested in Mann's theories and motivations concerning how and why WearComp will be used. Mann doesn't just want to invent the atomic bomb and then hand it over to the highest bidder. He has developed a very interesting philosophy concerning his inventions—a philosophy that situates WearComp on the cusp of the debate about what is "real" within the lifestyle culture continuum.

Central to Mann's thinking is the idea of surveillance

and counter-surveillance. Mann calls his theory the "inverse panopticon" after Jeremy Bentham's infamous prison design, the Panopticon, in which the prisoners live in barred cells and the guards watch their every move from a central tower. Influenced by the French philosopher Michel Foucault— whose thinking on the nature of power also utilized the panopticon model—Mann sees post-modern life as a kind of prison in which we live in our cells and are constantly observed. Implicit in this perspective on society is the fact that, in our earth-size prison, our perception of things is not important. It doesn't matter what we think we are doing, saying, watching; it only matters what our guards think we are doing, saying, watching. In other words, it doesn't matter how we respond to and partake of mass culture; it only matters how others perceive what we are doing—a perception that is mediated through the mass media, its various pundits, and their corporate sponsors.

For Mann, our inability to convey our reality through the mass media leaves us at a disadvantage. Thus, he is convinced that the only way we can escape the tyrannical effects of an ever more observed, controlled existence is to turn the tables. So, in much the same way that lifestyle culture is about reasserting our right to articulate our own lives out of the stuff of pop, Mann believes that everyone should be able surreptitiously to record and tape everyone else. Now, while I'm not able to invent a machine that cranks out blockbuster movies featuring your pet plot ("Ya know what would make a great movie . . ." slurs a drinking buddy of mine every time he sees me), Mann is able and willing to invent the technology that will let us all assert our various versions of reality as we see them looped through the gaze of our computer/camera/sunglasses.

"Would it not make sense to have your own record," he asks rhetorically, "your own side of the story, just as a contract is signed and both parties get a copy? . . . When there are differing accounts of reality presented, then at least it allows us to scrutinize the portions of the video in which the accounts differ."

So much for the old handshake. To demonstrate how this kind of constant recordkeeping would work, Mann evokes a school classroom in which the teacher can never be sure if he is being monitored and/or recorded by a child's parents. Another example of the efficacy of his system is his suggestion that, in the future, employees will monitor their bosses in the same way that bosses currently observe their workers. "But you know," he tells me, "it isn't even necessary that everybody has a personal safety system; it's only necessary that somebody *could* have a personal safety system."

Mann is a builder, a tinkerer. Nevertheless, he has constructed a theoretical framework for his countervailing individual recording devices, his "personal safety systems." This framework is articulated in a video he made when he was a doctoral candidate at M.I.T. (around the same time the U.S. media discovered him and he became, for a time, a minor celebrity—not for the video, but for the outlandish look, and economic potential, of his gadgetry). The video, called

Shooting Back, features Mann decked out in a computer vest going into department stores and complaining about being filmed by security cameras. He, of course, is surreptitiously recording the people he complains to. The irony becomes rapidly apparent when one worker angrily explains to him that only would-be criminals don't like being secretly filmed.

Another wacky Mann idea was to hook the camera up and broadcast his life on the Internet. You could log on to his website and see what Steve Mann was seeing that very moment through the camera lens of his cyber-sunglasses. "There was an explosion of interest, 30,000 hits a day," Mann says of the experiment. "I guess it was the sitcom effect . . . people would rather watch me live my life than live their own life." (Though others have provided and continue to provide voyeuristic websites featuring the insides of their homes, Mann's gimmick was that he was up and about; as he moved through the world, we saw what he saw, not just a single stationary camera angle.)

Mann's cynical labelling of interest in his website as a "sitcom effect" shouldn't surprise you; one might easily argue that his fairly bizarre explorations of social theory are, themselves, nothing more than a cynical smoke screen to obscure the fact that his wearable computers are intrusive gadgets that we neither want nor need but will, eventually, feel compelled to own. When I met with him, he evaded all questions concerning the price one of these computers might fetch, or what kind of corporate interest his wearable computers were garnering. At the same time, to be fair, it doesn't seem like Mann is just in it for the money. He does genuinely believe that giving us little people the opportunity to perpetually, surreptitiously, shoot our own never-ending home movies will be doing us a favour. Issues of profit-making potential aside, it is clear that for Mann many versions of reality are superior to a single, monolithic imposition of some corporate-sponsored "real."

■　■　■

We live in a *faux* land where everything is narrative, story, entertainment—all of it separate but very much part of the actual occurrences of our day-to-day lives. How to reconcile that fake world with our own mundane experiences? We attempt to inject our lives—our rote routine—into the fake world that is becoming the main portal into our spiritual life (our hopes, our dreams, our fears). We seek to find ways to believe in mass culture, and in that search we come to realize that our relationship to the figments of pop is one that permeates and changes our sense of reality. To argue that there is now a multiplicity of "reals," each one as valid as the next, does not speak to an inability to make the distinction between make-believe and actual. That distinction, in fact, is made moot by the way we use mass culture as something false that, nevertheless, we validate through not just our participation but our total immersion.

It might be argued that Steve Mann's idea of a multiplicity of "reals" has less to do with keeping an eye on those who are keeping an eye on us (thus theoretically subverting totalitarianism before it can really get started), and much more to do with each of us asserting our own sense of what is real within the shared expanse of mass culture. Thus, in lifestyle culture, as in Steve Mann's near-future world, the only reality is the one individuals agree to believe in. Playwright Daniel David Moses puts it this way: "We have all these competing realities, and this variety of realities is what we're taking to be real." Moses is, of course, speaking of reality in a cultural sense, reality as a kind of dogma. He isn't saying that I will look at a car and see a cockroach, and you will look at a car and see a horse and cart, and that we will both be right. What we're talking about here is reality as Mann sees it—as a document, as a version, as your assertion of what is real for you. "Reality is a process that involves our active participation," is how new-media critic Wade Rowland puts it.

In our lives, we don't experience fictional characters and events as real in the sense that we think that there actually is a Skipper on Gilligan's Island tormented by a klutz in a red shirt. We can and do make the distinction between the Skipper and the actor who played the Skipper. At the same time, as poet David McGimpsey's quote at the beginning of this chapter makes clear, we also know that there is a Skipper, and that the Skipper resides somewhere, his immortality prolonged for as long as twenty-somethings fondly speculate on the sexual politics of a certain desert island. "Gilligan's Island" isn't just a TV show. It isn't just a bunch of make-believe characters. McGimpsey titles the poem in tribute to the actor who played the Skipper (Alan Hale Jr.), but he is not confusing the two. He is, rather, recognizing the obvious: the Skipper and the man who played the Skipper are two separate things.

So the Skipper is real for us—he exists, is part of that which makes up our experiences and lives. Like so many other "characters," the Skipper is as real as, if not more real than, any number of actual people we've never met. Upon hearing that they were planning to cancel her favourite detective show, a viewer once wrote in to the network: "I totally enjoy 'Cagney and Lacey.' You are the best female cops TV has ever seen. I myself enjoy the show because I am going to the state police academy in a few months." Note the fluid movement from discussing the show, to addressing the characters, to discussing "real" life. "*You* are the best," the fan writes, and there is no doubt that she is fully aware that, in a corporeal sense, Cagney and Lacey don't exist. The incongruities don't bother her. Should they?

As the forces of mass media reduce our lives with a single monotonous picture (showing on innumerable channels), we "shoot" back by articulating our version of reality, by making pop culture iconography real in our conversations, in our actions, in the art the TV generations make. As a result, there are no longer any primary sources of information—everything is entertainment, everything is lifestyle, nobody is right or wrong, everybody is simply propagating a version of their reality. And yet there is a freedom to the idea that we are all making our ongoing home movie, a seamless blend of pop culture fantasies and personal myths and day-to-day routines. You have to think of reality as a kind of cultural democracy: you cast your vote by making a television show, cutting an album, publishing a zine, singing an opera, writing a short story; or, if you are unable to actively create, you cast your vote by collecting, by watching, by wearing, by "appearing" on talk radio and talk television and game shows.

The Detroit group AWOL, for instance, put together a photo exhibit and film entirely featuring G.I. Joe dolls engaged in realistic-looking battle. "The movie we made is our ultimate fantasy as kids for G.I. Joe," explains Greg Fadell of AWOL. "We tried to make our fantasy real; when we were making the film we kept saying to each other, yeah, remember when we used to do this or that? . . . If you look at it in a corporate way, some corporation made money off of G.I. Joe, but the way we look at it, you take what they offer and you change it—you make it your own. It's about your memories, not the product."

■ ■ ■

This need to manipulate and create your own "reality" through culture is complicated by the fact that our "real" experiences very often emerge from the not quite real world of mass culture in the first place. Members of the TV generations have come to find that many of our formative experiences were, in fact, not necessarily experiences per se but kind of fake experiences, events that happened without happening. What I mean is that many of our most defining memories are of events in which we did not have an actual physical experience; rather, they were "experienced" through the mass media. We watch a space shuttle take off, we watch a riot in another country, we watch the final episode of "M*A*S*H." These things affect us, but not in the same way they would if we were on the shuttle, in that riot, or part of the cast of the TV show. In fact, we aren't entirely sure how we are affected by the moments that mark important parts of our lives without actually being part of our lives. But we do know that we want to sanctify our everyday moments with that same kind of ripple in our reality. We want our lives to have the kind of importance mass culture confers on, say, a celebrity's birthday. So it's not surprising that we now seek to replicate this feeling by attempting to inject our lives, our realities, into the "reality" of mass culture.

This kind of theorizing is small comfort for the five-hundred-plus passengers and murdered pilot who, on a routine flight in Japan, found themselves held hostage by a deranged twenty-eight-year-old obsessed with flight-simulation computer games. "I wanted to soar through the air," stated the hijacker. In his mind, taking control of the plane allowed some crucial connection to be bridged between his real life and the "fake" life of mass culture. And yet the sum total of his actions adds up to a kind of pseudo-event. Something happened, he had an experience, but not in the same way that, for instance, losing your virginity was (is?) an experience.

I don't bring up virginity randomly. There is, in fact, a website palace erected to the experience of having sex for the first time. Called My First Time (www.myfirsttime.com), it is a brilliant scheme: people from all over the world can go there and read entries by other people in which they describe their first time having sex. "Hi. I'm Paul," starts one of the more interesting entries, in which a couple claim to be actually losing their virginity and recounting the tale as they go along. "Lori and I are going to have sex for the first time in a couple of minutes. We're alone in her room. We messed around a little last week and planned this for this week since her family is out of town. My First Time is our favourite inter-net site, and since we met on the web we thought this would be cool." These confessions range from the lustful to the loving to the harrowing. Some include all the graphic details, some do not. Those of you who think that erotica and sex out of wedlock are immoral will be offended; those of you who are interested in tapping into the zeitgeist of the twenty-first century will be fascinated. In the fall of 1999 there were over 20,000 entries on the site, and, unlike the stories in the back of *Hustler* (where the same anecdote is penned by a sexy co-ed from Newark in the U.S. edition and one from Laval in the Canadian version), the bulk of them, I am inclined to believe, are at least partially true. The question one is tempted to ask here is: why the hell would you want to put your private story on the Internet for millions to read?

The My First Time site is hardly alone in its confes-sional style. There is also *MonoZine*, dedicated to in-depth, graphic confessions of disgusting illnesses and health problems. The more horrific the surgery or pustulating the rash, the better. This process of creating your own story, your own document, your own indelible image, has a lot to do with the notion of our reality being nothing more than a composite of "events" that never took place, made real only through the layered process of being documented and made present to our collective consciousness. "Each work," warns our favourite dour philosopher Theodor Adorno, "insofar as it is intended for many, is already its own reproduction." "For whatever reason," writes the poet and playwright Jacob Wren, "images are all that we have left." My First Time demonstrates the extent to which we view many of our formative life experiences as real but false. Here, as in many other manifestations of lifestyle culture, we seek to validate ourselves, to enshrine our actual experiences in cultural forums. We create works that reproduce our lives, that sanction our lives the way we see that novels and sculptures and television shows and songs seem to sanction and, somehow, heighten the reality of all kinds of experiences, from the mundane to the unthinkable. At the same time, there is the loss we feel, a yearning quest for the authentic: the original experience buried under the layers of reproduction that make up our lives.

■   ■   ■

The louder we shout, hoping to hear our own voices somewhere in the monotonous babble of mass culture, the less we are heard. Partly as a result of this paradox, we announce what is real to us by picking and choosing from a whole host of already established simulacrum realities that shape our lives. In doing so, we silently assert power over that which is said to have power over us. In this scenario, your favourite movie, your favourite restaurant, the clothes you wear, the books you read (or buy but never read), are the signals you use to indicate who you are and who you want to be. These are decisions only you yourself can make—as opposed to, say, your ability to pick up foreign languages easily, your birth in the back seat of a cab, whether Penguin Books will publish that two-thousand-page manuscript on your personal quest to track down the Yeti. But, of course, these are also decisions that are made for us by the corporate entities that manufacture mass culture. So, despite all the choices we seem to have, we all end up listening to the same music, watching the same shows, wearing the same clothes.

There's a reason why we hear those stories of kids killing each other over Nike sneakers or see people living vastly beyond their means—staying at luxury hotels, eating at fancy restaurants, buying designer outfits on maxed-out MasterCards. It has to do with this desire to signal our power over our reality—which, in many cases, is connected to the imposition of a consumer ethos that rampages through all aspects of our lives. But I prefer, at least at this point, to highlight not those whose reality has been submerged in the "real" of commodity capitalism (the American dream reduced to nothing more than a relentless marketing ploy) but those who still fight the fight, attempting to preserve their reality, their version of events, by contorting the mainstream ideology (and, in the process, joining a select rank including the Tarzan fanatic and the Knievel expert). Anthropologist Yi-Fu Tuan calls the attempt to articulate our power over our surroundings—nothing less than the monolith of mass culture—escapism: "To see culture as escape or escapism is to share a disposition common to all who have had some experience in exercising power—a disposition that is unwilling to accept what is the case (reality) when it seems to them unjust or too severely constraining."

Tuan's escapism—an exercise of power when you have no power—is the increasingly prevalent belief that we can change who we are, no matter what our background, through the trappings of mass culture. In other words, what Tuan understands as escapism, I interpret as lifestyle culture. If our reality becomes too constraining, we can simply reinvent ourselves—by wearing different outfits, eating different foods, going to different places. Not only *can* we do this, but we have the *right* to do this. We use "plunder" to speak of and appropriate mass culture as an actual thing, as a part of our world. This language of plunder itself shapes our reality and how we convey what is real to us. Using this language, we tap into a complicated world of signs that signal other signs that signal other signs until, somewhere down the road of symbology, we are lighting beacons that, supposedly, declare who and how we want to be. Plunder is a language we use not just in writing books and making new forms of music; it is also the language of our everyday. We speak it when we choose to call up the bank of images mass culture provides us through various fads and fashions we carry on our person. The Tommy Hilfiger sweatshirt you are wearing says something about you. The Roots baseball cap you sport projects an attitude steeped in the rhetoric of a million ads. Your pink mohawk sends thousands of images through our brains, giving you an identity you can't control. When the brand of lipstick Monica Lewinsky wore for her TV interview with Barbara Walters sold out in stores all over North America the next day, critics pretended to be vaguely repulsed by how easy it is to manipulate the masses—and yet to me the message is the opposite from the one assumed. I mean, are we really to believe that the bulk of us want to be known the way Lewinsky is known? We don't adopt the look of celebrities because we want to be them; we do it because we want to bestow the aura of individuality on ourselves. Comments the style editor of *The New York Times Magazine*: "What we actually decide to put on our backs each day and venture out into the world in has nothing to do with trends or marketing. It has to do with who we want to show the world we are. Or who we want to convince ourselves we could be."

And yet, because of the long circling path we must embark on before our referents reach ground zero, what we are signalling—through a certain manner of dress or affecta-tion of a certain mannerism—is not always clear, even to us. "A sign does not simply exist as part of reality," explains one thinker. "It reflects and refracts other realities." "As we made increasing use of the flexible abstraction," warned Walter Kerr in the early 1960s, "we were forced to leave most of the referents, most of the real things, far, far behind."

Many of us don't stop at modifying what we wear, what we listen to, where we live, in order to signal our version of reality. Some of us go so far as to alter our actual appearance. The trend to altering one's physical characteristics reflects our increasing expectation (born—like a virus?—on the invisible winds of lifestyle culture) that we individuals should be allowed to determine who we are and what (or who) we look like. We dye and style our hair, stain our skin, starve our-selves, bulk up, chisel our nose down to a point, pierce our soft spots, all in the hope of accessing the authentic version of reality we wish to put forward. That this process often takes us farther and farther away from our own "real" appear-ance is one of the many ironies of lifestyle culture. Talk-show host Geraldo Rivera made this point abundantly clear when, in April 1992, he underwent liposuction on his television show. "Gobs of yellow fat were sucked from his buttocks and injected into his lips and around his eyes," is how one critic describes the event. As the chameleon-like host aptly demonstrated, external appearance is all part of public demeanour, and nothing, not even the act of altering one's appearance "live" in front of a studio audience, takes away from the illusion of possibility: we now have the opportunity to recast ourselves in whatever image we deem appropriate.

Even the kind of plastic surgery that brings us closer to the televised ideal doesn't cut it for many of those on the radical fringes of the lifestyle culture experience. Erik Sprague, twenty-seven, of Albany, New York, has "spent the last several years trying to turn himself into a lizard. So far he has had Teflon implants to enlarge his forehead and filed his teeth into fangs, while covering his body with tattoos of reptilian scales." Reported on as a freak in *Time*, Erik is, in my mind, less of a freak than those who have their looks surgically altered to conform to the "mono-real" vision of beauty. Still, it's two sides of the same coin, isn't it? Whether it's lizards or liposuction, those who feel the need to radically alter their physical form do so at the behest of mass culture: on the one hand, the facelift/nose job/breast enlargement in which we reinvent ourselves according to the monolithic reality of pop's beauty myth; on the other hand, piercings, tattoos, and surgeries that speak to our attempt to convey an individuality born out of the pop construct of the underground rebel. And so, either way, we are trapped in the mores of social contrivance exactly as they are articulated by our entertainment megacorps.

We are not all mini-corporations backed by a bevy of PR flacks, spin-doctor image consultants, and slick advertisements. We do not have a conscious goal we are constantly articulating—Vote for ME! Buy ME! over and over again, the mantra of the modern-day politician, charisma oozing off a name-brand hairdo. Ours is a more subtle struggle. We live in the entertainment universe, we work in it, we are its employees and its employers, we buy it and sell it, and we believe in it and can't make do without it. Its propaganda is our propaganda. At the same time, we are marginalized by a system that forces us to believe without providing ways for us to articulate that belief in a meaningful way. Once we've bought the product and its spinoff and its soundtrack and its collector's edition director's cut and its remix and its sticker album and its action figures and its collectibles monthly digest and its true-story paperback and its vintage reissue lunchbox— what's left for us? How are we supposed to use these products to make sense of our own mundane lives? How do we show that the stuff we buy and watch and listen to has become part of our real existence?

Here, where plunder meets the possibility of a new profusion of cultural realities, there is no final arbiter of what is real. If we can, at the very least, signal a change of who we are by presenting a new list of our favourite books, albums, and movies, by cutting our nose a different way, by altering where and how we live—what, then, can be said to be immutable? No wonder we must justify and, to some extent, validate our existence by putting it into the public sphere, by seeking to have it experienced as real by others the way we, collectively, experience stories, television characters, and celebrity personas as real. In the same way, our plunder art, itself hopelessly compromised, reaffirms the reality of our mass cultural experiences, while simultaneously using those experiences to connect to a possibly authentic past we all long to share.

Growing numbers of people are searching for something, anything, that might bridge the gap between the pop dream and their everyday lives. That search is taking us into the dangerous lifestyle space where artists and regular people become the same thing, challenging the old rules of cultural production by asserting our right to superimpose—record and project—our realities over mass culture's singular reality. This makes our crowned pundits nervous and upset. We can see this when critic Neil Gabler complains that the advent of the video camera resulted in a profusion of amateur dramatics: "People didn't wave or smile nervously at the video camera or bury their faces in their hands to hide from it, as they had done when confronted with the movie camera. People acted for it: they sang; they danced; they told jokes; they did tricks. Afterwards they could add titles and effects to professionalize the show. Some even edited the tapes to tighten them."

Smile, wave, tell jokes to your own camera. Plug your sunglasses in. Keep looking back over your shoulder. The dream is the truth of digital fibres coiled around your sculpted waist. We are the lost people, our lives in orbit around some awesome planetary imagination.

■   ■   ■

"**A**s visitors arrive at Tinseltown it is very evident that a major Hollywood-style event is taking place . . ." proclaims the promotional bumf for the Anaheim, California, fake movie studio/floor show Tinseltown. "A red carpet leads the guests past a corps of television press anxious for interviews. . . ." Members of the audience are paying for the privilege of pretending they are celebrities here, and one wonders what would happen if any of them actually stopped and disturbed the façade by consenting to a quick tête-à-tête with the people employed to shout questions and flash their flashes. But none of them does. Once guests make it past the media scrum, they are ushered into the dining room/ auditorium area where, over a "fresh salad," they peruse the Tinseltown program for the evening. Soon their faces will

California's Tinseltown, where everyone's a star!

appear on the big screen and their ordinary, unsculpted bodies will parade upon the stage as they accept "Oggie" awards for acts they were only peripherally involved in (just like real celebrities often do).

Now there's nothing wrong with Tinseltown—hell, it should probably be a government-subsidized program. Once a year, if only for a few hours, we regular people should get the godlike treatment given to our celebrities (who, like gods, are more often than not created out of thin air, their mercurial dispositions more relevant than their questionable talents). Anyway, I'm not interested in celebrities. What I am interested in is the way entertainments like Tinseltown up the ante of mediated reality. Is this, like the music of plunder-phonics, an inevitable dead end in which we finish up by parodying our desire to articulate the authentic fake?

Tinseltown is, purportedly, fun. (I haven't been, so I can't say.) But I will wager that no one believes that Tinseltown is real, any more than anyone believes that the Oscars every year pick the best movie made in the world and give it an award. So the point here is to suspend disbelief and have a good time. The subtext is: hey, there's really nothing at stake. Just as the Oscars market movies, Tinseltown markets the Oscars. Both events lack substance and are as forgettable as they are entertaining. But Tinseltown goes one step further: it endeavours to make us part of the show, demonstrating just how far the entertainment mono-real will go to manufac-ture pseudo-active entertainments that can meet our desire to be a part of the world of mass culture. Tinseltown is like

karaoke, a preplanned excursion into the world of mass culture that parodies the risks and rewards of creative action by
offering them in a safe context. Tinseltown's emphasis is on
theatre, spectacle, and, of course, fresh salads. We do not
participate in Tinseltown any more than we can be said to
participate in the Oscars or in "People's Court"; in all, we are
agreeably manipulated. "Guests will spend between two and
two and a half hours per visit experiencing the glamour of
Hollywood," promises the Tinseltown brochure.

The same phenomenon is seen in various theme parks
and entertainments, including laser-tag war arenas; bigger,
better Imax coliseum theatres with auto-tilt seats; and the relatively recent phenomenon of reality-based television shows,
including "Cops," "Rescue 911," "America's Funniest Home
Videos," "Trauma: Life in the ER," MTV's "Real World," and,
my favourites, the Fox network specials with titles like
"When Good Times Go Bad" and "When Animals Attack"
(not to mention the first wave: a whole host of judge shows,
talk shows, and game shows). All of these programs invite
us into their reality. In them, as in Tinseltown, we are the
spectacle, even though we have no control over how we will
appear on the big screen.

Whether it is a fake awards show, a game show, a collection of embarrassing accidents, or a string of footage showing car chases ending in tragedy, every single moment of
these programs is predetermined, preplanned. Each show
is carefully edited, marketed, and narrated to create the illusion of a multiplicity of participants with a multiplicity of

narratives, when in fact the show is expressing only the monolithic attitude of corporate entertainment. But we aren't fooled. We enjoy these shows, we like the way "regular" people take the place of the stylized actors, we laugh at "real" events as they take the place of formulaic plots. But do we see our lives reflected in the televised events? Do we actually think, gee whiz, they're really taking my life into consideration now, really thinking about how I might like to be an active participant in my nightly entertainment? With no characters and no plots, the entertainment formula is laid bare in a way that lets us see, for the first time, just how much of our lives are in opposition to reality as it is seen on TV. Writes one astute commentator: "Fleshed-out story lines and character development are scrapped; instead, the pace is ratcheted up with machine-gun editing and frenzied announcers. No matter what the footage, it is processed uniformly: a quick set-up (location, players, motive), followed by a period of escalating tension (a hostage situation, a chase or foot pursuit, an approaching tornado or shark), finished off with a 'money shot' (a crash, an attack or a rescue)."

In its approximation of spontaneity, reality-based television unwittingly parodies what is real about our own lives, adding yet another layer of "reality" and leaving us longing for the "spontaneous reaction" that Adorno describes as a "perennial paradox of art." Reality-TV, which came of age to answer the growing desire we had to participate in our culture, is a cynical ploy to distract us from what we really want: not access to reality-TV, but access to the media by which we can portray our own reality, shot before a live studio audience. Perennial TV talk-show host Ralph Benmergui puts it this way: "The impotency of the citizen is on the rise. The more we feel control of our world slipping away . . . the more we're anaesthetized by being able to call in and say how mad as hell we are." In other words, the talk show and other appearances by "regular" people on TV are just a sop to convince us that we, in fact, do have a say, when everyone—including us and certainly our hosts— knows just how little we can do to change the world around us. The mass media depend on our nonparticipation. But the more we wish to participate, the more we believe, the more "they" have to create the illusion of our participation— reality-TV, game shows, theme parks, instant online polls, letters to the editor, etc.—to make it seem as if we are participating, manufacturing our own reality. But, of course, all these things come with a formula, a price. After two hours in Tinseltown you instantly revert to your everyday limitations: letters to the editor must be two hundred words or less; you don't talk back to Judge Judy; your cute baby falling into a river and almost drowning on "America's Funniest Home Videos" is only funny until it is supplanted by next week's winner, a dog accidentally falling into a pit barbecue. Hilarious!

"Ordinary life is so dull that I get out of it as much as possible," Sex Pistol Steve Jones once said. We all now feel the desire for that heightened sense of artifice that Jones articulated, an escape from life into art that has, for us,

become the norm. Reality-TV is just further evidence of our
attraction to lifestyle culture, our desire to take the wheel, to
direct our own journey, to up the ante, to escape the ordinary, organized, surreal, violent, disconnected version of life
as seen in "Cops" by asserting our own more mundane reality, a linear narrative replete with detours that takes the
shape of Sadie Benning's *Flat is Beautiful* or Phil Petra's Tarzan
memorabilia collection. "There's something about the nature
of the tape, the grain of the image, the sputtering black-and-
white tones, the starkness," writes Don DeLillo in *Underworld*. "You think this is more real, truer-to-life than anything
around you. The things around you have a rehearsed and layered and cosmetic look." In lifestyle culture, we seek to
escape from the singular corporate version of our ugly lives
into the pure possibility of our lives when mediated by
expression, by narrative, by the arc of art. Writes Yi-Fu Tuan:
"It is daily life, with its messy details and frustrating lack of
definition and completion—its many inconclusive moves and
projects twisting and turning as in a fitful dream—that is
unreal. Real, by contrast, is the well-told story, the clear
image, the well-defined architectural space, the sacred ritual,
all of which give a heightened sense of self—a feeling of
aliveness." Thus our attraction to a pop reality we wish to
confer upon our lives. We are drawn to reality-TV, not
because of the way it situates us in the story, but because of
the way it suggests that we *could* be situated in the story. Pop
critic John Fiske argues that the appeal of "America's Most
Wanted" is its capacity to "show the fallibility of the official

system of law and order until 'ordinary people' come to its aid, and do for themselves what 'the system could not do for them.'" What "the system" cannot do for us is exactly what it wishes it could do for us: manufacture the illusion of a participatory culture, without actually relinquishing its grip on the pursestrings.

■　■　■

When two class losers in a Littleton, Colorado, high school opened fire during lunch hour, killing almost thirty teens, it was breathlessly reported that the duo always wore dark trench coats, and that they targeted blacks, Hispanics, Christians, and jocks. They singled out those who threatened their identity—those who had an identity more powerful than their own. In a world of subjective "reals," a reality shaped from the truth of pop culture is always tenuous. Despite our complicity, we have contempt in our hearts for the obsessive shopper, for the sci-fi geek, for the fanatical fan. How easy it is to deny a substantive reality to aberrant white boy geeks whose pathetic identity came not from the "real" world (of sports, race, and religion) but from the suspect world of Dungeons & Dragons and Nintendo and posing rock stars. The wearing of trench coats and the wielding of firearms, like the act of mass murder itself, was a symbolic one. We will not be denied our version of reality, these sad boys were saying. Branded losers, surrounded by the potency of violent imagery imbued with the instant pop potential for every loser to become a winner *à la* reality-TV, they lashed out, mindlessly, crazily, but not without a sense of the way in which their reality would spin out in "Reality" as showcased in the newspaper articles, magazine articles, television docudramas, movies, etc. True lifestyle culturites to the bitter end, the duo even left us a home video chronicling the build-up before the shooting. "The more it happens," a cultural anthropologist teaching at George Washington University told CNN, "the more it seems like an option." In violent death, the ultimate geek fantasy comes to life: you are noticed, respected, and, inevitably, followed. But you are also co-opted, turned into consumable objects before you are even remotely understood—a litany of clichés, a parade of talk-show guests and lipstick shades.

The acceptable argument is to say that the trench-coat boys were goaded by a violent mass culture. They listened to Marilyn Manson, played endless hours of violent video games, and constructed their own websites (in which they discussed the finer points of bomb-making). No wonder they went crazy. Look at it another way: they had all the outlets your average malaise-ridden outcast teen requires to act out and purge himself of his death-wish fantasies. So why do we still have murderous teens and hijacking pilot-wannabes? Why has our culture, our make-believe, failed us? One might say that these denizens of lifestyle culture understood all too well that the only way to articulate a reality is through acts of imagination that bridge the gap between the "real" of life and the "real" of mass culture. But what if you can't find an acceptable way to do this? What if your environment is so

acceptable way to do this? What if your environment is so totally hostile to who you want to pretend you are that you find yourself completely unable to assert the distinct reality, the imaginative safe zone, that you try desperately to build up all around you? You want to be a pilot more than anything, but everyone keeps telling you that you'll always be a passenger. In this way, the need to be seen, heard, believed, enters the world of multiple "reals" and the story plays out as an act of aggression against conformity, against the accepted version of reality, against the subsumed identity.

Meanwhile, the PR flaks tell us to go ahead, have your goofy fun, it's just a game, you'll grow out of it. The forces that unleash mass culture in the form of aggressive music, violent video games, and movies like *The Basketball Diaries* and *The Matrix* (cited as dangerous influences) attempt to deny that these things are real and, in doing so, subvert our capacity to use mass culture, to own a culture that acts out our truth. Satan worship is just more units of product now, the swastika a clever marketing campaign. The boys aren't having "real" formative experiences, they're just rebelling, just acting out, and the best thing to do is to make sure that they have enough pocket money to play out their adolescent fantasies—which aren't real, which *can't* be real. You crazy kids, here's another fifty, dear, why don't you buy some beer and act rebellious like we all did when we were your age?

So which is it? Are we pilots or passengers? Right now we're like flight attendants, trapped in the plane with no control over its destination but with responsibility for the well-being not just of ourselves but of others. When they were not allowed to take their culture seriously—not allowed their belief in it as part of themselves—the boys (we don't even remember their names any more, do we?) were propelled toward the attempt to assert their truth in the most graphic of ways. The myth of the underground, the collapse of the real, the search for authenticity of expression, lays claim to a mounting plane-wreck death toll.

"At the B.C. trial of teenagers for the murder of teenager Reena Virk . . . many people have commented on the apparent detachment of the young witnesses," writes *Globe and Mail* columnist Rick Salutin. "The kids can only vaguely recall the killing itself yet remember with brilliant clarity the labels on everybody's clothes. Well, how do you suppose kids are going to feel when the only future their society seriously holds out to them is the role of shopper?" It is not the lure of celebrity fame that inspires the teen killer; it is the frustration of not having access to the ability to articulate reality as identity.

Thumbing through the Calgary zine *In Grave Ink*, I come across a short story titled simply "Alanis." The story, by one "Kiki Bonbon," features two young department-store workers griping about pop star Alanis Morissette, her new album, and her trip to India in search of spiritual rejuvenation:

> "I can't go tripping off on spiritual pilgrimages around the globe cause I'm stuck working my ass off at the fucking Bay."
> "Yeah and like listening to this stupid satellite

radio all day with Alanis and her likes whining about their great therapy and giving head to losers and traipsing around raping so called exotic cultures for their own mental cleansing purposes makes it any better."

"I wish she'd gone to Africa to feed starving children instead and got malaria and died."

"I know like I'd totally love to assassinate her. You know just explode in fury right into her."

"Yeah, talk about real Canadian pop hero, it'd be like 'Disenfranchised Bay employee immolates Morissette in a ball of fire on her I-just-came-back-all-enlightened-and-pure-from-India-Tour.'"

The piece is a classic zine rant that gives voice to the frustrations we all feel when artistically challenged celebs climb up on the soapbox. Kiki is articulating a sensibility— found especially in a media-savvy, sophisticated new generation— that expresses our increasing anger and frustration with having the "real" of pop stars forced on us while avenues for expressing our own truth get narrower and narrower. In the same way, the serial killer or the killer who murders a celebrity are not doing what they do because they believe they will then become celebrities; they are doing what they do because their reality has been restricted by someone else's vision of that reality. They, like all of us, are in an invisible prison. We become frustrated with the fetters that restrict our movements, invisible bars holding us in invisible cells. And no matter what we do, what we say, we cannot get the guards to notice us.

The trench-coat boys are now just spectres. The moment our rampaging murderers disappear into death or jail is the moment their desperate war against the mono-real is lost. The irony is that these people who lash out as an attempt to establish their individual reality within the fake "real" of mass culture are the most likely to have their "real" imposed upon by the strictures of the state—shot by the police, executed, confined to a solitary cubicle for the duration of their sad lives. Sucked into the product world, any hope they had of asserting themselves as individuals with their own reality is lost; they have forfeited it. The celebrity assassin is a deluded, failed creature whose quest for reclamation and control through the contrivances of mass media is always rebuffed because such actions can end only in a total loss of control over the deluded reality the individual seeks to assert.

I'm watching it all go down on TV. I'm watching the tale of the Littleton shootings in all their grisly detail, teary interviews sandwiched between commercials. At a certain point the host says, in a complete non sequitur: "Read more about the tragedy in *People* magazine." Above her shoulder, the cover of the magazine appears, emblazoned with a headline. And so, even mass murder is absorbed by the dominant reality, converted into product and, in this way, understood, pacified, muted, forgotten.

■ ■ ■

Pundit Neil Gabler, in his book *Life: The Movie*, subtitled *How Entertainment Conquered Reality*, argues that our devotion to celebrity inspires the serial killer or the mass murderer who figures that his actions will be rewarded with everlasting fame. I'm arguing that much of what we do is an attempt to find a place for celebrity, and the other stereotypes of mass culture, in our lives. We search for the mental environment in which we can be happy just to be who we are—the unfamous, not the infamous. In Gabler's version, as in Neil Postman's, we are the deluded, confused citizenry; we are the trench-coat boys whose desire to view our lives as a show— or, as he puts it, a "life movie"—represents a loss of morality, the death of sustaining traditions, the victory of falsity over every aspect of our lives.

What Gabler fails to recognize is that our use of the language of plunder, our manner of comparing life to movie plots, our desire to participate in the manufacture of simulacrum narratives, is a sign of a battle only just joined. We *are* trapped in a singular movie, and it is our most fervent wish that we might find a way to distinguish ourselves from that movie, which threatens to overtake our lives. It's not that life is a movie or a TV show, but that the discourse of life now takes place on the level of movies, of entertainment. We must have access to that discourse if we are to have any hope of participating meaningfully in our own lives. The sad fact is that we are trapped in this world—which makes it easier for critics to blame us for the primacy and power pop has in our lives and to argue that the bulk of people have lost their sense of what they want, of what is important, of what is real. On the contrary, I say: those who do not deny that mass culture has found a resonance within our lives are the realists among us. They are the ones who assert that we have the right to make our own movies, free of the trappings of mass culture; that we have the right to use the language of plunder to allude not to pop and its celebrities, but to ourselves and who we feel ourselves to be in our world. This is an assertion of the reality of our experience when those experiences—pop moments that have somehow become lodged deep within us—are being constantly devalued by, among others, critics like Gabler. "To the post realist," he writes, "a life in which entertainment was the governing cosmology and all of existence an endless movie edged us closer to the possibility that we need never suffer life's hurts again." In other words, as far as Gabler is concerned, we are all just a big bunch of deluded idiots who use mass culture as a drug that forcibly alters reality and lets us stagger through life feeling no pain.

Gabler is horrified by the way in which reality is becoming a subjective entity that we each construe for ourselves; in a way we are all asking —who will organize our lives, decide on good or bad, provide us with helpful fashion tips? But in lifestyle culture, this subjectivity is the road to real freedom. The last thing that pop was supposed to do was to give us some sense that we can have control over our mental environment by doing what is natural to us: articulating our own reality. What is necessary, what is preferred, is to maintain the notion of a single, monolithic reality—the flickering TV screen you are expected to watch but not imagine, the stories you are expected to believe but not manifest in your life, the war you are expected to support without ever knowing whom you are fighting.

Meta-real, hyper-real, super-real, virtual real—all terms coined somewhere along the road to lifestyle culture. Terms thought up to try to differentiate between our lives and our cultural diversions, our false-real entertainments. And yet, inspired by the vigilance of Steve Mann's wearable cameras, informed by the grainy accessibility of the home movie, we sense that the truth in our lives is up to us to record, overdub, edit, and project. At the same time, we incur the wrath of culture's gatekeepers, who make us feel as if even our tentative, low-tech versions of our lives lack the certainty of the most hackneyed celebrity persona, the worst sitcom. This is not the big monolithic "life movie" Gabler conjures up with disgust. This is the redemptive, depressive future—a way to approach an understanding of our underground desires that reasserts the plundered life, not as product but as perspective; an engagement with the ever-diminishing but still apparent possibility of an infinite number of versions which gives us one last chance at expressing the degraded truth inherent in our real lives.

ARE WE REALLY DEPRESSED? MALAISE, IRONY, AND THE NEW MORALITY

CHAPTER FIVE

Many hours later I was back in the neighborhood. Incredibly hung-over, I felt great. My life sucked and things had to change. I would make them change. I'd start fresh and not base my future decisions on the mistakes of my past. I went home late that night and packed my bag. I filled a box with my books and letters and journals. I slipped the key under the locked door as I left. Behind the gun shop I found a shopping cart and tossed all my worldly possessions into it. The streets were empty. I didn't see a soul as I pushed my buggy along the cracked sidewalk. The only sound was the rattle of the wheels bouncing and echoing through the damp streets.

— Andy Healey, *I'm Johnny and I Don't Give a Fuck* zine

A guy in Regina, Saskatchewan, named Daniel occasionally sends me a batch of his tiny zines, an ongoing series of his own cryptic drawings and writings. ("—Sick, walking in summer stomach something the painting in Vancouver. Looking gone. Feeling well.") Why does Daniel put these books together and send them off? He says this: "Basically, making things makes me feel better. So that as little as I've done, it's not a complete waste." Where did we get this belief that our lives were wasted before they were ever begun? Or that obscure creative acts could reverse that process?

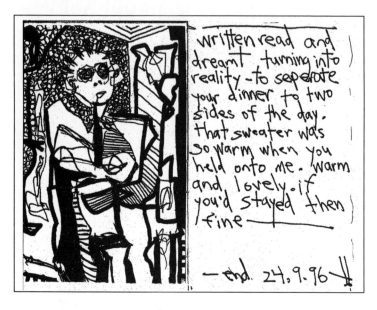

The work of enigmatic Saskatchewan zinester Daniel.

"I've been doing zines for eight years and the main reason I started was because I was depressed," says Brandon of St. Catharines, Ontario, publisher of *a.d.i.d.a.s.* (a.k.a. *all day I dream about suicide*). "Besides the music stuff, all the writing comes from being depressed. When I'm in a good mood, I hardly work on it. The last month has been great; I haven't written anything except CD reviews."

Prozac Girl, Happy Nightmare Baby, a.d.i.d.a.s., Full of Hate, Funeral Home Sandwiches, I'm Johnny and I Don't Give a Fuck, Sombre Souls on Prozac: these are just some of the many names our new generation of downbeat creatives are giving to their zines. At first glance, they seem like a portal

Depressed or defiant?
The zines of the
malaise era.

into that pop culture dimension where we (and television writers) establish our highly developed sense of cliché: "Full of hate?" gushes one Montreal zine. "Need to kill? We understand completely. Pervert? Freak?? Gore hound? Us also!!" At last, we think, our long-standing stereotype of adolescent depression can be confirmed: wan youths lacking even the will to sit up in bed long enough to eat six handfuls of pills; confused adolescents penning bad poetry, listening to Marilyn Manson, being ignored by their equally screwed-up fighting parents while moving zombie-like toward their fateful end as Prozac and suicide statistics.

And yet, these zines and so many more are hardly the depressive teen texts they seem to be. As is so often the case in lifestyle culture, the titles tell one story, the content tells another. Filled with bluster, bravado, bad poetry, and vaguely incoherent ramblings (not to mention the usual record reviews and laments for lost loves), these zines are, in fact, evidence of a latent lifestyle culture creative morality—a way to harness the vague sense of unease we all feel, trapped in lives that can never be as real, as powerful, as dramatic, as the lives we see on TV. These are our new texts, testaments to a society of the perpetually pampered, produced by lifestyle-culturites of all ages who mock the stereotype of listless hopelessness by embracing it as a way to explain away their futile desires. In the doldrums of the zine world, we find the stirring of a whole new world of post-ironic lifestyle culture creativity.

■   ■   ■

Depression is a serious illness, but it isn't what most young people mean when they claim that they are depressed. And to say that we are depressed somehow doesn't quite cut it when what we really mean to say is that our society as a whole seems ever more morbid, sarcastic, self-referential, ironic, and negative. Somehow, depression just doesn't capture the mood of pop culture's bastard children, forever shaping some kind of mythical future out of random acts of creativity nobody seems to notice.

Brandon says that when he feels "depressed" he tends to think and write and create. This is typical of many young artists and creatives—we are "depressed," so we talk and write and dabble. We get ourselves excited about our "depression," whereas the medical understanding of depression cites inactivity and passivity as the primary symptoms.

That's not to say that Brandon isn't occasionally unhappy, gripped by the swoon of some pervasive anxiety we all seem to share. Like Daniel and Brandon, we create in a strange state of denial, citing an unspecified mental pall as our inspiration. What is that pall? It's the pop culture promise much discussed in this book. Which is why what Brandon calls depression I would describe as "a vague sense of mental or moral ill-being."

This is not just another definition of depression. It's the dictionary definition of my favourite noun: malaise. Taken within the context of our lifestyle culture desires, malaise is a kind of ethical framework within which we try to address the difficulties of giving voice to a creativity that falls outside of the world of mass culture. To put it baldly, in the new morality of malaise, the best thing to do is to admit defeat before you even get started. "Thou shalt embrace a highly aware self-defeatism" is malaise commandment number one, carved in photocopy toner and cheap paper and dispensed, free of charge, to anyone who cares.

Malaise as a moral state is also a defence. When we are

confronted with our inability to give ourselves the voice pop culture promises, we like to tell ourselves that it doesn't matter, that we don't care, when, of course, it does matter and we do care—deeply, profoundly. We show this caring by channelling our frustration into creative acts that express our fear of failure by enacting a kind of displacement from the world around us. "We deflect emotions we long to feel by comparing them to something else, or by mocking ourselves for feeling them," says philosopher Mark Kingwell. "In this kind of self-consciousness, we make ourselves into the joke: here we are laughing at ourselves laughing." This, in a way, is an explanation for our growing fascination with the miscellany and trivia of pop culture, from soap opera enthusiasts to PEZ-dispenser collectors. But this is just the beginning of the process. We are still at the start of the long journey to lifestyle culture. To arrive is to lay the truth of our insecurities on the pyre of pop, to overcome our self-conscious joking by asking ourselves: are we really depressed?

■　■　■

Marshall McLuhan predicted a world of malaise-ridden lifestyle-culturites when he wrote that "electronic speed mingles the cultures of prehistory with the dregs of industrial marketeers, the non-literate with the semiliterate and the post-literate. Mental breakdown of varying degrees is the very common result of uprooting and inundation with endless new patterns of information."

Similarly, speed culture critic James Gleick speculates that the boredom given voice in malaise is the flipside of a manic world in which everything is frantic spectacle. In other words, there is nothing quite so boring as constant excitement. "Maybe boredom is a backwash within another mental state," he writes. ". . . [W]ithout mania, no boredom?"

The contrast between maniacal electronic speed and our bored, listless malaise is strangely familiar to us, in the same way Brandon's "depression" is recognizable. The thriller was exciting, but not long after we leave the theatre our paralytic inability to convey the energy we absorbed from the big-screen, big-sound spectacle begins to frustrate us. This creative frustration—an inability to make our lives live up to the overwrought electronic world, the pressing desire to make our nothing lives something—is malaise, the root structure of lifestyle culture. And yet we can't help but be somewhat muted in our celebration of our collective failure and dysfunction, living as we do off the bounty of a perpetually exciting electronic world. After all, what do most of us have to be down about? We're well fed, well educated, and generally pretty lucky. In contrast to those who, only a generation or two ago, suffered through the horrors of the Holocaust, Hiroshima, and other inconceivable tragedies, it seems almost ridiculous to admit that we are, collectively, a society plagued by a profound, petty sense of despair.

Perhaps the legacy of the past has left a tattoo on our skin. Maybe "mental breakdown" has as much to do with new, emerging generations being imprinted with the collective madness of the past century, a lasting legacy of assembly-line destruction representing the true impact of technology on our minds. The decade and century and even the millennium may have arrived and passed, but those consumed by the horrors of the Industrial Revolution still wander, haunting us in the aisles of our well-stocked grocery stores, fevered reflections of ghost-hollow faces glancing off the sides of wax-polished fruit. And what have we emerged into? A new thousand years to celebrate our lives, wedged between the optimistic rhetoric of our pundits and politicians—who speak of healing and renewal while gun-toting teens stalk high school libraries—and the high-energy promises of gleaming method actresses clutching new improved products to their new improved cleavages.

The web of history holds us in place while the spiders of industry descend to suck out our blood. How nice. And yet, the spider's limbs are soft, the web is silken, and we can be assured that our slow deaths will be oh so comfortable. We must make a life out of this comfortable degradation, and so our younger generations of lifestyle-culturites drink endless glasses of beer and chain-smoke cigarettes while they discuss the corrupt nature of corporate society.

Call it what you will, but evidence of our unease is everywhere. We distrust politicians, nations, corporations, institutions—anyone who claims to be on our side, working with us for a new future that sounds a lot like our pundit's evocation of a dimly recalled past, that returns to the old ways we are always hearing about. Meanwhile, our pop culture, with its emphasis on gore and destruction, has a distinctly apocalyptic feel to it that, ultimately, is less about vapid entertainment than about covering over the depth of doom with a veneer of bluster. Giant meteors fall, aliens invade, madmen drop bombs, cloned dinos take over, axe-wielding maniacs cut up fornicating teens, talking apes use humans as slaves to rebuild a crumbled earth, and we pay to see this stuff. The band Everclear sings: "We can live beside the ocean . . . and watch the world die."

■   ■   ■

Malaise is the legacy of the Generation X cliché in which we are portrayed wallowing in our existential pseudo-angst, drinking beer and clinging to our suburban childhoods. Like most pop platitudes, there is something compelling about the Gen X portrait, but we also realize that the essential truth eludes the magazine cover stories, newspaper features, and portentous movies. Malaise is a product of mass culture (and, as such, a precondition for lifestyle culture) and it is hardly limited to those who fall into the Gen X stereotype. In fact, malaise is a creative—not a pathetic—state. Vancouver cartoonist Brad Yung portrays young hipsters practising their apathy skills. "I don't care, I don't care, I don't care," one bespectacled young man repeats to himself over a cup of coffee. Such an act—not to mention imagining that act and drawing it—tells us that malaise is a proactive affliction; it isn't something that just happens, it's something you have to work at.

Vancouver cartoonist Brad Yung doesn't care.

Angela, creator of the suburban zine *Happy Nightmare Baby,* explains it this way: "I think for me being negative is much more accessible than writing something positive. . . . I don't think our art, books, and movies are meant to be depressing, but they do result in a pattern of frustration and rejection leading to depression. All of us try to make things positive in the process of doing what we do. Sadly, it disintegrates because it never ends the way we had hoped. We are caught up in the outside world and it affects what we do."

As Angela perceptively suggests, many who create from the ethic of malaise are expressing sentiments that go beyond society's ability or willingness to understand them. Malaise as a morality is complex. Though we are always willing—indeed, compelled—to try, we sense that most of our endeavours will end in abject failure. That's why the doing becomes so important, as does the talking about doing. Talk is a defence, a posture, a warning. Watch out, world, here I come. If I'm ever brave enough to get out from under the covers.

In malaise, your "depression" is always justified. The commercial world sucks; it won't allow you to create and exist on your own terms. You would be doing something—hell, you *are* doing something, you're burning up to articulate your vision, to get it done—but, unfortunately, you don't have the time, you can't afford a recording studio, your accordion is in hock, your novel is too strange and disparate for the profit-minded publishing houses. So why finish?

"There's a big FUCK YOU to loser psychologists who may consider me some sort of manic depressive because I tend to be dramatic in my zine," Angela tells me. "If they think I'm depressed, then everyone is depressed. My zines represent my feelings of resentment and denial at having to become someone or something. People are always surprised when they meet me after reading the zine. They assume I'm a depressed girl holding a candle, satin around my bloody wrists."

Pundits of earlier generations say we are whiners, warn that we are making life into a histrionic movie, and generally seem disgusted by the tell-all revelations evident in everything from Alanis Morissette songs to zines like Angela's. In contrast, the creatives of newer generations highlight their disaffection, proudly revealing the underground desires that haunt their too-public lives.

Steeped in the morality of malaise, a painting on the lurid backdrop of pop, we all have the potential to fulfil our dreams—though the odds are always against us, and we will never succeed. But, as Angela, Daniel, and Brandon will tell you, it doesn't matter. The wandering indie cartoonist Marc Bell has a wonderful panel that sums this all up. It shows a scruffy slacker lying on a futon staring up at the ceiling. A fat, defiant fist protrudes from his scrawny form and the boy says: "I'll fuggin show you, world—just as soon as I sleep this shitty

*Infamous roving Canadian cartoonist
Marc Bell sums it all up.*

day off and lie around for a few more and get the hell out of this place!!"

So you see how it is: a pallor, a fog, a gloom, a mist we squint through in hopes of catching a glimpse of our future. And make no mistake: in lifestyle culture there *is* a future. That's why we can say that it's malaise—not depression—that dominates the discourse of the TV generations. In the age of the atom bomb and ethnic cleansing and the Serial Killer™ line of skateboarding outfits, malaise is our new morality. It's our way of articulating the mores of a new relationship to our artificially stimulated, but no less real, world. It's depression-lite for the pseudo-underground, it's the moral fabric of our new plunder language, it's our attempt to assert the pop promise on our own terms—without, that is, actually admitting that we believe the promise.

Those who choose to ignore the predominance of malaise—or worse, find in it an absence, a lack, a negation of moral structure and possibility—choose to ignore a central shift in the way we communicate and understand each other and the world we live in. I'll fuggin show you, world! Maybe not today. Maybe not tomorrow. Maybe never. But soon!

■   ■   ■

Arising as it does from the hurly-burly of electronic life, malaise is different from its predecessor, angst. Now angst, I would argue, is the form of despondent communication favoured by an earlier generation of artists/pundits

influenced by the existentialism brought on by the Guten-
berg revolution, in which the invention of the printing press
made the Bible available to the world, with the result that
the ideas in the Bible could then be interpreted in almost
every possible way. I reject the angst label for newer generations in North America. Angst emerges from an existential
position in which, having discovered that God, country, and
relationships are at best subjective and at worst meaningless,
one is forced to face the solitude of the self in all its horrible emptiness. In other words, for us to be angst-ridden
would mean casting off our beliefs in, among other things,
the awesome power of the Almighty, the irrevocable primacy of family, the benevolent knowledge of government,
and so on. However, since we grew up in the speedy, amoral
world of pop culture, we never had the luxury of harbouring
such convictions; we no longer have much, if anything,
to reject.

There's a Tom Waits song on his long-awaited 1999
album *Mule Variations* entitled "Georgia Lee." A classic Waits
crooner, it talks about the tragic death of Georgia Lee, "found
in a small grove of trees" though "she's too young to be out
on the street." "Why wasn't God watching? Why wasn't God
listening? Why wasn't God there for Georgia Lee?" Waits
demands in a throaty groan of a prayer. And then, in the
second stanza, Waits sings these lines, the mother's lament:
"Ida said she couldn't keep Georgia/from dropping out of
school/I was doing the best that I could/but she kept running
away from this world/these children are so hard to raise

good." Now, without attributing ideas to the song that weren't intended, to me it always seems like a lament for newer generations of Georgia Lees, generations who have grown up without the privilege of faith—in God, in family, in school, in tradition. In my interpretation of the song, Waits sees the Georgia Lees of today as representing the lost generations, in which even the old faithful kiddie game of hide-and-seek is more terrifying than comforting. "Close your eyes and count to ten," he sings. "I will go hide but then be sure to find me. I want you to find me."

In Walter Kerr's early-1960s lament for the end of pleasure, he writes: "We have given up what used to be our pleasures in exchange for a set of assured values, only to discover that the values have vanished in the course of the transaction and that our old pleasures—when we glance back at them— merely confirm the void." At least his generation had the pleasure of looking back and seeing something. Today, we have only the moment, the immediate, the void that compels us toward the new morality of malaise. Try and find me. I want you to find me.

■ ■ ■

In malaise, just evoking the possibilities of the search for the self through creative action is a defence in itself. Leave me alone, goddamit, I'm an artist chasing the pop culture pot of gold. I don't have to *do* anything. The renowned child psychologist Otto Weininger (devoted to the teachings of Melanie Klein) sees the impetus for creativity as coming from our sense of loss and mourning when we are physically separated from our mothers at birth. He argues that the "creative process" is set in motion when we use "sublimation and reparation to cope with the experience of loss and mourning." If once the creative genius sought to "triumph over death itself through the immortality of art," now a multitude of anxious creatives seek to ascertain a way they can speak to the separation from the über-parent of mass culture that, like Mom, holds us all for a time in the nourishing womb, only to abruptly spit us out into the cruel world. But Mommy pop culture retains her hold over us, going so far as to treat our adult selves as children unable to assert our mastery over our own destiny.

Is the power of mass culture really as strong as the bond between a mother and child? I don't know. I hope not. But I think that the deep sadness so many of us struggle with—a creative tension, a depressive position that is not necessarily a depression—suggests that there is, indeed, a relationship between the moral ethos I call malaise and the forced separation from a collective reality that is our initial, parental relationship with mass culture. Raised by pop, we now search in vain for some way to identify with our parent. Seeking validation, we turn our most intimate dreams and despairs into self-negating pop tropes.

I'll quote here from a song written and released on cassette by a Toronto singer/songwriter named Kathy Goldman to show you what I mean. The tune is called "Prozac Song" and it is sung by Goldman with a jovial, repetitive lilt that the words as they appear on the page can only hint at. Still, you'll get the idea:

Its been years of stupid tears
I felt quite low
who wants to know?
but the psychiatric team said it would raise my self
esteem and give me a second chance to live and grow
and I am lovey dovey dovey . . .
I had bad R.E.M.
so I tried TM
I was disturbed
so I tried herbs
it's really very popular just ask your family doctor
but don't expect a new job or a raise
and I am lovey dovey dovey . . .

Goldman's stark honesty about her depression and her use of Prozac is wonderfully offset by her sarcastic attitude. In the song, she contrasts her clinical diagnosis of depression with the ironic inflections of malaise. This is notable because even the very serious difficulties many people encounter when wrestling with depression can be subject to the pseudo-joke of lifestyle culture and the blasé morality of malaise. While earlier generations might have sought to suppress the fact that they were on Prozac, Goldman and her cohorts display their flaws like medals of honour and dare us to demote them. ("I don't care. I don't care.") Goldman's song also demonstrates how it is that malaise culture turns the stereotype of depressives on Prozac into highly personal satire. In essence, the song is arguing that one of the few things that we still own completely and thoroughly is our pervasive sense of displacement and alienation. This is the essential tension between the pregnant possibility of creative action—our new religion—and the way that creativity must always be viewed through the prism of commercial culture, with all its futile and ephemeral labelling and sloganeering.

"As you watch," writes TV commentator Mark Crispin Miller, "there is no Big Brother out there watching you—not because there isn't a Big Brother, but because Big Brother is you, watching." It's Miller's suggestion of our complicity, as evoked in the work of unknown creatives like Goldman, Angela, and Brandon, that makes malaise such a central tenet of lifestyle culture expression. It's also what pushes it into the world of ironic refraction, where we discover that all we have is our ability to evoke our sense of our own devaluation. In other words, we have nothing but our expression of nothing (a.k.a. pop culture). But at least we still have that. And so, for better or worse, malaise becomes a kind of de facto morality. Irony at our own peril.

■   ■   ■

To speak about nothing in the land of plenty demands a new accounting of that strangest of terms, irony—

perhaps the most overused and overdetermined of the rhetorical conceits in our mass media arsenal. Poor irony, misunderstood and blamed for everything from the demise of morality to the rise of bad television. Even its apparent champions eventually turn on it, find in its rapid-fire undercutting of all that's sacred something insidious, dangerous. "I've been guilty of irony and cynicism," bleak post-rocker Beck tells *The New York Times*, "those things that are symptomatic of our times. You can't really blame anybody, in the way irony and cynicism are pounded into everybody's heads in every TV commercial, as if we're all insiders on the big joke here. But there's got to be more than just the joke."

Beck's transition from the overt irony of "I'm a loser baby" to the sly incandescence of *Mutations* is a telling one. The malaise ethos is irony in transit, sarcasm whirring by, a dream of a dream—despair in yearning moments that belie their ironic package: "There's got to be more than just the joke." In malaise, we evolve from a kind of generic irony— which, having been consumed by the marketers, has long since ceased to be an effective platform for rebellious outpourings—to a muted sadness in which the very doing, the very fact that we feel compelled to do, is dipped like a strawberry in the rich chocolate sauce of irony.

"We have to take the ironic laws of media evident in a postmodern world both seriously and not seriously," writes professor Wolfgang Schirmacher. "The self wants to overcome its separateness without losing its specialness." Which is to say that we want to find a way to articulate the communal depth of our despair, thereby defying our lonely "separate-ness," without jettisoning the individual possibilities of dissent that irony so expertly conveys—our "specialness." Hence Beck's transition from the ugly sarcasm of irony to a muted sadness, a repressed irony in which there can't even be a joke any more, because nobody knows what's funny.

Within the idea of malaise as a kind of morality, we can find a striving, a moving forward: we reject the soulless blanket irony of the beer commercial in favour of a less obvious, more strident malaise-irony that is intertwined with our language of plunder and our perceptions of the multiple real.

No less an authority than the nineteenth-century Danish philosopher Søren Kierkegaard has perceived the potential for de(con)struction that irony predicates. "For irony," he writes, "everything becomes nothing, but nothing can be taken in several ways. . . . The ironic nothing is the dead silence in which irony walks again and haunts (the latter word taken altogether ambiguously)." A hundred and fifty years later, philosopher Mark Kingwell warns us, writing on the moral turpitude of those who create "The Simpsons," that "the show's Harvard educated writers do not have the courage of their moral convictions. Instead of genuine satire—real social commentary that also happens to be funny—they offer a slyness that stands for nothing."

While there are certainly myriad TV shows and entertainments that do indeed serve up a kind of sly emptiness that is purely imitative, I think that the predominance (and popularity) of shows like "The Simpsons," "Seinfeld," "Beavis and Butthead," "South Park," and even their half-breed imitative cousins speaks to something more profound than just "a slyness that stands for nothing." The shows— and our reaction to those shows—speak to a moral imperative that is about the way to make nothing into something. This is the search that Beck alludes to when he tells *The New York Times* that there's "got to be more than just the joke." It's a search that marks a shift in the way we understand irony: from ghostly haunt of dissent, to jaded pseudo-inclusive marketing campaign, to, now, in lifestyle culture, its incarnation as something ethical and defensive, steeped in the ever-present "real" of pop, and, because of its undeniable potential as a nihilistic creative force, dangerous and subject to attack. Yes, it's true that, as the editor of the satiric website The Onion has explained, "Generation X is cynical and very afraid of doing something genuine or demonstrating a heartfelt belief in a cause or person." But is that necessarily a bad thing?

In searching for the essence of the new irony of malaise, I turned to an actual "Simpsons" co-producer/writer, former "Late Show with David Letterman" head writer Tim Long (he graduated from the University of Toronto, not Harvard). "Any show on network TV is in some way reinforcing the status quo," Long told me, on the phone from L.A., "but in defence of 'The Simpsons' it has done an amazing job of subverting a lot of the conventions that govern TV. The fact that the point of view is less definable and can't be reduced to a slogan doesn't mean it's not engaged. The ambiguity is good for comedy. Though I'm sure it drives the pinkos crazy."

"The Simpsons," with its clever attack on sitcom conventions and its appeal to our intelligence and our new plunder language, is a better, more inclusive and more challenging show than most. This is largely because its freewheeling use of an ever-present malaise-irony prevents us from taking each episode's inevitably trite conclusion seriously. Lisa succeeds in teaching her pals that girlhood is something to be cherished, but only when the school dance is flooded by the cafeteria grease Bart and Homer are trying to steal for lucrative resale. We learn nothing from this, but the nothing is far more instructive than the lame after-school-special tutorial found in, say, your average "Dawson's Creek" episode. "The Simpsons" and shows like it essentially mock the professorial view that one should learn from TV, that TV should refer to something other than . . . more TV. Tim Long and his cohorts know better. We do not learn from TV; we are entertained but never educated. This is the malaise ethos in practice: you bother to say something, even though you're pretty sure no one is listening, and no one cares. A troubling, entertaining, possibly liberating point of view.

Studies have shown (and who the hell knows how they study this stuff) that teenagers in conflict with society (their parents) tend to increase their VCR use *and* listen to more evil rock music. Now adults, we connect our guilty obsession with mass culture to illicit pleasure and juvenile rebellion.

And why shouldn't we? Pop culture is kids' stuff. To accept this is to admit that, contrary to established opinion, we often find a great deal of ashamed satisfaction in what we are and have become. We revel in the movies, and the hype about the movies, and the pompous, self-important commentaries that follow in the wake of the movies and their hype like smoke after fireworks. We wield armchair cynicism like a remote control, turning flagship shows "Entertainment Tonight" and "Fashion Television" into instruments of our dissent, conduits of our insecurities. We mock the corporate–entertainment synergy even as we bring it into our lives. Our TV shows offer up the facts of mass style with such glib assurance that they seem to invite our assumption that it's not just we viewers who are wasting our time, frittering away our lives, it's everyone—movie stars, super-enthused TV hosts, our most popular entertainment facilitators, and our most obscure semiotics academics. Like us, they've moved from a sense of standing outside of culture, from trying to *explain* culture, to, in fact, living within the overarching ironic paradigm of lifestyle culture, in which they smile and blink and publish and narrate how absolutely and totally full of shit they really are. And yet we watch. We do. We insist on our right to involve ourselves in this grand spectacle. We expect nothing and use the pulpit of capitalism to preach a frenzied brand of consumer existentialism. Everything is possible, everything is happening, and it all adds up to the meaningless moments that make up our lives. Yes, that's us exactly, all too aware that everything that had a value attached to it has long since been debased by the gods of capitalism. Still, we pursue our cultural fantasies, retain the über-pundit dream of carving our own instantly debased "ism" on the blank slate of the future.

In malaise—lifestyle culture's backbone—all creative acts are subject to the pop-up video treatment. "This is what we call irony," writes James Gleick. "The balloon layer mocks the original video, feeding off viewers' eagerness to smirk and wink and otherwise distance themselves from simple images that they accepted at face value just months before."

And so irony has evolved as a way to navigate the extremes: the plenty of pop culture versus the spiritual emptiness in which we long for that extra layer that includes us, that redeems us by keeping us in the joke; the relative comfort of our lives pitted against the recognition of our minute place in the product universe. When we "blame" the media for propagating evil and encouraging "copycat" acts of destruction, we are really blaming ourselves. (And what the hell is a copycat killing?—as if the play were being performed in a different city with a different cast; as if those were not individuals killing and being killed but pawns in the media continuum, imitators who weren't original enough to come up with their own act.) Similarly, when we "blame" irony and sarcastic indifference for instilling in us and others moral ambivalence and profound disaffection, we are essentially shooting the messenger we ourselves sent to bring back the news. After all, it's not as if "the media" is an entity that exists without us, despite us, or independent of us. And so the new irony works (always within the language of plunder), like "The Simpsons," to transgress decency and ensure our own complicity. In this way, we can articulate what is inside of us as though it were outside of us. In this way, we can speak about things as if we don't care, though we care very deeply. Malaise represents our collective attempt to reach that pure state in which irony is not a sarcastic, disembodied wanderer but a physical presence, a comforting hug, the lingering warmth of Mom's embrace.

■ ■ ■

If the morality of malaise can best be described as a kind of negative optimism in which we do things precisely because we know that they aren't going to make us famous (though we can still hope, can't we?), then perhaps one of its many subcultures—the campy, shrouded gloom of Goth—is a good place to reaffirm the fact that malaise is, essentially, the creative engine powering lifestyle culture. Goth is an interesting phenomenon, a mixture of eighteenth-century European sensibilities, certain kinds of New Wave music merging with certain kinds of electronica (1980s bands like Siouxsie and the Banshees and Sisters of Mercy come to mind), and a congenial interest in death and the occult. Practitioners wear black, dye their hair black, and paint their lips—you guessed it—black. And yet for all its celebration of doom and gloom and the way it was associated with the school shootings in Littleton, Goth is a nonviolent, almost pastoral subculture.

"I discovered Goth and became drawn to all of its beauties," explains Milena, who produces the Ontario-based zine *Sombre Souls on Prozac*. "Its dress, literature, music, and its fine arts. Sure, I had an ongoing romance with death, and perhaps the fact that Goth embraces that was a connecting force, but essentially I don't think it was the 'romance of death' which led me to actively seek a subculture that I felt a part of."

The message in Milena's statement is clear: Goth, like many alternative-music subculture scenes, does not romance death, just its trappings, thereby collectively confronting our greatest fears in a world where the crutches of religion and tradition have been cast aside, leaving us hobbling toward our uncertain fates. Goth (and other fusions of style and music, like the rave scene) nicely embodies another important tenet of malaise morality: malaise is demonstrably egotistical in nature. It is about us. You. Me. The ethos of malaise culture is to take our substantive fears and transmute them into the meaningless, ironic "nothing" that is our pop culture. The two aspects seem contradictory: communal, young, lively, exciting—yet increasingly morbid, solitary, devoted to mind-altering substances. Goth is just a single example, albeit one in which contrasts are at their most extreme: dress up, have fun, celebrate life and its many permutations rather than death and its singular inevitability. As the owner of a popular Toronto Goth club called Sanctuary puts it: "Goth is about being beautiful."

"There are many Goth-inclined people who do not experience depression," argues Milena. "They are drawn to its theatrics, its grace and love for the past. Some people simply love the music and dress in homage to their favourite bands. I think most people who are depressed are feeling too apathetic to go out and find something that interests them anyway. The seeming connection between Goth and depression is undeniable, but not the only truth."

In Goth, as in malaise culture in general, the intention is to join together and give voice and space to the collective unease the mass media alludes to but always papers over with pat plots and an assurance that cheerier news is "coming up next!" In that sense, malaise is more about catharsis than it is about finding solutions or becoming active in directly addressing society's problems. Malaise is about individuals finding a morality that allows them to express the multitude of insecurities that a frantic mass culture paves over and denies. As such, malaise is a complicated mixture of group dynamics and individual pioneers. When I try to explicate this, I keep coming back to a particular image by New York artist Eric Aurandt. There is a Super-8 film he made which shows him reclining in a coffin-shaped, slatted box. As he rests there, seemingly on guard against nothing, he calmly smokes cigarettes, eats crackers, and levels his rifle through gaps in the box and out at the unfriendly world. The message is one of sublime anachronism: as we seek to move back into the imagined self, the dreamy, simple pop world of heroes and antiheroes, we find that world's violent, malignant trappings within ourselves.

■　　■　　■

"A computer in every bedroom and a baseball cap on every head doesn't stop the alienation, which is why suicide is a leading cause of death among young people in the United States," lectures *The Globe and Mail*. All this product, all this misery. The steadily rising suicide rate among young people is the clearest evidence we have that lack of meaningful opportunities and a breakdown and absence of belief structures (family, God, state) create a cycle of exclusion that, in its conventional sense, starts with teen angst, moves on to depression, and ends, for some, in tragedy.

Malaise breaks that cycle by creating a cultural space that allows for and insists on doing and creating—even if we are creating nothing but words, Goth subcultures, safe havens of negativity where our pop culture obsessions and our creative impetus will be respected and understood as something that stands outside of the commercial sphere—a ghostly reverb irony that, however unappealing to some, is surely better than its alternative. In such a space we articulate what we feel, and cannot be told that it is unimportant or unappealing to the target market.

Perhaps we should be glad that our leaders are clueless, the economy is an engine pumping prosperity like carbon monoxide, and the old ways are just a rear-view-mirror impression. Freed from these increasingly dubious trappings, we can and are slowly beginning to commit to other endeavours and ways of living. To the casual observer these endeavours might seem pointless—obscure zines, indie tapes few ever hear, barely readable comics, grainy sixty-second movies—but when considered collectively they are infinitely more resonant than the bigger culture they are at once opposed to and consumed by.

Malaise is everywhere. Its surface message has already been taken up by huckster ad companies and cynical music executives in the form of the sly blanket irony Beck and Kingwell are right to lament. Warily we play along, secretly pleased to be finally getting some attention. But in our hearts we know it doesn't matter. Malaise cannot be invalidated by the pseudo-cultural space of consumerism. Built into our malaise is a profound and eternal distrust. Think of the Super-8 Aurandt forever guarding his shotgun coffin failure. Imagine what Brad Yung's hipster cartoon character would say ("I don't care!"). And does anybody who hears the band Everclear sing "We can live beside the ocean . . . and watch the world die" really give a fuck?

REACTION, REDUCTION: REINVENTING THE UNDERGROUND?

PART THREE

BEES STUCK IN HONEY: STUPID JOBS, POP-WORK, AND THE POST-WORK PHENOMENON

CHAPTER SIX

Sure there are perks working at a record store. Free tickets to shows, good discounts, free promo CDs and t-shirts are great . . . when it's actually something you want. But most of the stuff you get is crap and simply exists to try and help you forget the fact that you work at minimum wage with no chance of ever getting a raise.

— Jeannette Ordas, *Queen of the Universe* zine

I'm in New Mexico attending the sixth annual seminar of sabotage in the workplace. The desert swirls around the dude ranch/convention centre. Middle managers stinking of tequila stagger past prickly pear cactuses on their way to a buffet table heaped with tex-mex tortilla wraps. It's the closing barbecue and everyone is all smiles, despite the threatening sandstorm. We're confident, relaxed, and drunk. In a few hours we'll be soaring back to our various workplaces, hungover, fattened up, and prepared to encourage our subordinates to pilfer, borrow, and undermine.

"Encouraging your employees to steal," one organizer of the gathering tells me, "not only increases their productivity, but also enhances company loyalty. No employee wants their firm to fold when they think they're getting a 'free ride.'"

And so I am instructed, along with roughly three hundred other managers representing companies from the United States, Canada, Europe, and as far away as South Africa and South Korea, in the best ways to let employees think they are getting away with things. We are told to be sure and make it easy to pilfer retail stock, office supplies, and even, around major holidays such as Christmas and Easter, a little cash. The occasional long-distance phone call should be accidentally overlooked. Illicit use of company time and resources to pursue dream projects—like proposals for sitcoms that will never be made, and encyclopedic tomes on motorcycle stunt-jumpers that will never be published—should be permitted. Each employee should be allowed a certain amount of what is known in the corporate-sabotage handbook as "slack time." Slack proportions are determined on a case-by-case basis using a complex formula that includes dollar loss to the company from petty theft, equipment and merchandise "borrowing," and workplace stoppage, as well as employee rates of pay and production. Employees who exceed their allotted "slack" should be "found out" and either censured or terminated. According to the experts, this rarely happens.

In general, employees should be encouraged to be creative in their pursuit of quasi-illegal antics, which, studies have shown, will reaffirm their commitment to a job they consider "cushy" and "not demanding." The all-day lecture on "making your employees think their jobs are creative even though they're really not" was particularly helpful, providing insights into the way the post-modern worker is willing to trade rights—such as health care and job security and fair remuneration—for the illusion of freedom and originality in the new "info" environment of the post-work world.

The blood-red sun sets over the tan swirling sand of the desert as we drunkenly stagger onto the air-conditioned coaches queued up to take us to the airport. Doors swoosh shut and we're on our way to the highway, buses disappearing into the grainy maelstrom like the corporate-sanctioned, supposedly covert actions of our employees. We relax in our comfortable seats, secure in the knowledge that though we can't always see what our rapscallion underlings are up to, we can put measures in place to manage their petty subterfuge. Thanks to the sabotage conference, we have the tools to ensure that our employees do their jobs and treat us with a veneer of respect, even as we continue to nourish the vague sense of contempt and suspicion that characterizes the healthy workplace.

■   ■   ■

In actual fact, I've never been to New Mexico. The closest I've been to an employee seminar was a four-hour customer service training session when I was an usher (bring your own lunch, sodas provided). So why this sarcastic scenario?

For one thing, it has long been recognized that making

things up is just one of the many ways that we bring a spirit of creativity to our mundane, rote jobs. We falsify our time-cards, lie about our daily activities, nap on the job, call in sick when we're feeling fine, and, in more extreme cases, fabricate sales reports, invoices, receipts, and encounters with customers. We know we do these things, and our employers know we do these things. The amount of cash the poor corporations apparently lose as a result of workplace dishonesty is in the billions. Repressive efforts—like monitoring à la Steve Mann—largely fail to prevent us from indulging in inactivity, theft, and even deliberate destruction. Maybe the above scenario isn't that far-fetched. Taking their cue from the pseudo-rebellion evoked in pop culture, employers are starting to recognize that they are better off encouraging a little creative venting by their workers, looking the other way at certain instances of petty larceny, and, in general, creating an environment in which ersatz creativity (do the phrases "We want your input!" and "Our doors are always open!" sound familiar?) replaces the well-established traditions of employee sabotage and slack.

All this is to say that, though a certain amount of worker disgruntlement is natural and inevitable (and always will be), lifestyle culture is skewing the equation. We are increasingly at odds with the mundane nature of everyday life, which we participate in but do not accept as "real" for us. So, as more and more of us come to the lifestyle culture mantra—"We want some too!"—the nature of the job and our relationship to work is undergoing a radical shift. This is especially true for the newer generations, whose cup runneth over with the "useless" knowledge of an entertainment universe we all want to be part of. Thus, the question that really interests me is this: how does the workplace adjust to mass culture–inspired increases in the levels of disloyalty and disaffection we feel toward our jobs?

First, I suppose I'd have to make the case that attitudes toward work are shifting, that we are, indeed, becoming steadily more annoyed by the "opportunities" available to us in the workplace. Martin Sprouse, author of the 1992 book of anecdotes *Sabotage in the American Workplace*, writes in his introduction: "An interviewer asked what I thought could be done to solve the problem of sabotage. I told him I didn't see sabotage as a problem, but as a necessary and valid reaction to dissatisfaction caused by work. Since it's not a problem, there's no solution." Which is another way of saying that our workplace antics are a product, not of our general sloth and bad tempers, but of a mental environment that forces us to make a living in ways that are contrary to both our inclinations and our changing perceptions of the world around us. Sabotage isn't the problem; work is the problem. And if it's true that, where work is concerned, the collective "we" tends to be at the mercy of larger variables we have no hope of influencing except through what appear to be a limited number of predetermined "choices," then our relationship to work appears to be a lot like our relationship to mass culture. We are taught to pick and choose from a limited menu of possibilities, while at the same time we are told: The sky's the limit! Be your own person! Take the initiative! Show us what you've got! "You're a superstar," blurts Madonna, "you know you are!" These career-counsellor slogans rarely ring true when we attempt to apply them to our efforts to partic- ipate in the cultural sphere, or our efforts at finding mean- ingful employment (often the same thing). It seems as though a lot of attention is paid these days to the "construct" of the "corporate rebel." We are supposed to be comforted by the idea that there is such a thing as a company maverick who breaks the rules, takes risks, and makes pots of money for the firm while she's at it. But as we wait idly for our nose- ring to be noticed by the boss, somebody still has to answer the phone.

In "real" life we are expected to amalgamate ourselves into the corporate creature, serve its ends, and submerge our puddles of individuality into the ocean of memos and e-mails and meetings and flow charts and profit margins which make it clear that no one is greater or more important than the cor- porate entity (except the CEO, who makes twenty million a year to our twenty thousand). Like Mighty Morphin Power Rangers, who begin by flaunting their supposed individuality (out of costume, they are a racially diverse group of "normal" teens with different skills and abilities) and end by forming a single giant robotic dinosaur on the advice of a televised god figure who instructs them to tell no one of their powers, we must, every day, face the schism between individual and mass, independent and corporate. The tensions found in the workplace—ones that almost everyone, from the lowly gas station attendant to the wealthy middle manager, can relate to—are almost identical to the issues raised by our gradual immersion into the pop continuum. Creativity versus ersatz originality. Independence versus antagonistic dependence. The harsh truth of the commodity-state versus the opulent lie of the entertainment-nation.

So, we approach work the way we approach everything else in lifestyle culture, through the veil of malaise: as a forum for our struggle to consolidate selfhood and mass culture. Our work, like our pop culture, is both within and outside of us. The thing that engages most of our waking hours (with the exception of watching television, of course) is also the thing that we spend a lot of our waking hours complaining about, avoiding, and even deliberately undermining. This is the reality of the mass culture fantasy we half-believe in. Sprouse's theory that attitudes toward work stem from the overall construct of the way things are is extremely applicable to the lifestyle-culture struggle to alter our long-standing relationship with pop and, in the process, give the meaning to our lives that we used to find in work.

■　■　■

Even as mass culture has affected our approach to work, work's approach to us has also shifted. If we attempt to sabotage the company in small ways that are meant only to signal our not-yet-complete amalgamation into the corporate, the company (consisting of people a lot like us) will attempt to sabotage our sabotage by figuring out some way to harness those energies toward increased production and corporate loyalty. "Some firms are counting the costs of exhaustion-related accidents and errors, and encouraging workers to doze on the job," announces a headline I came across just a few days after imagining myself liquored up in the desert.

The debate is similar to the one in which all attempts to rebel through the contrivances of culture become the property of the culture industry. Thomas Frank's concept of the impossibility of dissent through the trappings of culture is, then, expanded to include dissent from within the workplace. "We're all in the company union now," he writes, "our needs for social justice served without having to go outside the system. Lifestyle capitalism comes complete with its own social justice and its own 'revolution.'"

Here, Frank repudiates "lifestyle" as it is seen from the point of view of the post-modern worker. Rather than take the outsider stance and work toward a strong union and employee rights, the worker prefers to, at least partially, reiterate the corporate ideology, believing that the company represents creative action in the same insidious way that brands stand not just for products but for generic values dubbed freedom, liberty, choice, rebellion, etc. It's a reminder that we can use the language of plunder to signal not just dissent but also assent. A sort of yawning "Yeah, yeah, we know all about that, but I've got an all-right job here and I'm making good coin, so what the hell?" (Even though I'm tired,

unhappy, constantly stressed, afraid for my job and livelihood, and spending the majority of my days doing something very much like nothing.) Work is one of those places
where we exchange the rebellion of principle for the rebellion of lifestyle culture, in which hobby obsessions and
minor sabotages become signals, *faux* revolutions shoring up
the system that attacks us from within after we hack off the
occasional tentacle and eat it when no one's looking.

And yet, as the entertainment/infotainment industry continues to expand and encompass everything from news to
advertising to marketing to toys to literature, it might actually be argued that there are more "creative" jobs available.
Within the system that I'm describing, in which we are
eagerly reluctant participants in our own demise, there is an
unbelievable demand for more stories, images, trinkets, spin-
offs, stores to sell all this stuff in, and ways to get people to
buy it. The result? One is, now, far more likely to be working
in "culture"—the holy grail of employment for newer generations spurred on by the hollow optimism of pop—than ever
before. Says one academic: "Intellectual properties of all sorts
are being produced and acquired at a delirious pitch in the
expectation that the envisioned media technologies to come
will require a simply colossal amount of product to transmit.
Thus, if anything, one may anticipate the production and
distribution of more mass art in the approaching future than
ever before."

Consider the case of Toronto poet and linguist Christian
Bök. In 1997 he was commissioned to compose a new language

for the shlocky sci-fi series "Earth: Final Conflict." "The Taelons speak a whispery language that often seems nonsensical when translated into English," Bök writes with the evident delight of a university professor asked to expound on a pet theory. He then details not just how the alien language functions but what the functioning of that language says about the species' culture—a terrific, technically complex act of imagination made all the more poignant by Bök's perception that poetry itself is "now nothing more than an alien idiom." What strange opportunities the culture industry provides. In moving from the alien language of poetry to the alien language of a TV race, Bök shows us to what extent the reality of working in a mass culture can impose itself on the desires of the individual. Bök has invented another language just as, once upon a time, Klingon was written down, spoken out loud, brought into this world to the delight of that first gaggle of overweight Trekkie guys sporting greasy ponytails, who knew—even as the first throat-clearing battle-grunt echoed over the bridge of the Starship *Enterprise*—that they could forever perpetuate their lost childhoods (no matter what they might do for a day job). Somewhere, in the deepest outer space of our minds, the Taelons whisper their ambiguous, polysemic language. Back on earth, where one might be tempted to see a life's work compromised by the entertainment juggernaut, one can also find the fragile, crystalline beauty of the enduring imagination—the poet eking out a living on the margins of the culture industry.

Work, far from being the last vestige of the old ways, the

only hope by which the still sane aspects of society can inject the morality of tradition and ethics into a lawless, feckless youth, is in fact at the front lines of our lifestyle culture fantasy world. Our work is both the source of lifestyle attitudes propagated through the auspices of the various culture industries and the place where these attitudes come home to roost. The workplace is where the luxury of our dissatisfaction is felt most keenly, where the opposing values of mass culture are jammed into individual expectations, where we struggle for a version of reality that includes us, and encompasses the ironic cynicism, overt posturing, and moral distance of malaise.

The longer it takes to get a job, the longer it takes to get a promotion from assistant pencil-sharpener; the more education we have by the time we get a "real" job (whether it's in the form of an elaborate knowledge of techno bands from Finland or a trail of degrees in philosophy), the less likely we are to want and appreciate and enjoy the jobs we do finally end up in. "Horrible work isn't, of course, new," writes Carellin Brooks in the introduction to *Bad Jobs*, a 1999 compendium of workplace horror stories. "What's happening now is that people who never thought they'd have to settle for a bad job are finding that's all they can get. The old education/work connection isn't holding up." "Though the unemployment rate has fallen from a peak of 11.3 percent in 1992," reports *Canadian Forum* magazine, "the increase in number of jobs has appeared to come at the expense of quality. Only 40 percent of new jobs created in 1998 were

WE WANT SOME TOO

full time." Between 1989 and 1997, eight out of every ten new jobs constituted some form of self-employment, even though, on average, self-employed Canadians earn 30 percent less than other full-time workers.

Clearly, the post-work age is upon us. Couple our lack of interest in taking up our worker-bee perches in an ergonomically incorrect hive with the fact that, in the dying days of the industrial age, there are quite obviously far more people than jobs that need doing, and you can see why a life lived through pop culture is starting to look more and more enticing. It's probably worthwhile noting here that technological innovation has had the dual effect of, on the one hand, eliminating jobs and, on the other hand, making many of the jobs that remain more mundane than ever before: "In many fast food restaurants you will not find numbered keypads on cash registers but pictures of hamburgers, french fries and milkshakes. . . . A central theme in the time-honoured ideology of progress, the belief that technological development and the enhancement of human abilities move forward together, is now effectively undermined by innumerable systems that successfully decouple those two ends through design programs that assume most working people are incompetent." And for this job, now designed for idiots, employers require experience and a college degree.

No wonder we'd rather be working in the world of culture, where, as manufacturers of the narratives that make not just the fast-food worker but fast food acceptable, we perceive ourselves to be in control of the invisible forces that

240

shape our collective identity. From pimply-faced record clerks to all kinds of film production workers (grips, extras, caterers) to web designers and a whole host of communications spin-doctor specialists, the number of jobs that seem at the same time essential, incomprehensible, and completely useless is on the rise.

And make no mistake: business is booming. I've never talked to workers more harried and busy than agents, publishers, publicists, record executives, television producers, and their myriad of assistants. One Halifax-based indie record company maven recently told me, with pride in his voice, that if he left his office for two hours, he would return to find his voice-mail completely full. Those who occupy the big offices in the upper floors of the cultural industry are on the go, non-stop, can't stop, can't believe how busy I am. There is, of course, a contradiction here: everyone claims to be busy. Horribly busy. Don't have time to watch TV. Don't have time to read. Don't have time to cook. And yet, the culture industries—from eco-tourism to video gambling to TV cooking shows—are proliferating at an exponential rate. If we are all so busy—if, as conventional wisdom has it, the information age has brought us not more leisure time to pursue and create our realities but, in fact, longer hours of labour—who is finding time for all this leisure that our culture industry executives must somehow produce as they jog along an endless treadmill of more books, more records, more CD-ROMs, more video games, more sporting events, more raves, more more more? "In reality," James Gleick tells us, claims of a work explosion are unsupportable . . . where did that monumental slab of new work time come from? Has leisure given way? Not television watching time. Not time on the stair-master. Not time spent driving. Not time spent figuring out how to program the VCR. Not time spent playing computer games. Not time at national parks. Not time spent gambling. . . . We do have time, free or not, that we like to fill with recreation.

In the long lead-up to actually having some kind of career, we are likely to fill our free time with antics ranging from anarchism to amateur theatre to ultimate Frisbee. These "interests," as we've seen in extreme and not-so-extreme cases presented in this book, often border on obsession, prompting Thomas Frank and others to dismiss them as being contrary to a struggle that we should theoretically be engaged in. (Whether that's the struggle to return to the "old ways" or the struggle to smash all vestiges of the "old ways" depends on your pedagogical make-up.) Nonetheless, these interests have become an integral part of our lives. They are our memories, our surrogate parents, our alphabet. The cold truth of logic is unlikely to divest us of them. The fact that we will not find our interests, obsessions, and passions addressed in that which we must do for a living does not make our urge toward lifestyle culture disappear. We subsequently live in a schism in which our hobbies and obsessions are, arguably, more real to us than the jobs (the lives) we are forced to perform. As

Marshall McLuhan wrote: "[T]he TV child expects involvement and doesn't want a specialist job in the future. He does
want a role and a deep commitment to his society."

The creepy realist paintings by artist Chris Woods (of
Chilliwack, B.C.) portray fast-food workers in gestures of
anachronistic confidence. Healthy, glowing young people
parade around dressed in perfectly pressed, stain-free Dairy
Queen uniforms. Two McWorkers stand in a McDonald's
parking lot, each one holding on to the corner of a bag of
takeout; they stare into each other's eyes and salute. A stern
manager proffers a KFC cardboard box, and a young worker
swears some imaginary oath over a box of the best chicken
the Colonel has to offer. This compelling series of paintings
conveys neither anger nor even bewilderment. There is, instead, an opulent confidence in Woods's images. He doesn't
ask "what have we done?" as much as he wonders "what are
we doing?" I talked to him and he gave me the typical line,
telling me that "consumerism is the opiate of North American society," but for me his paintings aren't at all about consumerism. They're about our desire to re-imagine what we
do for a living in terms of the pop promise. In their portrayal of bold, strong, powerful fast-food workers, they
speak to this developing understanding of identity and
work merging into one mass culture whole, which redeems
us by allowing each and every one of us to feel as valuable
and glitzy and speedy and universal and comforting as a
Happy Meal.

For now, in our work, we must resign ourselves to our

Preserve, Protect and Defend *by B.C. artist Chris Woods.*

"specialist" roles. This gives way to the awkward grafting of our lifestyle culture ambitions onto the realities of our everyday lives. We all know the familiar cliché of the waiter who is really an actor/writer/sculptor. But what about the consultant who's really a film critic? The convenience store clerk who's really an expert on Harley-Davidsons? The number-cruncher who's really a zine publisher? What about Joseph Boudreault, the Prince Edward Island hospital worker who spent $7,000 publishing a thousand copies of his giant, five-hundred-page novel after it had been repeatedly rejected by publishers? What about Stanley Won, computer programmer for the Bank of Montreal, who spends $5,000 to $8,000 a year on Star Wars memorabilia and has twenty cartons of merchandise stored in the house he lives in with his parents?

What about the computer programmer who goes by the name "Porsupah" and is "something of an elder statesman within the furry community"? (The furry community, by the way, is a subculture community made up of those fascinated by "all things anthropomorphic . . . fiction, films, comics, zines, cartoons, fan art . . . where animals have human characteristics and minds.")

We rarely hear about these people, though they exist in ever-increasing numbers: those of us who address the fundamental desire inherent in lifestyle culture by treating our jobs as hobbies and our hobbies as jobs.

■ ■ ■

When you apply lifestyle culture to work, you tend to find something very revealing: as McLuhan suggested, some members of the TV generations seem to have the unholy idea that work should relate in some way to our interests and, dare I say it, values. So, unlike our parents and their parents before them, we don't just want to get jobs because everybody gets a job, raises a family, retires, lives off a meagre but sufficient pension, and dies a comfy death in a hospital bed paid for by the government. No, the growing consensus is that we should be able to find jobs that reflect our interests, even passions. We must live life to its fullest, our pop pundits tell us. And yet, our cities are populated by despondent workaholics who trudge through life like it's a duty. Our cash-starved universities supplant studies of the humanities with expensive

MBA programs designed to crank out drone-like middle managers addicted to Prozac, martinis, and the stock market.

Nice Job! is "the guide to cool, odd, risky, and gruesome ways to make a living." It's a partially sarcastic catalogue of weird jobs that run the gamut from Pet Groomer to Human Guinea Pig to Geisha to Bigfoot Research Director to Army Food Technologist. An entertaining book, its subtext is that, in the new global leisure economy, life and job can be one and the same. I spoke with one of the writer/editors of the book, twenty-four-year-old Jake Brooks of Boston. "One of the really encouraging things that we found," he tells me, "was how people aren't willing to settle for having their primary interest in life not be their job. People want their interests to be what they do most of their waking hours. The philosophical goal of the book was getting people to think creatively about what they want to do in terms of a job—let it spark your imagination."

What an idea! Scandalously liberal claptrap not at all reminiscent of the old days in which your job was a duty, something to endure, not enjoy. Where did this attitude, propagated by the young turks of the information age, come from? By the end of the nineteenth century, the skilled worker who performed a variety of tasks was being replaced by the unskilled worker who did the same thing over and over again, unless you got to run the machines or be the boss. Most of our ancestors weren't the bosses and had no idea how the machines worked, just as most of us today aren't the boss and can barely figure out how to turn our workstation on, let alone open it up and make it function again after we've spilled a can of Jolt on it (damn, there goes an entire afternoon of e-mail, Tetris, and surfing the Internet). Anyway, by the beginning of the twentieth century, we were all pretty much stuck in mechanistic, boring jobs in which the same tasks were performed every day, whether we're talking about the assembly line or the office. There was one thing, though: we had become the middle classes. The mass production of stuff also produced a surplus of cash with which to buy the stuff we were spending our days making—how else to sustain the constant production of goods? We were making money and we wanted to spend our excess money on entertainment and luxury, contrivances and unnecessaries that would show that we were still individuals with distinct interests and desires, not slaves but free people who worked hard and partied hard. "At the end of the workday," writes Neil Gabler, "workers left their factories wanting to have a good time and wishing to declare their independence off-hours in ways they were prohibited from doing when on the clock."

"I slept all day resting up for the job," answers Charles Bukowski in his 1971 classic *Post Office*. "On weekends, I had to drink in order to forget it."

The job looms each morning, occupying our time and invading our minds, giving us dizzy spells and stress attacks and chest pains. I could be at home drinking myself to death. I could be working on my collection of vintage baseball cards. The job as an end unto itself has faded. Now, the job, which provides access to the trappings of lifestyle, is just something to get through. "For a growing number of Quebecers," writes Jean Mercier, professor of Political Science at Laval University, "work is becoming increasingly what one does between going to the movies, listening to CDs or any other two cultural events. We need look no further for the postmodern society: we're already there."

Of course, many of us still have jobs, but how many of us actually believe in our jobs, want to hold them for the rest of our lives, seek the satisfactions one associates with the good life in work? "For the first time," claims a City University of New York professor in an essay titled "Technology and the Future of Work," "work and play are identical for occupations beyond those of artists and scientists." Well, that sounds a little optimistic. Maybe we can restate the maxim in this way: for the first time, we *want* work and play to be identical occupations. Most of us are unable to achieve this goal. Frustrated, we choose play over work. We revert to sabotage, the dreamy idealism of malaise—mass cultural obsessions, binge-boozing at happy hour. We spend countless hours e-mailing our fellow labourers, discussing the latest movies and lamenting our heavy workloads.

The aspiring lifestyle-culturite, then, has the following options. 1: Work as little as possible at a variety of "stupid jobs" and pursue cultural directions on a part-time, freelance basis until it's possible to make a living doing only what we "really" want to do. 2: Get a job in the culture industry and try to work our way up through the ranks from assistant to the editors, directors, publishers, programmers, etc., to the point where one actually has a job that provides some modicum of self-respect in the form of sanctioned expressions of creativity and personal vision. 3: Work a nine-to-five job and actively "play" whenever it is feasible to do so—on the weekends, on breaks, when the boss is away, after work, etc.

These scenarios, of course, assume that one has come to the conclusion that work is not an end but a dead end; what you do with yourself is no longer just a matter of pursuing that which will help you acquire the most capital (though making money is not necessarily excluded from any of the chosen alternatives) but a matter of living a lifestyle that can assert the particular reality you have taken on as your own.

STUPID JOBS

In 1998 I wrote an article for the leftie *This Magazine* that I called "Stupid Jobs Are Good To Relax With." The article touched a nerve. Even though, up to that point, my vague ramblings on the subject of youth culture had gone unnoticed, the article was reprinted in another magazine and anthologized, and later appeared as both television and radio pieces. Even better, I received letters and e-mail from young people who felt that someone had, at last, successfully articulated their approach to the workplace.

I was surprised by all the attention the article received, since the overall theory that "Stupid Jobs" touched on was something that came out of my head almost as an afterthought. What I really wanted to do was contrast my personal experiences as a low-level, part-time flunky with two university degrees with my father's experience as a high-level, full-time flunky with three university degrees. At the time I was writing the piece, Dad had recently taken early retirement after working with the same bureaucratic entity for fifteen years. He felt cheated that his work had never been recognized, his path to senior management levels remaining permanently blocked. As for me, I was biding my time as an angst-ridden young artist unsure of how to make a living or go about becoming what I so badly wanted to be—a full-time writer/thinker/slacker on no one's payroll. What the article became, however, was a manifesto directly related to what would become my theory of lifestyle culture. In the "stupid" jobs I was working back then, I was encountering a plethora of recent university grads who were, like me, biding time while they pursued or talked of pursuing a variety of highly infeasible antics. So it dawned on me that, essentially, what we were doing was deliberately choosing part-time, meaningless employment over full-time, lucrative employment. We were valuing lifestyle over work.

The concept of the feckless, angst-ridden, lazy slacker/artist is hardly new. The bohemians of the 1920s left us the indelible image of wine-swilling hyper-romantics swooning around lush countryside and living off their rich, semi-disapproving pals. Jumping ahead, the term "slacker" was coined sometime in the late 1980s and used, of course, most famously in the 1991 Richard Linklater movie of the same name, which featured twenty-somethings wandering around a sun-parched town clutching jars of Madonna piss to their scrawny, ripped T-shirt chests. The now hopelessly tired pseudo-cult The Church of SubGenius placed "slack" at the centre of their new "religion," declaring in the meaningless ironic profundity popular in the late 1980s: "Slack is like freedom, but unlike freedom it brings no responsibility." (I'm a loser baby . . .) And yet the concept of slack continues to be reinvented, evolving and finding relevance in this cowardly brave new age of malaise. As our lifestyle culture urges us to tackle an ever more fundamental element in our lives, the stupid-job attitude is found to be increasingly prevalent. Even academics have taken to analysing this new philosophy: "What slack offers . . . is a philosophy of laziness as a positive attribute," explains one leftie prof.

Every city in North America has its ever-growing collection of people who, quite simply, do as little as possible in terms of lucrative employment. They search out and accept low-paying, menial jobs with flexible hours that demand nothing of them but their physical presence. If things get more demanding, they quit and get a different stupid job. They do this because they usually have some other goal they are pursuing—a degree in Marxist thought, a band, a novel, a collection of Pepsi-Cola cans from around the world. Keep in mind that we aren't talking about geniuses here, or even, for the most part, artists. I've met all kinds of people who deliberately avoid work that engages the mind, people who are, in fact, not artists but mass culture enthusiasts, well versed in anarchist thought, punk bands, sitcoms, and the novels of Philip K. Dick. These are full-fledged members of the TV generations who are content to sit around and theorize, let their minds float free, unencumbered by the hassles of daily life they see going on around them. They are our lifestyle dreamers, individuals who aren't exactly dropping out or working for change or, in fact, trying to be subversive at all. They just, quite simply, don't see the point of full-time employment when it is obvious to them that they have better things to do—like pursuing cultural visions that are, after all, very much part of the same socialization that values gainful employment over almost everything except prepackaged stereotypes of originality and freedom.

"The feeling that I'm a prisoner of whatever work I'm doing," writes Paul Levine in an article entitled "My Brilliant Career," which appeared on the now defunct Vancouver-based webzine *Barbed Wire*, "and my instinct to avoid the requirements of the job description have never really left me. The solution, I have slowly discovered, is to work for someone who understands my reluctance to work, gives me plenty of time off, pays me well and truly appreciates whatever small efforts I eventually do get around to putting in. This is why I work for myself."

Paul not only describes the feeling of imprisonment many of us feel when we become too engaged in meaningless work on behalf of others, he also quite adequately sums up the ultimate goal of most of those who work stupid jobs as an aside to more fruitful endeavours: the drive to make a living in the cultural workplace on one's own terms.

One city where you will find the stupid-job approach noticeably practised is Montreal. With its traditionally sky-high unemployment rates and its booming spoken-word and comic art scenes (two developing genres of expression that provide great examples of plunder and malaise culture at work), Montreal is a microcosm of shifting attitudes toward work. "These anglophone Montrealers in their 20s and early 30s have . . . lots of education, decidedly little employment prospects, and no plans to go anywhere else," writes a reporter for *The Globe and Mail*. "For this subset of Montrealers, underemployment can be a conscious—and unashamed—choice." What the article doesn't say, of course, is how the underemployed deal with all their free time when they're not chain-smoking and drinking lattes. As Zoe Whittal, a Montreal spoken-word performer and writer, puts it in a short story about life in post-referendum Montreal: "Maybe tumultuous times breed passionate creations. Or maybe we're just reluctant to leave somewhere with such low expectations." After dumpster-diving for pumpernickel, the characters in the story "Go home and make cinnamon toast for hundreds. . . . Plan a canoe trip. A bilingual performance cabaret. A juggling troop. A publishing house. Then a detailed plan on how to rob a Brinks truck."

"Is it worth giving up lifestyle for career?" wonders the *Globe* reporter (in a line reminiscent of something that would come out of a marketing campaign designed by hyper-ironic twenty-somethings to bring everything from soap to soda pop to the attention of their peers). That the reporter, herself no doubt a twenty-something trolling the lifestyle beat of the business-oriented *Globe*, could even consider the question represents the extent to which the shift away from work toward "lifestyle" has permeated our social awareness.

Now you might be tempted to make the case that these are just isolated examples, Paul's article in the *Barbed Wire* e-zine being just one man's opinion; you might even argue that Montreal slackers are in a unique position because of that city's unique (de)composition. But, in fact, I've met people who share the stupid-job attitude in every job I've ever had. In addition, there are many, many zines that articulate similar sensibilities, including classics like *Dishwasher*, by the guy who plans to work as a dishwasher in every state in the U.S., *Temp Slave!*, *McJob*, *working for the man*, and *American Job*. These are just some of the zines that actively propagate an anti-job, or at the very least post-work, attitude.

They are also zines that are engaged in a relentless campaign against a central reality in which we are nothing more than workers endlessly collecting pollen for the queen bee. Countless other zines not exclusively dedicated to work, such as *Barbed Wire*, feature the occasional workplace confessional in which writers discuss workplace satisfaction, quitting jobs in favour of different ways of life, and, of course, our old friend on-the-job sabotage.

Mind you, of all the scenarios I've put forward, the stupid-jobs scheme is the one whose adherents are least likely to engage in work sabotage. The stupid-job practitioner usually just does what he or she is told. Nothing more, nothing less. Sabotage involves too much effort. Those truly committed to the stupid-job lifestyle usually have something else that they are focusing their mental and physical energies on. Their energy is not spent on hating their job or reforming the workplace, but on whatever they hope to achieve when they aren't at their job—which is, after all, so undemanding and uninteresting that it is easy to forget. "While at one time working organizations rallied to preserve the 'dignity of labour,'" explains zine theorist Stephen Duncombe, "in the new, deskilled, service economy, zine writers feel there's nothing left to preserve."

AT PLAY IN THE CULTURE INDUSTRY

Not everyone has the fortitude to wade through the world of bad jobs. We can't all be content as bottom-feeders waiting for our dedication to Inuit throat-singing, Tarzan, or science fiction to hit paydirt. When we reach a certain level of frustration (or, in rarer cases, success), many of us are tempted into pursuing our cultural ambitions by assuming low-level jobs in the booming culture industry. Jobs in culture offer a status that jobs in, say, the food industry do not. A minor assistant at a prestigious publishing house holds her head up high, while her stupid-job counterpart at Burger King is generally considered a failure. You serve coffee in a uniform, you're a loser; you ring up records in a ripped T-shirt, you're cool. A friend of mine, security guard at an upscale gallery, has a master's degree in cultural theory he puts to good use when the occasional visitor accidentally asks him to explain something about the art on the walls. I can imagine him happily patrolling the aisles of the art world, but can't see him pulling night watch at a factory or mall.

It is extremely rare and difficult for "us" to penetrate the culture industry in such a way as to actually have an effect on what becomes sanctioned mass culture product and what doesn't. For every Tim Long—whose aggressively marketable sarcastic genius propelled him from head writer for "Late Show with David Letterman" to "Simpsons" associate producer before he was thirty—there are countless interns and assistants in their late twenties, thirties, and even forties still slaving away in the culture industry for little pay, in the hopes that some senior editor will have a heart attack or slip up and publish something too freaky and get sacked (only to, of course, immediately reemerge at some other publishing house, his vision reasserted through a briskly selling series of calendar-style cookbooks adorned with cute housepets). Even if you did, like Long, manage to ascend the ranks, I suspect that you would still find yourself cloistered by the confines of an industry in which inspiration is subject to endless rounds of focus groups and marketing meetings. Meanwhile, you make zines, movies, and songs about your experiences, hoping that your superiors will see these as evidence of your creative malleability, not your discontent.

Aspiring indie filmmaker Malcolm Fraser made a short film and publishes a zine based on his experiences as a film industry flunky in charge of securing parking spaces for the large production trailers that seem to sprout up like summer weeds in Canadian cities. The film is, for the most part, an account of his experience setting up orange pylons and bull-shitting with his co-workers, and it captures the essentially mundane, time-wasting occupation of the low-level culture worker. Why make a film about an uneventful, boring job in the movies? As a way to reassure himself that this dull occupation on the bottom rungs of the film industry is just the beginning. Jeannette Ordas of Vancouver wrote an article in her zine *Queen of the Universe* called "I was a Record Store Ho," which nicely sums up both her four years working at various record stores and the allure and disappointment of the culture flunky.

> I had to quit my job. I hated every single working min-ute of it: the boredom, the emptiness, the inescap-ability. Was it a work farm where I toiled away my very soul? Perhaps not, but I can imagine the feelings are similar. I worked in record store hell. "Surely you jest," I am told, "Everyone wants to work in a record store." Exactly. Competitiveness for that crappy job is tremendously high and the employers know it. They know that dozens of kids will scramble for a chance at a "cool" job in a record store. We are probably the most expendable employees out there and are penal-ized a decent living wage because the Management knows every un(der) employed sap wants our job.

In recounting the nature of her record store job, Ordas makes an important point about the nature of the stupid job in culture: the coolness of work even tangentially related to the culture industry is such that people are willing to be exploited in order to have symbolic access to a power structure that many of us, nevertheless, are smart enough to disdain even as we claw at the gates. Cineplex Odeon put a plan together that has volunteers receive free tickets and concessions in exchange for evaluating the service and quality of the movie-going experience. "Club members have surprised Cineplex by playing amateur movie critic, offering spirited film commentary. This despite the fact that Cineplex is seeking only an evaluation of the theatre, not Adam Sandler's performance."

Similarly, the practice of recruiting teens from urban neighbourhoods to go around putting up posters and stickers and creating hype for rap and hip-hop releases is proliferating. Posses are formed and participants are eager to show their worth, hoping for a way into an industry that isn't exactly known for offering management opportunities to young black men. Some of the multinational, billion-dollar-grossing record companies pay their workers a marginal sum. Others simply pay in free CDs and cachet, knowing that we will always be willing to do corporate dirty work in exchange for even a tangential association to celebrity that, in some small way, raises us above our peers.

Another, much stranger example: when a production company decided to solicit volunteers to spend a year surviving on an uninhabited island "under the prying eyes of British

TV cameras," they received six hundred volunteers willing to drop everything and head off to the island, including a Montrealer. Why? Again, the allure of the culture industry, the possibility of dipping one's hand in the honey-pot of fame and coming up with a sweet fingertip.

Of course it isn't all free work and retail drudgery. It's not at all unheard of to actually get semi-creative jobs in the culture industry. "You're seeing a lot of integration between business fields and creative fields," *Nice Job!*'s Jake Brooks tells me. "The demand for creative talent is definitely growing. Whether it's writing for TV and movies or working on Internet stuff, there's a demand for artists: visual literacy is growing as a culture, more complexity is needed in magazine advertising, there's more demand for quality written and visual content because of a boom in the entertainment, advertising, and marketing fields." These are the optimum jobs, the jobs that make us bite our tongues with envy as we froth the milk for your double diet cappuccino. They are also the most demanding jobs in the culture industry, jobs that very often whittle you down to nothing.

"The studied hipness of new media is a fascinating and rather devious cultural illusion," comments journalist Clive Thompson on the profusion of software creators and website designers and computer programmers.

These ultra-cool offices cover up a seldom-discussed truth: that the jobs themselves are often deeply exploitative, demanding intense work and devotion for relatively low pay and zero security. Ironically, the coolness of the new media marketplace is an essential part of the exploitation. By making work more like play, employers neatly erase the division of the two, which ensures that their young employees almost never leave the office. . . . [New] media employees are so desperate to believe that they are not, in fact, workers: that their work can be play, that they can control it and that their employers are bending over backward to please them. Instead of the other way around.

I've worked as an usher at a concert hall, an intern at a big publishing house (where they were nice to me and let me read manuscripts and pretended to care about my opinion), and as a flunky at a literary agency (where they quite rightly viewed me with suspicion and eventually got rid of me). I took this work not to make a living—there were better jobs I could have gotten, and the intern position didn't even pay—but because I knew that as disgusted and desperate as I felt while ushering people to their seats or misfiling a high-earning author's royalty statements, I would have felt even more disappointed with my position in life had I been the clerk at a law firm or the usher at a hardware trade show. At least at Massey Hall I could claim to have seen great shows (well, two or three) and even interacted with entertainment history once or twice—like the time Bruce Springsteen kicked off his world tour there and I had to deal with the drunk patron whose wild clapping and hooting was distracting Bruce from a series of sombre songs about the plight of the Mexican migrant worker.

But that, as they say, is another story. As in the stupid-jobs scenario, the central conflict here is between our desire to touch the brass ring of pop, and the rigid strata of the corporate world, which makes sure to keep us anxious hordes of pop acolytes at bay, driving us, inadvertently, to sabotage, disaffection, malaise, and finally, hopefully, independent creative pursuits that function, as much as possible, outside the vagaries of the marketplace.

Wilson Lee is a reporter with "CityPulse News", found on Toronto's slavishly entertaining Citytv. He is singular among those who have already achieved near-pundit status for choosing the bold, brave route of self-publishing his critiques of the very news show he is employed by. In the invaluable zine *minute:thirty* ("the length of most news stories on most nightly newscasts," writes Lee in the introduction) he provides us with gripping accounts of the stories he is sent out to cover. His revelations are telling. In one issue, Lee is confronted with the hostile reaction of a group of stunned teenagers he is trying to interview about their friend's accidental death at a high school in Oakville. "The students started swearing and throwing things at us," Lee writes. Though it's clear that nobody wanted to be a City photo-op that day, reporter Lee persisted long enough to find students who would talk to him and assist him in his eventually fruitless search for a high school yearbook photo of the dead student. "The story came in at one minute and twelve seconds," is Lee's remarkably honest conclusion. In a later issue, he describes being called into his boss's office and subjected to a severe browbeating for a supposed indiscretion he committed when quoting a Toronto politician. Wilson is pulled off the hot crime and politics stories and reassigned to the softer stuff that comes later in the news, when everybody has already switched to "Jerry Springer." Typically deadpan, Lee comments that he is enjoying his move to light news, which is less hectic.

Jeff Yamaguchi writes in the zine *working for the man* of his struggle to keep up with the newsroom fax machine and the spools and spools of press releases it cranked out. Jeff was spending so much time figuring out who should get what fax that he eventually just gave up. "Towards the

working for the man
stories from behind the cubicle wall

To _remember to write this down_
Date: ___ ↓ Time ___ ↓
WHILE YOU WERE OUT...
M _Ask for the correct spelling!_
of _ask just in case!!_
Phone ( ) _read the # back_
TELEPHONED   PLEASE CALL
CALLED TO SEE YOU   WILL CALL AGAIN
WANTS TO SEE YOU   URGENT
        RETURNED CALL
Message ___
Ask what the call is regarding,
even when the caller acts impatient..
better safe than sorry.
        DON'T FORGET _to initial!!!_
            oper.

$2

end of my time as the news clerk," he writes, "I just took all the faxes and threw them into the recycling bin. No one ever said anything. No one ever cared."

I contacted twenty-eight-year-old Jeff in New York, where he was now working in the marketing department of a publishing house, and asked him about the reasons for writing his stories down and keeping the zine going over the years.

> Part of my reason behind doing the zine is it's your way to have your own micro business. Even though it might not be making any money, it satisfies the need to have creative control, to sacrifice yourself, make your own decisions. Especially in book publishing I think you're definitely going to find that people get frustrated. You're twenty-five, twenty-six, twenty-seven, and you're an assistant editor, you're doing very mundane things, and if you're a creative person you're going to need more.

Again, the idea of asserting control over your life through independent cultural expression comes to the fore:

> There's a subtext to all the stories in the zine which is, if you don't like your job you can do something about it, you take the steps to get out of it. I think what I've found is that—it's not a cure-all—but one of the things that I like to tell people is "read my zine

at work, while you're on the clock." It's that kind of subversiveness, it's taking a little control back, not letting work reach in and take over your entire life. That's what it's done for me personally.

The ability to produce one's own narrative, one's own "real," is our version of controlling our lives. No wonder we are drawn to the image factories to make a living. At the same time, all too often we emerge from our mundane culture industry jobs stunned by the greedy complacency that is at the heart of corporate mass culture. It's no different from any other business, we are forced to admit. We might as well be making and selling widgets. But we aren't. And we don't. Because in our minds the culture industry, for all its crass devotion to the bottom line, isn't a factory—it's a place where the cotton candy of our lifestyle dreams is first spun in fluffy pink clouds. We eat the myth of pop, and it melts in our mouth.

WORKING FOR THE MAN

Not all of us are willing to go hungry. Many, the majority, suppress our cultural urges, those low-current ambitions that surge just below the surface of our lives, in favour of traditional full-time employment. In doing so, we capitulate to the forces of the work ethic, relegating our valueless pop obsessions to the back of the bus that drags us to our daily labours. Of course, nobody can be blamed for making such a decision. Economics, insecurities, social expectations, and the excruciating lengths one has to go to in order to survive as a creative individual both at stupid jobs and within the culture industry are all factors that challenge our predisposition toward a total submergence in lifestyle culture. Jeff Yamaguchi described the pressures to get a full-time, "real" job in this way:

> At twenty-five, money, it doesn't matter so much, you're paying rent, you go out with your friends, you can comfortably say I just want to have fun and I don't care about money. But when you start to get a little older, you feel a little pressure, you maybe get married, maybe you want to own your house, and you feel financial pressure. I think it's an age situation. In your early twenties maybe you want to be an artist. In your mind you're willing to do whatever you have to do, but as you start making that shift toward your thirties, you start feeling the pressure, you start having to make compromises—and the more power to people who don't, but at the same time the realities you face create that pressure.

The number of us who harbour the desire to strive toward aesthetic achievements and cultural accomplishments that are ludicrous and distant to our parents but seem, to us, tantalizingly possible, dancing before us on TV every day like an oasis mirage the desert has no intention of producing, continues to amaze me, considering the social pressures that Jeff pinpoints. The desire to not just consume but actually create pop narratives comes from the perception, instilled in us by mass culture, that aesthetic creation is a direct route to freedom and possibility. That said, our actual ambitions do not necessarily come out as "frivolous" acts of fleeting pop. I've met dancers, sculptors, and philosophers who have given up, frustrated by the obstacles put in their way. In an illustrated feature in indie-culture digest *Broken Pencil* entitled "What We Do For Money," one twenty-nine-year-old aspiring thinker/poet says: "If I don't get anywhere with my ideas, like a steady, stable income in an area that I enjoy, then I might as well get a corporate job." Before he became a full-time commercial lawyer, my brother got a master's degree in Middle East Studies and dreamed of writing a complete account of the history of Jerusalem. What happened to that lofty ambition? Our dreams don't disappear, they just get pushed further and further down until they are lodged in the netherworld of workplace dissatisfaction we confront with therapy, antidepressants, whiskey, and hockey pools. "So why was I dishonest and subversive?" asks Brendan Bartholomew in the zine *Temp Slave!*, discussing his relatively cushy job in customer relations. "Well, I've been sabotaging employers for so long, it's become second nature. It's in my blood. I couldn't stop if I wanted to."

You might shiver at the chilling lack of responsibility, but, as this chapter has argued, it makes sense: prevented from doing what you want to do, from being who you

want to be, you become frustrated and lash out. But, in a lifestyle culture in which we are constantly attempting to restate our reality through the contrivances of pop, that in itself isn't enough. You assert yourself in typical lifestyle fashion by putting a narrative forward that reaffirms your claim to your own life. This narrative—a zine, a short video, a short story—is often more meaningful and lasting than the act of sabotage itself. It is only when we become forced to work the stupid job full-time—which happens when we think we need more cash or when we find that our stupid job has accidentally become a real job—that we tend to revert to petty sabotage to vent our frustrations. In other words, it is when we feel our lives slipping away from us that we revert to asserting our "real" in ways that reveal the dark side of malaise—a malevolent creativity that consists of fleeting outbursts and short-lived satisfactions.

This can be seen in the example of one anonymous commentator who identifies himself as "Kinko" after the workplace he so loved to hate: "I started to utilize covert actions in my quest to make myself feel better about the job," he writes. Covert actions that included ruining large orders, giving friends and even strangers free copying and massive discounts, faxing resumés to prospective employers on company time, and printing 150 colour prints of his personal slides—at a cost to the company of "about 5 bucks each."

■ ■ ■

The growing trend toward employee sabotage represents an evolution: from the frustration and anger of earlier generations, lashing out at rote employment that makes life meaningless, to the canny, self-disgusted antics of the frustrated lifestyle-culturite, whose sabotages are more likely to involve photocopying a zine on the job than throwing wrenches into the rollers of the assembly line. If, in the stupid-jobs scenario, we are too engaged in our busy lives to bother screwing up the works, and in the culture scenario, too busy trying to impress our superiors, hoping for a raise and a promotion, or just hoping to hold on to our hip jobs, then it falls to the daily grind of full-time employment to account for the full extent of our dissatisfaction with work. Remember Jeannette, publisher of the zine *Queen of the Universe*, who hated her job at a record store? Well, in a later edition of her zine, she reports that she's moved on to her first ever full-time office job. The pay is better, there's a fridge with snacks and drinks, and Jeannette feels appreciated by her employers. "Yup, I'm good at my job," she writes. "So why does this bother me? Can I really get excited about people telling me what an excellent and professional phone voice I have? Does it really matter whether I can fax and chew gum at the same time? Of course it's nice to have people comment on what a good job I'm doing, but is this something I really want to be good at? Sure, I like my job and it's good for now, but babies, this ain't gonna be forever!"

Once, a good phone manner was the key to job satisfaction. Today, such niceties pale when compared with the vertiginous possibilities of pop. Like so many of us, Jeannette has tasted from the honey-pot of mass culture and now she's just biding her time, waiting for her chance. She doesn't want to be a secretary or a record store cashier or even an administrative assistant. She wants to be queen bee of the universe—publisher, writer, musician, thinker, film critic, and pop historian. So what's stopping her?

OBEY! THIS IS MALL LIFE

CHAPTER SEVEN

Evidence of the rise in U.S. shit-industry output—musical sun visor, Austin 3:16 foam can coolers, PepsiMan II video games for the Sony PlayStation, and new toilet-training postponement diapers for toddlers previously thought to be well over the age at which one should be allowed to continue defecating in one's pants—is everywhere. Yet the prospect of federally legislated shit-stupidity limits remains controversial, raising many questions: In a free society, do citizens have a constitutional right to be as stupid as they wish? How stupid is too stupid? What about the enormous profits generated by incredibly stupid shit? And are the limits even realistic given the ever-growing consumer demand for stupider and stupider shit?

— from The Onion website, 1999,
"Should the U.S. Impose Limits On Incredibly Stupid Shit?"

I n 1999, twenty-nine-year-old Shepard Fairey celebrated the ten-year anniversary of his supremely successful marketing campaign, Giant. You might have noticed it: posters pasted on walls, stickers on a friend's guitar case, articles in magazines and newspapers, product placement in movies and music videos. Perhaps you saw the documentary Fairey made and showed at film festivals around the world? Or maybe you attended his gallery exhibit of smartly designed related paraphernalia? A self-motivated self-starter, Fairey has taken every opportunity to propel his vision into the public sphere. He's distributed over a million and a half stickers and five thousand posters. And, after ten years, Fairey's entrepreneurial spirit has paid off. His design company is thriving, thanks to the big corporations anxious to tap into his grassroots, ground-level savvy. He even got a gig to rework the look of the Mountain Dew can so it would better appeal to the TV generations on their endless search for that all-important after-school sugar/caffeine/citrus high.

The amazing thing about Fairey's unprecedented success is how difficult it is to find what he's selling. You can't buy it at the mall. It isn't at underground record stores, it isn't at hip boutiques, it doesn't pop up late at night on The Home Shopping Network. It isn't available through mail-order, you can't order it with a credit card off a website, and you won't find it even in the most obscure catalogue dedicated to counterculture product.

You see a poster wrapped around a telephone post exhorting you to "Obey Giant." You stop, stare, spend some time with the oddly familiar visage, a face you think you remember from your adolescent days as a more than casual fan of the World Wrestling Federation circa 1985. Okay, you think. Looks cool. Gotta check that out.

But there is no Giant. There's nothing to buy.

"There's no concept," Fairey explains, taking time out of his busy workday to talk to me on the phone from Black Market, his San Diego–based design firm. "It's totally reflexive. It's a total experiment in how far you can take an absurd idea using all the devices of advertising, and whatever other propaganda is used to infiltrate a society."

Write to Fairey, send him a couple of bucks, and you'll get a package of stickers featuring the slightly bastardized visage of dead wrestling superstar Andre the Giant (best known for his role as the gentle behemoth in *The Princess Bride*). The stickers feature an ominous, generic version of Andre staring out at you, deep-set eyes bulging above a protruding nose. Underneath the image a few choice, enigmatic words. The most popular stickers and posters show Andre's black-and-white image and exhort us to, quite simply, "Obey Giant." It's a captivating marketing scheme that at once intrigues, informs, and mocks.

"Over the years," says Fairey, "I've simplified the face to make it very iconic so you don't even have to know it's Andre the Giant any more. Because it's not really about Andre at all. It's a way to comment on how monolithic everything is. I'm taking it over the top; my work is black comedy. My idea isn't to go on some speaking tour and talk about what I do. It's more like if you get it you get it, [and] hopefully you'll talk about the issues it raises; if you're pissed off about it, you might talk about it instead of cruising through life in a haze."

The Giant campaign is a sly reflection on how we perceive the world, what it offers us, and what we have to offer it. It's a commentary on the increasingly prepackaged way we approach the proliferation of ads in our life. "Information is

Images from Shepard Fairey's
ongoing Giant campaign. Obey!

the crucial commodity," McLuhan informed us. "Solid products are merely incidental to information movement." Fairey's Giant project is a case in point. But is this really what McLuhan was preparing us to look forward to?

"It's amazing how much it just freaks people out that I'm not working for somebody, making money," says Fairey. "I'm actually spending my own money doing this. When the cops arrest me for putting up posters, they always want to know who I'm working for."

So much time and energy expended to sell nothing. Such an effort is almost inconceivable to us. As much as we are "media savvy" and "cynical" about ad campaigns, they still manage to penetrate our defences. This is because we are taught to perceive our social milieu as a place where every image carries with it the demands of product; a place where every act, every billboard, every sign, becomes nothing more than a stand-in for stuff. We see a poster or sticker or bill-board set up in public space and we immediately assume that somewhere, somehow, there is a product. Maybe we don't actually plan to buy it, but we certainly want to know what it is. Nothing annoys us more—or attracts our attention more effectively—than an ad that cleverly strings us along, refusing to come clean and tell us what's for sale.

Increasingly, as in the Giant campaign, there is nothing for sale. Fairey is, essentially, updating an argument made by situationist Guy Debord (creator of the film *Society of the Spectacle*) in his 1967 manifesto, in which he writes, "all that was once directly lived has become mere representation." In other words, Giant, like almost everything that is marketed through ads and posters and T-shirts and sun visors, repre-sents something that isn't. McLuhan saw great possibility in the shift toward a world replete with symbolic products also known as information. Debord, on the other hand, saw a world populace reduced to its lowest-common-denominator illusions, in which the manufactured consent of the people is achieved by offering us the opportunity to choose from a handful of predetermined, virtually indistinguishable, ultimately meaningless icons—not unlike the "stupid shit" that *faux*-news website The Onion so adeptly skewers. And somewhere between Debord and McLuhan there is Shepard Fairey, who, in typical lifestyle culture fashion, straddles the faultline shift from product to phantom product, while also demonstrating that, for what it's worth, the individual still has the power to throw "stupid shit" against the mall and make it stick.

∎ ∎ ∎

The standard argument against the marketing package so expertly crafted by Madison Avenue goes like this. As the forces of marketing permeate our everyday lives, we lose our capacity to connect to the essential truths of who we are and what we want and why we want it; we become disdainful of anything that doesn't come to us borne on the airbrushed wings of a fancy marketing campaign designed to show us that something is cool and thus necessary to our carefully crafted persona. In other words, as a Manhattan ad agency executive told *The New York Times*: "It's not just about the ad anymore. It's about the message behind the company, the brand and the ad."

But what if what we want is what they are offering? The advertiser has succeeded. The lifestyle-culturite is a buyer.

Yeah, sure, we want fame, riches, privilege, power—we want
to be on TV, to be glamorous, to be head of the class, to not
have to take the bus to work. We're convinced. We want
what style promises. We're willing to buy it, to give up almost
anything to be able to afford it. But where is it?

The Giant campaign, featuring false ads for a pseudo-
product, is meant to convey something entirely opposite
from its surface message. Similar campaigns, for everything
from prescription drugs to perfumes to Pop-Tarts, now make
regular appearances in the sophisticated ad campaigns of
North America's most rapacious industries. Our lifestyle culture strivings for an ironic authenticity are borne on the
winds of symbolic manipulation orchestrated by the marketing machine. In the process of wallpapering our brains with
slogans, of getting us to perceive as true that which we
know to be false, the ad world has promised what we want—
but it cannot deliver. It has become, like TV, entertainment-
information: shaping our world, our lives, but leaving us
hollow and anxious underneath the façade. We want what
they promise—a voice, an identity, a style. But the promise is
as empty as a global village in a cyber world.

■   ■   ■

I met Bart Bonikowski, twenty-year-old film student at
Kingston's Queen's University, while we were both
working on our 1999 summer jobs. I was watching TV and
hanging out in Wal-Mart for the air conditioning—

"research"—and he was working as a project manager at an
ad agency that was focusing mainly on hawking Internet
advertising. Bart's summer project was the launch of
Toronto-Dominion Bank's new "interactive" website,
Greenville. He was looking for youth-oriented sites to put
TD banners on, and he called me to see if my zine's website
would like to participate, for a per-hit fee, of course. I
politely declined, but asked him if we could meet to talk
about his job as a cog in the marketing machinery. Bart, who
seemed surprisingly eager to talk, agreed.

"What they want is to make TD look fun and cool by
making a TD community called Greenville. One of the mot-
toes of Greenville is that everyone in Greenville is perfectly
happy because they are all using TD banking. They are trying
to make it fun, look fresh; it's like this is not really an ad for
a product."

So what exactly is "in" Greenville? I asked Bart.

"You're on this website, you see flashy colours, you're
bombarded by multimedia. The destination page features
these fun boxes. One fun box has a girl and you click on her
and get her to dance in different ways. So it's fun. She's
wearing a TD Visa T-shirt. From there you can go right into
TD and sign up. This whole campaign is really about trying
to be fun."

In other words, like Giant, like the "stupid shit" we buy
every day, there's a whole lot of nothing in Greenville, a
place where you can see the latest web multimedia tricks,
play various games, make an animated character dance

around. If you want, no pressure, you can visit the actual TD banking services site. But only if you want. You're in Greenville. It's delightful.

"Greenville's supposed to be a TD city where everybody's happy," says Bart. "That's really scary. It's like they're saying that all you need is to commit yourself to the corporation and your life will be perfect. It's complete greed," he says, dropping his voice even though we are behind the closed doors of a mini-conference room. "Just jump on whatever you can. This business I work at started as outdoor billboards. Now they are doing ads on bank machines, Internet—there's always a new way—ads on garbage cans, new ways to advertise without people noticing it or becoming conscious of the fact that they are being brainwashed."

All of this is as McLuhan predicted. "The product matters less as audience participation increases," he wrote. Which is why dominant "spaces" in our society, such as television and malls and streets, are packaged up with frenzied sales pitches in ubiquitous ads that, after a while, become inseparable from our daily lives. An ad campaign for Calvin Klein perfume features a series of sexy models you can send e-mail to. Your e-mail is answered as if the "character" were a real person, a friend of yours. You get e-mail from, say, Tia, who tells you about her imaginary life with her imaginary friends, who are also featured in the campaign and will also send you e-mail. Tia and her cologne-soaked buddies— all liberally doused in "the fragrance for a man or a woman"—are your friends too. What does this have to do with perfume? What does dancing user-friendly character animation have to do with banking?

These are questions that young Bart Bonikowski, for all his perceptive insight into the inner workings of the marketing mind, can't answer. All he can tell me is that he doesn't particularly like his job, he doesn't plan to get into it as a career, but he has tuition to pay in the fall and had to take the best offer he could find. "Consumer culture is insane," he sighs, "and it's now the model for everything all over the world."

■ ■ ■

What really bothers Bart about Greenville isn't the buying and selling necessary to the workings of everyday commerce. What really gets to him is the way what is for sale is no longer a product but a fantasy—the pop promise that penetrates every aspect of our lives. Buying is a given in our world. Now the marketeers focus on maintaining and extending what we can call the, uh, positive marketing environment. A news item on the homeless followed by an ad for frozen chocolate cake is not a positive marketing environment. The answer isn't to work toward ameliorating the homeless situation, but to eradicate reports on the homeless. Remove them from the picture. Obliterate their reality. Then sell cake. There's a reason why, since 1989 (the year Shepard Fairey started his Giant project), the number of billboard spots in Canada "has soared by 42 percent." Public relations, advertising, marketing—these are all booming businesses hard at work smoothing down the bumps in the road of lifestyle culture. The Canadian Association of Ice Industries, the Canadian Association of Financial Planners, the Canadian Association of Gift Planners, the Canadian Association of Japanese Automobile Dealers, the Canadian Association of Specialty Foods—they all exist to foster the correct marketing environment for their products. Someone says cars are polluting the air? Call up the Canadian Association of Environmentally Friendly, Totally Safe and Enjoyable Personal Transport Systems and they will tell you that it's just not so.

The protection of the positive marketing environment can and does extend to even the most trivial encroachments on the corporate territory of manufactured entertainment. For instance, Russell Oliver, a Toronto jeweller well known locally for his extravagant late-night commercials on local TV, was sued in the summer of 1999 by DC Comics for dressing up in red-and-blue tights and calling himself "Cashman." DC Comics, a division of Time Warner, stated that Oliver was "depreciating the value of the Superman franchise." The portly Oliver, clearly relishing the publicity and not too worried about the $300,000 Superman's defenders want in damages, has responded to the suit by announcing that Cashman is "too fat to fly."

Another example of the way the patina of marketing glosses common sense: network television's consistent refusal to run anti-commercials put together by Vancouver-based

Adbusters Media Foundation. The CBC, for instance, has been approached several times and has not allowed the Media Foundation to purchase ad space exhorting people to turn off their TVs or buy less stuff. Why does the CBC refuse to run the ads? After all, the Media Foundation is a paying customer. The answer is, of course, to protect the other advertisers whose messages would be clouded by the bad-news rhetoric of the anti-consumer ads. (CNN finally broke their long-standing ban on Adbusters ads, using the broadcasts as a publicity ploy. But the CBC stays the course.)

Clearly, Greenville and our new pal Tia are shaping the agenda. The goal is not just to prevent the expression of differing opinions and possibilities but to prevent the expression of the *possibility* that there are differing opinions.

To further illustrate how the steam-roller of marketing flattens out our fledgling lifestyle culture attempts to assert ourselves as something other than the products of various immensely profitable industries, we can look at the example of that ubiquitous community fixture, the mall. One of the great innovations of the century, and long a fixture in Canadian history (from the first trading post/garrison to the all-but-forgotten, once grand Eaton's chain), the mall has always been a pseudo-public space that is carefully designed to appear homey and fun while maximizing sales and the number of stores you have to walk past to get back to your car after you've made your purchase.

In movies and TV shows the mall is portrayed as a fun-loving, good-times place dedicated to cheap goods standing in upward mobility. In our lives, however, the mall is a place where human existence is anecdotal. Here is a place where everything we want is available, accessed in total comfort, total control. The mall—like marketing and reality-TV shows—is essentially a parody of our lifestyle culture ambitions. You want to take control of your stuff? You want to assert your individuality by reshaping your possessions? Well come on down, it's all here in our sanitized environs.

It's no coincidence that malls are moving toward their true destiny, not as shopping spaces but as entertainment emporiums. In the same way that in entertainment centres like Disneyland, Wonderland, and Tinseltown you are never more than a stone's throw away from a kiosk offering everything from cheesy mementos to overpriced sun screen, restaurants like the Hard Rock Café, Gretzky's, and the Rainforest Café are now incorporating ever more mall-like displays of tie-in products. Divisions between mall, street, school, restaurant, arcade, airport, and entertainment centre are deliberately blurred. At Tinseltown, which will set you back $44.50 (US) for dinner and a show, the first thing you see when you step into the lobby is the adjacent "2,400 square foot 'Prop Shop' offering Tinseltown merchandise." The ideal, you see, is a kind of real-life Greenville, where good times and shopping are one and the same, all the time. The West Edmonton Mall, Canada's largest shopping centre, is moving slowly but surely away from retail and toward entertainment. When it opened in 1981, the water park and

roller coaster and other fun features occupied about 10 percent of the mall terrain, and were intended only to lure shoppers to the wares. Now 35 percent of the mall is occupied
with entertainment, and the number is steadily rising. It's as
if, writes one cultural commentator, "old-fashioned 'buying'
at a 'store' were a hopelessly archaic notion."

The effect is similar to the effect of blurring news and
entertainment, allowing us to watch "Beavis and Butthead"
and "The National" with the same mind-set. Indeed, it's not
at all difficult to compare the mall to television. Like television, the mall is a place where poverty and desperation do
not exist. Both spaces provide "a site secured against all
threatening juxtaposition." In TV and in the mall, "management denies all dissident groups the right to leaflet in the
antiseptic corridors." Like television, in the mall you can pretend you are choosing your entertainment, you can pretend
you are an active agent in your own passivity, even as you
tread elaborately marked paths that make sure you have no
chance of going somewhere "they" don't want you to. In TV
and in the mall, as in marketing overall, the trend is toward
a captivating, if specious, *faux* interactivity: ride the roller
coaster, slurp the soda, record your thoughts in a booth for
potential broadcast on a Speaker's Corner–type TV show.
Buy a pair of ski goggles on your way out. Head home and
watch a perfectly timed real-life execution of a convict on
your digitally enhanced wide-screen idiot box. The idea of
presenting a sanitized, glossy image has even spread to the
penal system. When one U.S. state recently revived the

grand old tradition of the death penalty, they assembled a crack team who "rehearsed everything . . . right down to the color-coordinated outfits worn by the team (white jump-suits, 'so it's nice and neat and clean')." The only thing miss-ing is the gift shop.

■   ■   ■

The market for happiness through the acquisition of use-less stuff has never been better. Get out there! In lifestyle culture we respond to this clarion call, we do exactly what we are told, we obey. You see this in the ever-growing ranks of our avid collectors—post-modern hunter-gatherers who try to spear the product world even as they are swallowed into the belly of the beast.

"What drives someone to place not one but six plastic rotary phones, each a different colour, on her coffee table and wire them to ring simultaneously?" begins a whimsical article on an obsessive graphic designer found in the design glossy *Metropolis* (one of a plethora of recently incarnated specialized magazines on lifestyle). The article goes on to discuss what exactly thirty-year-old Keira Alexander finds so fascinating about the cardboard mantel pieces, Fisher-Price people, and exotic canned foods crammed into every cranny of her apartment. "Alexander embraces plastic's fakeness, and generally prefers the simulated to the real. [As she says:] 'I remember walking down the street one night when I first moved to New York and I said *God that moon tonight is out of a movie.* I'm probably more into the fake of the movie more than just admitting that it's nature doing its wonder.'"

Pioneer semiotician Roland Barthes wrote in his classic *Mythologies*: "We constantly drift between the object and its demystification, powerless to render its wholeness. For if we penetrate the object, we liberate it but destroy it; and if we acknowledge its full weight, we respect it, but restore it to a state which is still mystified."

From Barthes, we learn that we collect to "penetrate" the myth, only to restore the myth of product to an even more exalted state (merging it, in this case, with the myth of a liberating underground). We destroy the unexplained events in life—from sudden company bankruptcies that put us out of a job to sudden celebrity deaths that leave us with one less hero—by situating them on our doorstep. In doing so, we shape the random of mass culture into some kind of fantasy order. We portray the marketing world's empty promise and endless barrage of stuff as a soon-to-be-revealed secret only we know. We collect, demystify through ownership, and end up mystified owners. "Hundreds of people flocked to Connecticut this past weekend to celebrate a three-calorie, fruit-flavoured candy and the colourful, collectible dispensers it comes in," goes the newspaper report. "It's those dispensers—in characters that range from Fred Flintstone to Spider-Man to Kermit the Frog—that supply the mystique. Some collectors have so many they've lost count; others have spent as much as $850 for a single PEZ dispenser." As Barthes suggests, the process of collecting—whether we're collecting conspiracy theories or Godzilla comics or expressionists—only serves to remythologize. Like pop culture itself, the myth can never be destroyed; it can only be beaten down until it returns in a stronger, more pervasive cycle.

We see this not just in straightforward collections of pop iconography but in the way the TV generations collect pop experiences. Zines regularly evoke the myth of forgotten pop the way high-minded academics might rhapsodize on discovering a chest of abandoned index cards scribbled by the philosopher Ludwig Wittgenstein. Vancouver's *Sockamagee!* exhumes best-forgotten blaxploitation flicks of the 1970s. Toronto's *Rivet* chronicles the exploits of Le Pétomane, a top attraction in Paris in the late nineteenth century, whose act was, and I quote, "the anal emission of gas." In the same issue, our zine-creator punk-spaceman-scenester Stacey Case tells of coming face to face with his adolescent wrestling idol, the now-forgotten Abdullah the Butcher. The Butcher, reduced to the regional wrestling circuit, was found performing in Appleby's Sports Bar & Grill, located in a nondescript suburban strip mall that could, let's face it, be anywhere in North America.

As we reinvent and collage and collect our experiences—our images—we discover that the myth is a toddler buried in the pet cemetery out back: it lives on and on and gets weirder and nastier and ever more personal. Eventually, we don't have just another tragic, confusing moment in history; we have a story we can all tell, we can all own. We're proud of that story, though it is a dubious tale, is probably,

in fact, a lie, in the same way we lie when we assign worth
to an object with no inherent value other than how many of
us would like to own it. As Walter Kerr asks: "Does man's
astonishing capacity for controlling reality through the use
of abstractions also lead, in some similarly perverse fashion,
to his losing his grip on reality?" "The match was a blood-

288

bath," answers Stacey Case. "Did Abdullah win? Who cares!"

Taken outside of the marketing world of mass culture, the idea of our lives merging with our fantasies in the form of G.I. Joe artworks and PEZ dispenser collections seems silly and trivial. But in lifestyle culture, it all makes sense. We are answering Fairey's order ("Obey Giant"), blindly accumulating and giving worth to that which we accumulate. To expose the lie is to leave us without meaning—which is why almost everybody admits to buying stuff they don't need, to watching too much TV, but very few of us actually change our ways. Mass culture allows us a world without meaning, without value, without judges, juries, and executioners. Once upon a time in the real-life fairy tale we are stuck in, a man discovered that his collection of five thousand Barbie dolls had been stolen. "They meant everything to me," he told a reporter. "I could do without eating. I don't know if I can live without them."

■　■　■

In trying to understand how we move from art to conspiracy to collectibles and back again while still maintaining at least the illusion of a beneficial society working and living together, I came across *Artistamp News*, a Vancouver-based newsletter that provides all kinds of info about "artist" stamps—postage-stamp-like stickers made as art, not as a way to defraud the postal system.

With the artistamp, the translation of mass myth to

individual realities, the move from commodity to culture and back again, occurs seamlessly. Here, collectibility meets the renewed possibilities of a meaningful creativity. You can look at an artistamp and understand it as a thing you lick and stick on an envelope, or as a representation of some aspect of lifestyle culture's collective need for myth, or as an artwork in the classic sense of a sheet of stamps representing the transcendent vision of the individual brought to bear on a particular canvas, whether it's holy ceilings or the sides of buses. Artistamps are fun, they are beautiful, they are mass produced in limited quantities, and they provide instant commentary on an abstract culture adorned with the highly personalized mythologies of conspiracy and collectibility. For only twenty dollars, the publisher of *Artistamp News* will sell you his "Di Dies!" sheet commemorating "the death of Princess Diana and consequent media frenzy." Comes in colour, sheets are signed and numbered, and the stamps are available on either gummed or archival paper, all, of course, pinhole perforated.

With one lick, the authoritarian postal service, the authoritarian world of art, and the wacky libertarian world of collectibles are merged. And yet, even artistamps have a trade publication, occasional gatherings, an informal society, and an ethical stance that disapproves of the use of their stamps as real stamps passing through the postal system. It's an anarchic art form about lifestyle culture and the reassertion of individuality that reaffirms the human need for community. Is this as good as it gets? "Along with artistamps," says *Artistamp*

News publisher Ed Varney, "people create their own imaginary country, they create their own authority to define their own culture, to define their own borders, to define even what's valued in some sense. The stamps allow you to do that. They commemorate in the sense that. They say these things have been important to us, so you can say I have my own heroes—and they're not the heroes of officialdom."

In 1993 Ed Varney commemorated the fifty-year anniversary of the discovery of LSD with a sheet of stamps issued by the mythical empire of "Canadada." "Each one was different," Ed advises. "Some people didn't notice at first."

Whether it's stamps or pieces of the Berlin Wall or bad art, we seek to commodify the narrative of our lives through the process we have available to us to control our world of information, our world of figments, our world of art. We buy and sell, and

Ed Varney's LSD stamps.
Look closely, each one is different.

in our function as collectors and as creators of things to collect, we're really functioning as de facto art curators; we're
creating our own little galleries of hippo figurines and first
editions and decorative tea cosies. Our mini-museums are
about what is absent in our world and what lifestyle culture
seems to provide: a sense of control, of ownership and mastery over something, no matter how inconsequential. But
what happens when we finally acquire the all-important
object? When we find out the truth about the Kennedy
assassination? When we put that last stamp in the album?

■   ■   ■

"People think the Giant thing is cool because of the way
they come to it," says Shepard Fairey. "Giant isn't marketed through the same channels that say 'buy buy buy, you
are the consumer,' it's a little more subtle than that. A lot of
people are a little weary of having stuff sold to them, so it's
all how they hear of it initially—when it becomes part of the
persona, it's too late to reject it. They get the stickers and
then they find out there's a T-shirt and they think that's cool,
but if someone had started out saying that they wanted to
buy them a T-shirt, it wouldn't have been cool."

Fairey could probably earn big bucks paying lip service
to these kinds of theories at desert conferences. Aren't the
marketing types always trying to convince us that what
they have to sell isn't jeans or perfume but Obsession and
Guess? (Not product, but persona.) And aren't we forever

disappointed that our outfits don't make us look slimmer, that our magazines can't really solve our problems and help us get ahead, that our frozen dinners don't really taste like they were carefully plucked and prepared fresh by the Green Giant himself? We're not stupid. We already know this, and we buy anyway, somehow never prepared for the pang of disappointment and loss we feel when, inevitably, we realize that we have been fooled—again. So what interests me in Fairey's project is this notion of the impossibility of escape, of a particular marketing campaign becoming part of us in such a way that, even once we realize we've been duped, we find it's "too late to reject it."

There's something triumphantly sad about this perception. Fairey's analysis of his project and what it says about the nature of our society reminds me of the classic "Twilight Zone" episode in which a petty criminal thinks he's died and gone to Heaven. He wakes out of unconsciousness to find himself in a hotel where every luxury is free, and every bet is a winner. But when he gets tired of always winning and tries to leave, he finds out where he really is: in Hell. Such are the contortions of the marketplace, where contradicting surface reflections endlessly entrance us with a light-saber duel to the death (until the inevitable prequel reincarnation).

So, okay, the idea of marketing is to create an environment that lets us think we always lack something that we can buy. This is old-school criticism straight from Theodor Adorno. What is fascinating is how we respond to the world of marketing that has, at this point, completely colonized our minds, preventing dissent by giving us everything we want, even if we don't want it. The marketing behemoth gives birth to Fairey, to artistamp maven Ed Varney, and to the many other lifestyle tricksters whose urge to fuck shit up at least keeps things interesting. It also gives birth to the millions of collectors who make it clear how difficult it is to act upon our lifestyle needs in a world where the promised product— despite our ardent willingness to buy—does not exist.

And yet, there is a tendency to soft-shoe our dance with the marketing behemoth, conduit to all the "stupid shit" we could ever want. As an editorial in free Toronto weekly *eye* argues: "Most of us expect our public amusements to come covered in logos . . . is there harm in this? Very little, in our opinion. As citizens/consumers, we have agreed to tolerate (sometimes grudgingly) the ubiquity of brand advertising as a convenient way to pay for public goods." In other words, c'mon now, marketing isn't all that bad. People have product and they want to sell it. People have money and they want to buy stuff. It's only natural that there should be methods by which these mutually beneficial desires should be united in an orgy of shopping and selling, not to mention the spinoff benefits of occasionally providing us with "free" content, like weekly newspapers and corporate-sponsored concerts, festivals, and TV shows. In this scenario, marketing is ultimately about meeting the consumer's demands, helping us to find the products that will improve and enhance our lives. "You may not know it," goes the *Teen Tribute* magalogue available free at movie theatres across Canada, "but you have more power to influence what companies sell and how they advertise than ever before . . . fashion, video games, snack food, soda pop, and sneakers. . . . Your power to shape consumer patterns is nothing to sneeze at."

Critics from Adorno to Neil Postman have responded to this sort of idiocy by noting that when you are "choosing" cultural product from the mass market, what you are actually doing is choosing from preselected, prepackaged brands. But, I interject, aren't some of these brands entertaining, fun, tasty? We all know that slipping into the comfortable tropes of the sitcom, the love song, the thriller, the bag of BBQ chips, can be enjoyable, beneficial, relaxing. Observes philosopher Noel Carroll: "What critics condemn as a failing of mass art—formulaic repetition—is actually a design feature that ensures that people will be able to understand mass art by becoming familiar with its conventions and formulas." In other words, the sheer accessibility that Postman reviles is what allows us to come to lifestyle culture, to speak the language of plunder and search endlessly for the holy grail of unpopular pop.

The more we "become familiar" with pop's "formulas," however, and the more pop's "formulas" are applied to our everyday lives—work, shopping, the news in the newspaper—the more those formulas come to predetermine our own mental engagements with them. That is, when pop literally becomes an ad for itself, we lose our ability to respond to it, to create it, to apply it to the project of our self. Try applying Carroll's defence of "mass art" to the TV-for-toddlers hallucination "Teletubbies." The show features a bevy of spherical, brightly coloured baby aliens who wander around a lush landscape and spend the majority of the twenty-minute episode waving hello or bye-bye. It's not a show that attempts to inform or educate or in any way promulgate anything other than the kind of active passivity everyone finds so appealing in infants. Here is the perfect introduction to a seemingly easy, carefree pop world, a world in which most of us are first exposed to the possibilities of free will, imagination, and the ease of the passive aesthetic experience. It is in this mass culture world that we first develop our shared plunder language and assimilate the values of our society (however skewed and pig-headed they might be). The immense popularity of "Teletubbies" suggests not only that even babies can and should be able to appreciate "mass art," but that the stranglehold of a pastel-coloured, generic mass market culture is making considerable inroads in the minds of our youngest, most impressionable future shoppers. Here I reach the point where I reluctantly join forces with the mass culture doom-mongers and naysayers: "Teletubbies" isn't a work of mass culture, it's a steam-roller, paving the way for the marketing machine. (Can you wave bye-bye?)

Not that we necessarily need such advanced techniques in social control. When I was growing up, we didn't have the "Teletubbies." In fact, I was the kid whose parents wouldn't let him watch TV during the week. I still remember what it was like to pretend during recess that I had seen a certain sitcom or movie. "Oh yeah, yeah, that was great!" I would gush along with my eleven-year-old companions. Just like the ad that doesn't tell us what it sells, I was intrigued, obsessed, hooked. Even when you are missing out on it, pop culture exerts its power. A longing was instilled in me—to see everything, to know everything, to be part of everything. Obey!

In dismissing the marketing promise, our critics dismiss the promise of mass culture that keeps us going. It's not the promise I object to, it's not the easy formula of pop that offends; it's the inability of our "product" to *realize* the promise. We bought the soda, we spritzed the perfume, we let Tia take us out and show us a good time—but we are as alone as ever. To object to mass culture is to object to a major foundation of our shared experience in this increasingly fragmented and confused world. As McLuhan wrote, "to lament that the packaged tour, like the photograph, cheapens and degrades by making all places easy of access, is to miss most of the game." The game we play willingly; but the sides have become uneven. The mass market illusion is everywhere, stuck in our minds, preventing us from exploring our own creative impulses and from accessing and appreciating the cultural output of those working outside the mainstream pop model. Says Stuart Ewen, historian and author of *PR! A Social History of Spin*: "My problem is not that we live in a society infused with publicity, but that the publicity is a one-trick pony. It represents only one voice." The effects of this singular voice are seen when young Bart Bonikowski laments the surprisingly closed-minded nature of his film school peers: "People in film class who are there to learn about film and filmmaking will see an avant-garde film and go, 'Wow, that was crap.' They are so brainwashed, they only see things from a mainstream perspective."

We become suspicious of things that are grainy, dirty, too personal, too political. We unconsciously shy away from independent culture because we have been subtly indoctrinated with a mall glitz that assures us that everything can and should look like it just hopped off the TV set and into the living room. We no longer believe that we can or even should engage in creative acts that might actually fulfil the pop promise of realized potential and individual empowerment. As new-media commentator Wade Rowland puts it: "Man as a consumer has plenty of choices, granted, but almost all of them are trivial, falling as they do into the category of 'selections': his freedom is illusory."

The critics are wrong. There's nothing wrong with pop culture. It's the ad world, chauffeuring pop directly into our brains, that is eroding our capacity for choice, our right to respond to and play with our own mental environment. The sum effect of the marketing barrage that takes place every day, twenty-four hours a day, is to create an illusory freedom. To look at marketing as it relates to our desire to assert ourselves as cultural interlocutors is to examine the way that marketing creates mythical product and, in the process, forces us to constantly reassess our own sense of self. Pinch me; am I still here? Marketing is at the front lines, decorating our wart-ridden consciousness with sparkles and neon-hued plastic and pink-coloured popcorn. It is the marketing process, not the product it hawks, by which we are divested of our capacity for original and free thought and turned into the consumptive drones that Debord predicted.

Why won't Braino ever get accepted as fun-loving musical innovators whose music isn't nearly as weird or abrasive as it seems? What's stopping twenty-something record store clerk Jeannette Ordas and so many like her from realizing their culturally inspired dreams? We have to point the finger at the profusion of banners, billboards, window displays, perfume-scented ad spreads, and malls that linger in our perception of what things should be like until, as with those who unwittingly fall prey to the mystique of Fairey's Giant campaign, it becomes too late to divest ourselves of the notion that things which appear unmasked and unpackaged are, in some fundamental way, unworthy.

■ ■ ■

Once upon a time, I was asked to appear on Pamela Wallin's CBC TV talk show. Sure, I thought. What fun! I'll propagate my subversive ideas and exchange barbs with that grande dame of schmaltzy news-speak, the Barbara Walters of Canada.

I went on the show to talk about zines. Accompanying me was Maggie MacDonald, who was living in Cornwall,

Ontario, at the time, attending high school and producing the zine *Saucy*. (Maggie had a subsequent brush with fame when, as a university undergrad, she ran, unsuccessfully, as an NDP candidate in the 1999 Ontario provincial election.) Earlier in the month, I had submitted to several hours of pre-interviewing done by a producer who, presumably, prepared a lengthy brief on the subject of zines for Wallin. We were supposed to be on for the last fifteen minutes of the show, but, to the frustration of the producer of the zine segment, Wallin couldn't seem to pull herself away from her conversation with the author of yet another insightful book on relations between the sexes. When we were finally hustled onto the set, there wasn't much left of the hour-long show. Wallin, after commenting enthusiastically on Maggie's bright red (dyed) hair, began the very brief discussion by asking something along the lines of: aren't zines just a fad?

Needless to say, I was disappointed. My appearance had been a sham. A waste of time and, even worse, kind of embarrassing. At one point I remember holding up a copy of *Broken Pencil*, my zine about zines, and very enthusiastically waving it in the air for all of Canada to see. Only after, when I saw the tape, did I realize that the camera had been trained on my face the whole time. I had neither the chance to expound on my views about independent publishing nor the opportunity to do a little national marketing courtesy of the CBC. But hey, what did I expect? What did I think was going to happen?

Part of the way the mall-life ideal is implanted in us is through the marketing machine's most effective tool: the media. By now, we should all know the story of media monopolies and consolidated interests in North America. But what we don't necessarily realize is the extent to which the media minimizes and ignores cultural efforts outside of the world of marketing. Harried entertainment reporters take their cues from the corporate publicists and professional go-betweens who feed them information. Undeniably, every vehicle of the media—from the TV news to the papers to the "alternative" weeklies to radio—focuses the bulk of its coverage on the celebrities and products that come out of the marketing apparatus. I don't think this is a planned assault on our freedom of expression, but that's what it amounts to. That increasingly singular entity we call the media conspires with the corporate entertainment juggernaut to shut out the vast majority of our lifestyle culture antics.

When the media does cover zines, and independent culture in general, they comment on it as if its purveyors were somehow outside of the entertainment continuum we live our lives in—radicals who are ruining everything by not playing along, by not fostering a positive marketing environment. Zines, and other manifestations of indie culture, can never be equal partners whose approach to pop is an effective challenge to the synergistic monopolies that serve up our culture like just another order of fries.

I would argue that the absence of even limited representations of indie culture doings in the mass media is the main reason for our insecurities regarding our own malaise-ridden, fledgling, tentative, hopeful exercises in aesthetic expression.

One wonders how many part-time zine makers, filmmakers, artists, and writers there might be if people were encouraged to create, rather than just pretend to participate. Ben Bagdikian comments in the preface to the fourth edition of his excellent book *The Media Monopoly* that "concentrated corporate control is somewhat discounted" because many people see it as purely an entertainment matter; the synergies the mass media occupy don't have to do with politics but with pop, which, aside from high school slaughters and teen beatings, is generally considered to be unimportant. "But," Bagdikian writes,

> entertainment does more than just entertain. Not only does it crystalize popular culture, reflecting and confirming what already exists, but by selective emphasis and de-emphasis, and by creating self serving images and celebrities of its own, it can also create its own version of popular culture. A popular culture, quickly and universally transmitted to the whole society, and uniformly designed for the quick and profitable selling of goods, has a profound effect on social values.

We can apply Bagdikian's perceptions of an increasingly self-contained and self-perpetuated mental environment to the growing, worldwide trend of using a narrow range of pop culture "events," as dispensed through the media, to form de facto national (even global) identities. You see this happening not just in the "new world" of Canada and the United States, but in the countries of Central and South America, of Africa, and even in a country like Israel, which, in spite of its rich, divisive cultural history, struggles, like so many "new" countries, to produce a kind of generic, easily marketed blanket pop culture environment that will appeal to everyone and no one. Intrinsic in these attempts to superimpose a pop culture over older, less transferable, less product-based, indigenous cultures are the all-too-willing efforts of the media in these countries, who fall upon each modest pop success with a fervour meant to convey that their country, too, can produce American-style, just-add-water instant superstars. Independent, indigenous, anything that doesn't refer to the marketing veneer—it all has to go.

"I'd say that mainstream articles have been almost uniformly inane, error-laden, superficial, treating zines as 'flavour of the month,' wacky, faddish," says Minneapolis-based librarian and zine crusader Chris Dodge, who keeps a zine-ography of articles and essays on zines. According to Dodge, the articles will generally start off with a spurious definition of zines, then move on to list some wacky titles and quote from a few youngsters in the newspaper's constituent region. My own reading of articles on zines suggests that the articles will often include the following assumptions:

1 Zines are flash-in-the-pan, not a lasting phenomenon. From *St. Petersburg Times*: "Zines are

monetary sacrifices for their owners, and many publications go out of business after a few issues. A major problem is trying to sell subscriptions and ads with only a handful of unpaid staffers." From *Louisville Magazine*: "Many of them would never survive as regular magazines."

2 Zines are all on fringe topics and bizarre obsessions, and most of their creators are weird if not outright nutso. Nobody really takes zines seriously as anything but a hobby. From *The Globe and Mail*: "Since each of these publications is a reflection of someone's private obsession, the diversity is not really surprising." From *The Toronto Star*: "On Saturday, Dysfunctional Family will be on display. As will Tranzine, aimed at transsexuals, transvestites and other 'transgendered' people, put together by Amanda Kelly, a male cross-dressing suburban postal worker."

3 Zines are put out by kids in their teens and twenties whose lack of traditional/established writing or publishing credentials suggests they are amateurs, writer/publisher-wannabes. From *Arizona Daily Sun*: "It takes years of hard work and dedication for people to earn a shot at being a magazine publisher. Now all it takes is a photocopier." From *Los Angeles Times*: "Thanks to the increasing

affordability of photocopying and desktop publishing equipment, practically anyone can be an
ersatz Citizen Kane."

Tellingly, most articles on zines never mention details
like where one can find them, the addresses of the zines discussed, or the specific attitudes the editors have toward
mainstream media beyond one or two clichéd sentences
about free expression. So the double whammy goes like this:
zines are outside of the normal spheres of pop culture, inaccessible to the general public, the products of revolutionaries who are challenging a social order that, let's face it,
keeps most of us pretty comfortable; at the same time, zines
are mini-ads for corporate culture, as their amateur efforts
serve to enhance the primacy of authentic, professional,
mass entertainment. It isn't much of a stretch to argue that
zines are not exactly given kudos and respect from the mass
media.

The same kind of "coverage" can be found across the
indie cultural spectrum. Is it an accident that grants to the
independent arts are shrinking, that audiences are disappearing, that arts councils and governments are trumpeting syn-
ergetic partnerships between the arts and big business?
Montreal cartoonist Rick Trembles recounts in an issue of the
great zine *Fish Piss* his experience of doing an interview
with the local CBC TV news about an animation project he
was working on. Of course, they weren't interested in his
work as an artist; they were looking for weird projects that

had received grants from the Canada Council so they could disparage the idea of arts funding. When the reporter wanted to know what Trembles would tell people who think the money he got should have been spent on hospitals, the cartoonist knew he was in trouble. Despite trying desperately to add context to the interview and, finally, trying to have his participation pulled, the segment aired after an evening of sensational promo ads stating "You may not like it, but your tax dollars are paying for it . . ." Naturally, Trembles's worst fears were confirmed. The show portrayed him as a pretentious pervert, quoting him out of context saying that his work was about "the sexual history of a character from masturbation on" and then sniggering.

Vancouver rock pioneer and writer Jean Smith recounts a similar episode, though her tale played out almost a decade earlier. It was the early 1990s and the media was all worked up about the Riot Grrrl phenomenon, a sort of tie-in to an overextended love affair with grunge rock, Generation X, and all things flannel. Anyway, Jean, singer for the band Mecca Normal, was cited as an inspiration by many of the groups being featured, so she was often contacted by the mainstream to discuss her take on "women in rock." She reports that, invariably, her comments were misrepresented and, despite lengthy interviews, boiled down to one or two sentences. At one point Jean even appeared on an American TV talk show on its "women in rock" panel. Writes Smith:

I was flown out to Boston, put up in a fancy hotel and taken by limo to the studio. Audience member Tim Alborn of Harriet Records (and a history professor at Harvard) later told me that the studio audience had been jacked-up on sugar, then warned that we "Riot Grrrls" ran foul at the mouth and didn't shave our legs! During the commercial breaks the producers came out and encouraged us to interrupt each other, and to elaborate on personal victimization.

The media takes its cues from the dominant culture of marketing glitz, in which executions are colour-coordinated and gleaming billboards sell nothing but more billboards. The media—international, national, local—by now a generic feature in every city in North America, clearly fear the implications of an indie culture revolution, for exactly the same reasons that the larger culture monopolies and their marketing schemes do. These reasons are suggested when, for instance, *Toronto Star* journalist Antonia Zerbisias attempts to comment on Canadian independent arts and culture magazines such as *Geist* and *Fuse*, writing, proudly, "most of the time I can't figure out what they're on about," then proceeding to trash all "cockamamie cultural magazines" and, by extension, all zines, announcing that "most of us will never buy these." Are we to believe that veteran journalist Zerbisias really didn't understand these magazines? Or is it more likely that she understood them, and what they represented, all too well?

Either way, her argument is a self-fulfilling prophecy, since most of us will never buy anything that we don't know exists, or know of only in a negative context as obscure, fringe, weird, self-indulgent. But the prophecy of a weird, threatening indie culture also serves to patch up the deepening cracks in the cultural monotony. When Zerbisias argues that alternative magazines are outside the marketplace, she's saying that it is not normal to crave unfettered free expression, any more than it is to devote time and energy and money to something that does not bring financial reward. It is not normal to engage in creative acts not sanctioned by the mainstream establishment in the form of promised remuneration.

The less we get to hear about ourselves, the more our "life" and "entertainment" reports consist of the antics of generic celebrities (a bizarre oxymoron that itself suggests the media's willing complicity), the more we crave news about our lives outside of the trappings of power and commodity. "Newspapers no longer write about the achievement of ordinary people," warned veteran reporter John Miller in his lament for the Canadian newspaper industry, *Yesterday's News*. "How many 'regular' people do you see on television?" wonders Stephen Duncombe. By refusing to report meaningfully on independent cultural endeavours while burying us in an entertainment monoculture that preaches *faux* self-determination and sound-bite solutions, the mass media literally forces us to create our own modes of communication. In response to our lifestyle culture desires, the media become even more conservative, withdrawn, inaccessible—falling back on the shaky construct of "underground" culture to keep down what cannot be easily understood.

■   ■   ■

Having succeeded beyond the dreams of even the most rabid proponent of laissez-faire capitalism, the giant marketing machine cannot stop. "Just as we now try to control atom-bomb fallout," warned McLuhan, "so we will one day try to control media fallout." Young Bart Bonikowski's analysis of the ever-creeping tentacles of ad placement is chilling and makes it clear that the fallout from the marketing machine is spreading, killing dissent and co-opting our lifestyle culture ambitions.

Fairey's Giant project is the marketer's dream—to appeal to both our urge to be part of something and our urge to reject the group in favour of hedonistic individualism. Corporations love featuring generic, meaningless slogans that attempt to include and embrace as many people as possible. The Indigo book chain embarked on a series of ads with the exhortation, "Blue Your Mind." Coca-Cola is among the pioneers in this field, from its "I'd like to buy the world a Coke" days to its "Always Coca-Cola, always the real thing" campaign, which has no inherent content and, essentially, functions on the same principle as "Obey Giant," except that Coke is not portrayed as a kind of hip, retro-slacker mystery but as a steadfast wonder beverage that always was and always will be—a bubbly sip of the authentic experience in this fake, plastic world.

We don't even have to leave the soft drink industry to come up with more specific examples of the way the marketing milieu attempts to penetrate the last small pockets of token resistance. Remember the zine *Salvation Army*? In it, Scott Treleaven tells of getting a letter from a company called Perspective Marketing. They'd "read the zine and wanted our help in creating a national 'non-mainstream' publication" for one of their clients, writes Scott. Curious and sceptical, Scott got on the phone with a guy named Greg, who was "terribly enthusiastic" and kept optimistically referring to "the project" even after Scott reminded him that *Salvation Army* was mostly about "theft, sodomy, and ritual bloodletting." Greg, however, was "unfazed." Finally, after Scott asked "for the sixth or seventh time who this client was," Greg buckled and admitted that he was working for Pepsi. "After a hardy, but friendly, 'fuck you,'" writes Scott, "I put the phone down on Greg and possibly a lot of money."

A while back, I got a letter from a division of the multi-national marketing research group Angus Reid asking me to participate in something called the *PopCulture Report*. "As part of our research methodology we will be contacting experts in the major cultural purveying industries to conduct interviews focussing on perceptions of pop culture today in North America. We are particularly interested in cutting edge opinions. That's where you come in."

In 1998, I attended the launch of a book called *Chips*

& *Pop, decoding the nexus generation.* "Nexus" is a code word for Generation X or slacker or whatever you want to call it. The book is the product of a Toronto marketing firm called D-code, and is a slavish portrayal of the rapidly aging "youth" market, an attempt to create a direct conduit between corporate desire to access our pocketbooks and the supposed need to "understand" what "we" are "all about" via a bevy of statistics and half-baked philosophies. Why does the corporation think we don't want product but the glamour of product? Because the experts they hire, the D-coders, tell them that "Nexus consumers are looking for more than just 'stuff.' They're looking for an experience." Which is why the launch juxtaposed pretentious placement of Nexus influences—Atari, Twister, Monopoly, an album by The Cure—with a Royal Bank info table and free beer from Carlsberg. Am I having "an experience" yet?

Marketing fosters an environment in which "cool" is just a way of recycling a previous decade's cultural product. So where does that leave us? Are we ripe for the plucking, grinding, and packaging that was so successful with the baby-boomer generation? Everything we do is consumed and spat out again, a masticated, formless pulp that mocks our intentions. Is it any wonder that people will go to outrageous lengths just to be noticed, let alone understood? If you have to go to sporting events wearing a rainbow afro, so be it. If that doesn't work, take hostages. Do something, anything, that can't be decoded and marketed back to you.

Rather than take risks on actual artistic ventures,

companies tightly control the product image and then unleash their forces: they hire "street teams" of urban (that is, black) youth to randomly plaster corridors of North American cities with stickers and posters meant to appear like "the enthusiastic handiwork of actual fans." Also a good corporate move is the focus-grouping of pop songs. Get a bunch of kids together and ask 'em: Do you like the song better this way or that way? Should this be the hit single, or that? Capitol Records even has a focus-group sign-up sheet on the Internet. "What do you think about Beck?" you are asked. You can choose only from parameters including "Like It a Lot" to "Tired of that Band." Beck would probably deny having had his songs focus-grouped—even if groups of fifteen-year-olds did, at one point, get to fill out surveys on the quality of his plunder stylings. Says a vice-president from our friends at Angus Reid: "I've done market research for bands who virtually swore us to secrecy that we would never reveal their identity. If you're a rock 'n' roll rebel, you don't want to be seen to be doing market research."

Meanwhile, the trend in "independent" film is to mimic the long-standing Hollywood practice of having companies pay to have their products placed in the movie (who can forget the shrivelled E.T.'s inexplicable love for Reese's Pieces?). Explains the director of marketing for The Shooting Gallery, an independent production company responsible for, among others, the movie *Sling Blade*: "The key is not only to find opportunities to seamlessly place products, but more importantly to associate brand to the entire film relevance." Isn't that a nice way of putting it? I long to see movies that surreptitiously feature products associated with "entire film relevance" almost as much as I can't wait to go out and get my hands on the latest focus-grouped single by some prepubescent quartet of crooning corn-fed siblings. Is it any wonder that even the most cynical of us cannot help but associate certain corporate products with certain memories and moments in our lives? Is it any wonder that we are confused, that our values are up for grabs, that we drift through life unable to connect to anyone or anything that might cut through the façade that has us hiding behind cool like a pair of sunglasses? What's for sale is nothing. Is everything. Excuse me, do you sell "entire film relevance" here? A soothing, gentle AT&T voice wants to know: "Have you ever tucked in your kid from a phone booth? Have you ever read a book from two thousand miles away? Have you ever faxed someone from the beach?" Naturally, we don't get to reply. "You will," proclaims the voice, full of triumphant indulgence at our innocent amazement. Here again is the idea of connectivity, of family, of good times, contrasted with the cold, clinical precision of tucking your kid in from a phone booth—an idea that, quite frankly, makes me want to puke.

"All media exist to invest our lives with an artificial perception and arbitrary values," McLuhan confidently assures us. In other words: no reason to panic. Only, we are starting to panic, to crack, because the relentless fluff of marketing makes it impossible to convey who we actually are, what we feel, and why we are angry and disappointed and dissatisfied. Worst of all, we are unable to recognize other ways and possibilities, so that even when someone like Shepard Fairey comes along and does, quite brilliantly, parody the post-modern marketing campaign, his victory seems hollow and at our expense.

Fairey and Giant at least show us how easy it is to break the monotony and get those who notice to recognize the chimera of marketing that dominates our mental environment. The malaise and the ironic inflections of nothing that dominate our jaded discourse and inspire Fairey to new heights of anti-achievement are confusing, not just to those who are perpetrating these minor acts of lifestyle rebellion but also to those who so desperately seek to hold on to the keys to the gate. Who are we? What do we want? These were questions that, once upon a time, seemed simple and easy. We are handy age groups divided into pie charts. We want different variations of the same thing. So when did it get so complicated? When did it become a billion-dollar business to understand the kids? Full-time thought police monitor our every purchase, swear word, and cult obsession. But in a world where we are all artists, creators, thinkers, there is too much to keep track of, too much information to pave over with an endless array of stupid shit.

■　　■　　■

How, then, should the fledgling lifestyle-culturite respond to the marketing behemoth? Throughout this book we've met artists, thinkers, and collectors who have picked up on

Fairey's legacy by chronicling the ways we've tried to reclaim the world of billboards and Greenville websites as our own. Our zinesters, our stupid-job workers, our obsessive hobbyists, all crave the same thing, inspired by a world of fakes in which we crave authenticity. At the same time, as Giant shows us, no one can give us what we want except ourselves. Fairey's decade-long, ongoing commitment to his project tells us that we are adrift in a swirl of imagined images, each one attempting to touch the essential nature of who we are and who we want to be. And this, in turn, suggests that in the McLuhanesque information age there will be no truth, no product, no "real thing." Which means that we all have an equal capacity to reinvent and to be reinvented. We are, each one of us, out on our own, on an equal footing with the big boys, who, for all their desperate machinations, will eventually succeed only in adding to the confusion and permeability of a marketing environment obsessed with conveying an aura of authenticity and individuality. It's a conflicting environment that negates the indie operator even as it offers Fairey—and us—the opportunity to obey our own vision of the true lie of style.

WACKY, WEIRD, AND PROBABLY DANGEROUS: THE DEATH OF BRAINO AND THE BIRTH OF A NEW CULTURE

A CONCLUSION

I've been accused of being part of the paparazzi, a CIA stooge, an exploitative motherfucker, a merchant of sleaze, a purveyor of lies, a right-wing co-conspirator and on and on. At other times I've been thanked for supporting the democratic process, exposing bureaucratic inefficiency, being fearless, a socialist, and anti-authoritarian and on and on.

— Wilson Lee on his job as a news reporter with Citytv

Braino broke up not long before I finished this book. Well, maybe I should say that they parted ways, amicably as far as I can tell, drifted apart the way people do when they are bonded not by family or friendship but by convictions as difficult to express as they are to advance. In fact, none of the members of the band has even been willing to say that the group has disbanded. A hiatus they call it. A vacation. Nevertheless, it is clear that the band's legacy—a devastatingly long two-hour CD launch, an abruptly truncated six years—was too much to sustain, too much to believe in, and the boys drifted away, their faith in Braino compromised by the pressures of a world in which we must always be speeding toward new challenges, new dreams, new successes.

317

Who knows how many creative acts have been lost in the wilderness of lifestyle culture or, worse, left sucking exhaust, caught in the traffic jam of pop? Was Braino a failure? Not really. Not any more than our frustrating everyday lives can be described as failures. Don't we all strive for a kind of accomplishment that falls just outside the parameters of what our society calls success? And yet, we soldier on. For the boys of Braino—for all of us—there will be more bands, more acts of hopeless, necessary hubris that shore up our identity in the anonymous, arbitrary world of mass culture. We are creatures of our times, guilty of irony and sarcasm even as we cast our tinted gaze toward a future we insist on every time we dust our curios or scrawl the lyrics to the rock songs we will never sing in a tattered notebook we keep underneath the bed. At night we dream multiplex big-screen Technicolor Dolby SurroundSound dreams—giant, impossible, gratuitous dreams that, though they cannot be fulfilled, aren't the worst promise a culture can give new generations.

Despite the inevitable setbacks and the inordinate amount of rhetorical anger vented on our ambitions, we continue to create and discuss and rearrange our pop inheritance. The project of lifestyle culture moves on, a car with no brakes rolling down a hill that seems to have no end.

Or maybe there is an end, but it's one that merely conveys a sense of the new beginnings and new possibilities that we are in search of. Not a conclusion, but the end of this awkward phase of life in North America, where, somehow, we have become controlled and manipulated by our stuff, as opposed to the other way around. An end to a strange century in which stuff has come to represent ambitions and hopes for which there can be no tangible analogous object— no perfume that offers us escape, no car that promises freedom, no pair of jeans that assures us of desire. And so we return to art—not Art in the traditional, cloistered sense, but an art available to us all in endless permutations, an art that defies prepackaged, mass-marketed interpretations of who we are. The end—and the beginning—is in the founding of such an art as the populist, self-validating, self-perpetuating birthright of the information age. An art that can convey our fragile individuality, without denying the potency of our collective mass bluster. An art that breaks down nationalities without refuting heritages, all the while reassuring us that we can—despite everything—find meaning and real identity in a society of fragmented TV moments and Tarzan obsessives.

Where will we find this new beginning, this dramatic restatement of our lives through the art of a lifestyle culture age? More important, how do we create a space for this art to thrive and grow?

For the last five years, I've spent time, money, and immense amounts of energy exploring zines. In the summer of 1995 a friend and I scraped together the cash and put out the premier issue of our zine review digest, which we called *Broken Pencil*. It was an act of vanity that I'd rather forget. The first issue of the magazine—after hours of drunken arguments and weeks of all too sober debates—cost just over two thousand dollars to print. I had just graduated from university with the always useful combination of English Literature and Philosophy, and so, naturally, I was working part-time as an usher and van driver. Co-founder Hilary Clark was a bartender. We each put in a thousand bucks, convinced, without the slightest bit of research or real understanding of the small press business in Canada, that we would recoup, double, triple—no, quadruple our outlay. How could anyone resist a chronicle of the zines and underground endeavours of the hyperborean? Even now I look back at our innocence, our stupidity, and our enthusiasm with amazement. What were we thinking? What compelled us?

Of course that was the question that I wrote this book to try to answer. But at the time, before starting this long odyssey, a journey through the hinterlands of pop in search of a way back home, we only knew, as writers and readers,

The first issue of Broken Pencil, guide to Canadian zines.

that something had to be done. Too much activity was going unfound, unread, unrepresented. The best new creative minds in Canada were coming up through the ranks of the zines, micro-presses, and indie journals that we wanted to trumpet and represent in *Broken Pencil*. So what the hell? We put together a magazine. And then we waited.

That summer, somewhat unsure of my direction in life and why I had gone to all the trouble and expense of printing two thousand copies of a magazine issue that, as it turned out, would reach fewer than five hundred people, I headed off to graduate school. There, I honed my drinking abilities and continued searching for someone or something to give me some sign that our little fledgling publishing attempt had been noticed. One morning, I opened an e-mail from an editor at the then independently owned and still feisty *London Free Press* of London, Ontario (the newspaper has since been swallowed up by one of Canada's handful of media monopolies). He said he had seen *Broken Pencil* and was intrigued. He asked me if I would consider writing an article on zines for their Focus section. Sure, I said. He gave me a word count and a dollar amount and a deadline and away I went, eventually producing a zine opus that was double the length requested and virulent in its opposition to the cultural hegemony that relegates independent creative action to the bottom of the barrel.

He liked it. It was published in its entirety, spanning the first two pages of the Saturday Focus section, complete with covers of zines, interviews with zine creators, and contact info for the zine publishers discussed in the piece.

It was that moment, not the moment when we got the first issue of *Broken Pencil* back from the printer, that spoke to me about the power of independent culture: I had written about the "underground" in an intelligent, considered way and my ideas had been taken seriously. And how had this miracle come about? Because I had put myself forward, produced an ephemeral document speaking to my passions and obsessions that, unknown to me at the time, also gave me the kind of credibility that the "mainstream" (whatever that is) could accept. As a magazine editor I was an expert—fitting fodder for a Focus section that probably would not have returned my calls a few months earlier. I had created, through my barely understood lifestyle culture ambitions, a space for myself and the zinesters I wrote about, a space in which we could express a truth that would otherwise not have existed.

So I began to contribute to various newspapers and magazines. It was better money than van driving (just barely) and far more self-validating. We continued to publish *Broken Pencil*, and I continued to agitate from inside the monolithic media tower—even writing a column on zines for the *National Post*, flagship vehicle of Conrad Black's right-wing newspaper monopoly. The experience taught me that you can present a meaningful discussion about independent culture both within the confines of the mainstream press and outside of it, in the form of indie endeavours. As Citytv's Wilson Lee well knows, the media—monolithic, profit-obsessed, evil—is also run by individuals who are, for the most part, interested, benevolent, and eager to bring new ideas to readers.

Nevertheless, my experience with the now cruelly diminished *Free Press*, the *National Post*, and other media outlets could and should be considered an exception. As I've argued quite belligerently in this book, one rarely sees substantive articles on zines or independent culture in a climate where all arts reporting is driven by the marketing machine that feeds a steady stream of prepackaged mass entertainment products and, most important, accompanying ads to editors only too happy to have their job (determining what cultural events are significant to the reading public) done for them.

And that, too, is why we are still plugging away at *Broken Pencil*—a publication about as likely to make a profit as an eight-year-old's lemonade stand—and why I am still writing about zines and indie culture in the mainstream press. Asserting an alternative reality, a collective and personal truth different from the dominant conception of the way things are, demands that we convey our own impressions and desires on our own terms. We must hold our own anti-press conferences and develop our own celebratory events; we cannot rely on others to give us a voice. I've been interviewed by many mainstream media representatives from TV, print, and radio. As was the case on the Pamela Wallin show, when I get hold of the finished product, only rarely do I find my spiel (and by now it is a spiel) adequately represented. On most occasions my experience is eerily similar to that of Mecca Normal singer Jean Smith: lengthy comments are whittled down to a sentence that makes me sound like either a reactionary maniac or a hopeless idealist (I'm both and neither). The resulting articles or TV segments pay lip service to the idea of independent culture, but it's clear that their architects are, for the most part, just going through the motions.

I've published *Broken Pencil* all this time because the world of mass culture is our world; we belong to it and it belongs to us. I've written for the mainstream press to convey the same message. My driving force has been to create a public mental space (just as the Active Resisters want to liberate physical public space) that can assert the primacy of lifestyle culture, of this new kind of art that speaks to our abstract desires in a way that the world of stuff—a world that often subsumes even the most well-intentioned editors, reporters, publishers, and creators—simply cannot do. What I found in investigating and agitating for this space is that what most affects our sense of self in relation to our mass culture is not the products we buy but how we encounter our products, how we are taught to encounter the exclusionary, alienating world of televised experts sporting larger-than-life lives that we can never measure up to. And so, I continue to agitate for a space, a free zone, where we can recognize the effects these things have on our lives without denying that our lives have been profoundly changed by pop—in both good and bad ways.

It's clear that the structure of mass culture and synergistic media monopolies is counter to the interests of
independent culture. Which is to say that, as I've argued
throughout this book, that structure is counter to the interests of all of us who have grown up within the mass culture
continuum, but without a language and a place to speak
about the slippery, near-incomprehensible legacy of a bold
new electronic information age. We all—whether we recognize our need or not—want to be involved with our culture
in a meaningful way. So far, we've blundered about, searching
for a way to assert our involvement. I started a zine, the
Braino boys held weekly collaborative song-writing jams
where they incorporated punk and free jazz and TV theme
songs, but the majority of us respond more passively to our
lifestyle culture urges—collecting, buying, tattooing, arguing, taking stupid jobs running errands for the producers of
made-for-TV movies. In all these efforts, we seek the space to
express our reality, our truth, our malaise-ridden hopeful
indifference. These forays have met with varying degrees of
success. Braino is on hiatus, but their particular take on the
swirling eddies of pop will no doubt resurface, just as plunderphonics has inspired new voices. Your interest in film noir,
poetry, soap operas, stamps, zines, furries, antiques, ultra-
violent computer games has led you to meet people with similar interests, and together you understand and validate each
other, providing not answers but a silent acceptance of the
way that we all latch on to something—however ephemeral
and seemingly stupid—that can help us understand and

control the world around us. *Broken Pencil* continues, makes enough money to just about pay for itself, and has fostered a space—however small—where lifestyle culture creators at the front lines can meet each other and the world.

Still, there are the countless many of us who, mired in depression and substance abuse, chase an ideal that never was and become immersed in a mass culture world from which we don't emerge. We must blame ourselves for the growing number who don't find a way to reflect their truth in the minute space we have available to us, the widening crack between individual conception and mass reality. For too long we have happily allowed our greed and indifference to be validated, reflected back to us in the media, the same way one day soon we will use Steve Mann computer glasses to show us only the world we want to see. In recognizing that the real violence perpetuated in the media doesn't come in the form of gunshots or karate chops, but in the form of systematic repression of our right to assert our "real" by telling our own stories to ourselves, we must also recognize the way that each and every one of us plays a part in this reduction of human beings to ciphers, units of consumption we use and then discard.

And so the search for a space—physical and mental— where we can say what we have to say and be the way we have to be, in order to reach a new understanding of the way we live, continues with increasing urgency. It continues because mass culture's relentless synergy of entertainment and information has rewritten our conception of our own lives. Because to be able to supply ourselves with our own perspectives, we need to re-imagine a world where we are all artists, critics, thinkers, dreamers. Because when we actually try to step into the looking glass of this dreamy, seedy panorama, we are branded as wacky, weird, and probably dangerous; we are prevented from realizing that basking in the ultraviolet rays of the false dawn entertainment economy is only a small part of what could be the western world's real sunrise: a cultural renaissance of unprecedented proportions.

NOTES

CHAPTER ONE

19   Jennifer Brook, *Under the Stars*, #2.

27   Michael O'Neill, quoted in John Miller, *Yesterday's News* (Halifax: Fernwood, 1998), p. 266.

29   "What's Wrong With TV? Just Do the Math," Jeff Mac-Gregor, *The New York Times* (August 9, 1998), p. 27.

32   Max Horkheimer and Theodor Adorno, *Dialectic of Enlightenment* (New York: Herder and Herder, 1972), p. 139.

33   Noel Carroll, *A Philosophy of Mass Art* (New York: Oxford University Press, 1998), p. 4.

34   Herbert Blumer and Philip M. Hauser, quoted in Noel Carroll, *A Philosophy of Mass Art*.

34–35   Fredric Wertham, quoted in Les Daniels, *Superman: The Complete History* (San Francisco: Chronicle Books, 1998), p. 131.

35   Dwight MacDonald, "A Theory of Mass Culture," *The Popular Arts in America*, eds. Bernard Rosenberg and David Manning White (New York: Free Press, 1957), p. 59.

35–36   Neil Postman, *Amusing Ourselves to Death* (New York: Penguin, 1985), p. 156.

36   Tom Henighan, *The Presumption of Culture* (Vancouver: Raincoast Books, 1996), p. 28.

36   Theodor Adorno, *Aesthetic Theory* (Minneapolis: University of Minnesota Press, 1997), p. 17.

36–37   Marshall McLuhan, *Understanding Media* (New York: McGraw-Hill, 1964), p. 199.

39–40   Anonymous Chapters bookstore patron, quoted in Josh Brown, "Freeloading Readers Always Welcome," *The Toronto Star* (March 20, 1999), J14.

40   Jeffery Conway, "The Album That Changed My Life," *Poetry in Motion*, eds. Todd Swift and Regi Cabico (Montreal: Véhicule Press, 1999), p. 291.

43   T. S. Eliot, *Notes Toward a Definition of Culture* (London: Faber and Faber, 1962), p. 34.

43–44   John McCabe, *Stickleback* (London: Granta Books, 1998), pp. 21–22.

44   Jude Lane, quoted in J. D. Biersdorfer, "Star Wars Fanatics, The Trailer Is With You," *The New York Times* (November 22, 1998), p. 17.

45   Karen Coker, *Cashiers du Cinemart*, #9.

45   McLuhan, *Understanding Media*, p. 166.

47   "Live long and prosper, eh," *People Weekly* (November 9, 1998), p. 16.

48   Evan Solomon, quoted in Dre Dee, "Paper, Scissors, Shock," *Ryerson Review of Journalism* (Spring 1997), p. 78.

48   Matthew Arnold, quoted in Raymond Williams, *Culture and Society* (London: Chatto & Windus, 1958).

49   Kalle Lasn, *Adbusters* (Winter 1999), p. 20.

50   Jean-Paul Sartre, quoted in Dick Hebdige, *Subculture, the Meaning of Style* (London: Routledge, 1979), p. 167.

51–52 Eliot, *Notes*, p 31.

57   Michael Comeau, *Radio Free Elvis*, #2.

59   Walter Kerr, *The Decline of Pleasure* (New York: Simon and Schuster, 1962), p. 13.

64   Jeffrey Mackie, *Junkfood Architecture*.

65–66 Steve Mandich, *Heinous*, #5.

66   Chris McDougall, "My Main Man Tarzan," *The New York Times Magazine* (October 25, 1998), p. 25.

69   Sarah Bayliss, *The New York Times* (December 6, 1998), p. 43.

70   Matthew Stadler, "I Think I'm Dumb," Bliss Conference Lecture (May 19, 1994).

74   Stephen Duncombe, *Notes from Underground: Zines and the Politics of Alternative Culture* (London: Verso, 1997), p. 107.

74   Hebdige, *Subculture*, p. 111.

74   Duncombe, *Zines*, p. 95.

74–75 Rick McCallum, quoted in Stephen Cole, "Even bad reviews can't stop menace," *National Post* (May 12, 1999), A1.

75   George Comstock, *Television and the American Child* (San Diego: American Press, 1991), Preface.

CHAPTER TWO

79   Scott Treleaven, *Salivation Army*, final issue.

81   Tom Godfrey, "Anarchy in the Streets?" *Toronto Sun* (August 12, 1998), p. 5.

87   Douglas Rushkoff, *Media Virus! Hidden Agendas in Popular Culture* (New York: Ballantine Publishing Group, 1994), p. 5.

89   John Fiske, *Understanding Popular Culture* (London: Routledge,1989), pp. 148–49.

91   Tim Yohannon, quoted in Carl Wilson, "Dead Punks On Hope," *This Magazine* (August, 1994), p. 15.

93   Marcia Tucker, "Museums experiment with new exhibition strategies," *The New York Times* (January 10, 1999).

93   Greil Marcus, *Lipstick Traces* (Cambridge: Harvard University Press, 1989), p. 3.

94   David Samuels, "Rock is Dead: Sex, Drugs and Raw Sewage at Woodstock '99," *Harper's Magazine* (November, 1999), p. 82.

101   Dick Hebdige, *Subculture, the Meaning of Style* (London: Routledge, 1979), p. 96.

102   William Burroughs, quoted in Hebdige, *Subculture*, p. 23.

108   Thomas Frank, "The End of Hip," *We the Media: A Citizen's Guide to Fighting for Media Democracy*, eds. Don Hazen and Julie Winokur (New York: The New Press, 1997), p. 52.

109   Leah McLaren, "Woodstock Dream As Dead As Sixties Idealism," *The Globe and Mail* (July 24, 1999).

110–11 Stephen Duncombe, *Notes from Underground: Zines and the Politics of Alternative Culture* (London: Verso, 1997), p. 151.

111   Chad Hensley, "The Essence of Repugnance," *Panik* (November, 1999), p. 31.

113   John Miller, *Yesterday's News* (Halifax: Fernwood, 1998), p. 18.

114–15 Treleaven, *Salivation Army*, final issue.

CHAPTER THREE

119 Beck, "Cyanide Breath Mint," *One Foot in the Grave* (K Records, 1994).

121–22 James Gleick, *Faster: The Acceleration of Just About Everything* (New York: Pantheon, 1999), p. 177.

122 MTV president of animation, quoted in Gleick, *Faster*, p. 190.

125 Umberto Eco, *Travels in Hyperreality* (New York: Picador, 1987), p. 136.

126 Marshall McLuhan, *Understanding Media* (New York: McGraw-Hill, 1964), p. 335.

130 WTRA founder Mbanna, quoted in Ron Sakolsky, "Frequencies of Resistance," *Seizing the Airwaves: A Free Radio Handbook*, eds. Ron Sakolsky and Stephen Dunifer (San Francisco: AK Press, 1998), p. 76.

130–31 Tricia Rose, "Give Me A (break) Beat: Sampling and Repetition in Rap Production," *Culture on the Brink*, eds. Gretchen Bender and Timothy Druckrey (Seattle: Bay Press, 1994), p. 249.

131 Bill Graham, quoted in Andrew Goodwin, "Sample and Hold," *On Record: Rock, Pop and the Written Word*, eds. Simon Frith and Andrew Goodwin (London: Routledge, 1990), p. 269.

131–32 Bruce Springsteen, quoted in Chet Flippo, "Interview with Bruce Springsteen," *Musician* (November, 1984), p. 54.

133 Andrew Jones, *Plunderphonics, Pataphysics and Pop Mechanics* (London: SAF, 1995), p. 132.

133   John Oswald, quoted in Jones, *Plunderphonics*, p. 132.

134   Ibid.

135   Andrew Goodwin, "Sample and Hold," *On Record*, p. 263.

136   "In Negativland's plus column," *The Washington Post* (September 20, 1998), p. 64.

137   Chris Cutler, quoted in Jones, *Plunderphonics*, p. 26.

137   Eco, *Travels*, p. 31.

141   Beck, "Sleeping Bag," *One Foot in the Grave* (K Records, 1994).

141   Beck, quoted in Jon Pareles, "A Pop Post-Modernist Gives Up on Irony," *The New York Times* (November 8, 1998), p. 33.

144   David Bryant, quoted in "godspeed you black emperor!" *Exclaim* (March, 1999), p. 22.

147   Neil Postman, *Technopoly* (New York: Random House, 1992), p. 16.

148   Elyse Gasco, *Can You Wave Bye Bye, Baby?* (Toronto: McClelland & Stewart, 1999), p. 3.

148   Golda Fried, *Darkness Then a Blown Kiss* (Toronto: Gutter Press, 1998), p. 11.

149–50 Sonja Ahlers, *Temper, Temper* (Toronto: Insomniac Press, 1998).

150   Sonja Ahlers, quoted in Hilary Clark, "Temper, Temper," *Broken Pencil* (Winter 1999), p. 12.

152   John Fiske, *Understanding Popular Culture* (London: Routledge, 1989), p. 112.

156   Greil Marcus, *Invisible Republic* (New York: Henry Holt, 1997), p. 21.

157 Jon Katz, "I Want My MP3," *Shift* (March, 1999), p. 34.

157 Robert Levine, quoted in Gleick, *Faster*, p. 183.

CHAPTER FOUR

161 David McGimpsey, *Lardcake* (Toronto: ECW Press, 1996), p. 49.

161 Marilyn Morley, "Technology to Wear," *Montreal Gazette* (May 29, 1999), J8.

168 Daniel David Moses, quoted in Bert Archer, "Canada Book Day with an Irreverent Little Twist," *NOW* (April 22, 1999), p. 82.

168 Wade Rowland, *Ockham's Razor: A Search for Wonder in an Age of Doubt* (Toronto: Key Porter, 1999), p. 168.

169 Fan letter, quoted in John Fiske, *Understanding Popular Culture* (London: Routledge, 1989), p. 67.

171 Juliet Hindell, "Hijacker Obsessed With Flight Simulation Video Games," *National Post* (July 24, 1999).

173 Theodor Adorno, *Aesthetic Theory* (Minneapolis: University of Minnesota Press, 1997), p. 33.

173 Jacob Wren, *Unrehearsed Beauty* (Toronto: Coach House Books, 1998), p. 29.

175 Yi-Fu Tuan, *Escapism* (Baltimore: Johns Hopkins University Press, 1998), p. 27.

176 Amy M. Spindler, "What Your Clothes Make of You: Dressing and Identity," *The New York Times Magazine* (November 14, 1999).

177 V. N. Volosinov, quoted in Dick Hebdige, *Subculture, the Meaning of Style* (London: Routledge, 1979), p. 13.

177 Walter Kerr, *The Decline of Pleasure* (New York: Simon and Schuster, 1962), p. 121.

177 Simon Penny, "Virtual Reality as the Completion of the Enlightenment Project," *Culture on the Brink*, eds. Gretchen Bender and Timothy Druckrey (Seattle: Bay Press, 1994), p. 241.

178 Jeffrey Ressner, "Brand New Bodies," *Time* (September 13, 1999), p. 52.

180 Neil Gabler, *Life: The Movie* (New York: Knopf, 1999), p. 234.

184 Tom Vanderbilt, "When Animals Attack, Cars Crash and Stunts Go Bad," *The New York Times* (December 6, 1998), pp. 50–51.

184 Adorno, *Aesthetic Theory*, p. 33.

185 Ralph Benmergui, quoted in Mitch Potter, "Talk TV Leans on a Tiny, Familiar, Chattering Class," *The Toronto Star* (October 25, 1998), D16.

185 Steve Jones, quoted in Hebdige, *Subculture*, p. 27.

186 Don DeLillo, *Underworld* (New York: Scribner, 1997), p. 157.

186 Yi-Fu Tuan, *Escapism*, p. 7.

186–87 John Fiske, *Media Matters* (Minneapolis: University of Minnesota Press, 1994), p. 33.

188 Phillip Scher, quoted on CNN (April 21, 1999).

190 Rick Salutin, "Too Many Explanations for Teen Violence, Not Too Few," *The Globe and Mail* (May 6, 1999).

190–91 Kiki Bonbon, *In Grave Ink*, #1.

193–95 Gabler, *Life*, p. 244.

CHAPTER FIVE

197   Andy Healey, *I'm Johnny and I Don't Give a Fuck*, #2.

199   Chloe Kitten, *Full of Hate*, #1.

202   Mark Kingwell, *Dreams of Millennium* (Toronto: Viking, 1996), p. 321.

202   Marshall McLuhan, *Understanding Media* (New York: McGraw-Hill, 1964), p. 16.

203   James Gleick, *Faster: The Acceleration of Just About Everything* (New York: Pantheon, 1999), p. 270.

210–11 Tom Waits, *Mule Variations* (Epitaph Records, 1999).

211   Walter Kerr, *The Decline of Pleasure* (New York: Simon and Schuster, 1962), p. 104.

212   Otto Weininger, *The Clinical Psychology of Melanie Klein* (Springfield: Charles C. Thomas Publishing, 1984), p. 50.

213   Kathy Goldman, "Prozac Song," untitled recording (self-released, 1998).

214   Mark Crispin Miller, *Boxed In* (Chicago: Northwestern University Press, 1988), p. 331.

215   Beck, quoted in Jon Pareles, "A Pop Post-Modernist Gives Up on Irony," *The New York Times* (November 8, 1998), p. 40.

215   Wolfgang Schirmacher, "Homogenerator: Media and Postmodern Technology," *Culture on the Brink*, eds. Gretchen Bender and Timothy Druckrey (Seattle: Bay Press, 1994), p. 77.

216   Søren Kierkegaard, *The Concept of Irony*, trans. Edna Hong (Princeton: Princeton University Press, 1998), p. 258.

216   Kingwell, *Dreams*, p. 325.

217   Scott Dikkers, editor of The Onion website, quoted in Ryan Bigge, "Sauteeing the Media," *Shift* (April, 1999), p. 36.

220   Gleick, *Faster*, p. 196.

223   Owner of Sanctuary, quoted in Leah Rumack, "Goth Shock," *NOW* (April 29, 1999), p. 20.

224   Andrew Cohen, "Epicentre of Anguish and Disbelief," *The Globe and Mail* (April 23, 1999).

CHAPTER SIX

229   Jeannette Ordas, *Queen of the Universe*.

233   Martin Sprouse, *Sabotage in the American Workplace* (San Francisco: Pressure Drop Press, 1992), p. 6.

236   Caitlin Kelly, "Catnapping on Company Time," *The Globe and Mail* (May 15, 1999).

236   Thomas Frank, "When Class Disappears," *The Baffler* (#9, 1997), p. 8.

237   Noel Carroll, *A Philosophy of Mass Art* (New York: Oxford University Press, 1998), p. 173.

238   Christian Bök, "Speaking with the Aliens," *Brick* (#60, Fall 1998), p. 10.

239   Carellin Brooks (ed.), *Bad Jobs* (Vancouver: Arsenal Pulp Press, 1999), p. 11.

239–40 "Forum File," *Canadian Forum* (June, 1999), p. 48.

240   Langdon Winner, "Three Paradoxes of the Information Age," *Culture on the Brink*, eds. Gretchen Bender and Timothy Druckrey (Seattle: Bay Press, 1994), p. 193.

241–42 James Gleick, *Faster: The Acceleration of Just About Everything* (New York: Pantheon, 1999), p. 159.

242–43 Marshall McLuhan, *Understanding Media* (New York: McGraw-Hill, 1964), p. 335:

245 Bob Boster, "Furry Friends," *Stay Free* (#16, Summer 1999), p. 56.

246 Jake Brooks, Nicholas Corman, Chuck Kapelke, Sara Smith, and Michelle Sullivan (eds.), *Nice Job! The Guide to Cool, Odd, Risky, and Gruesome Ways to Make a Living* (Berkeley: Ten Speed Press, 1999).

247 Neil Gabler, *Life: The Movie* (New York: Knopf, 1999), p. 145.

247 Charles Bukowski, *Post Office* (San Francisco: Black Sparrow Press, 1971), p. 104.

248 Jean Mercier, "A Look at Some 1998 Films," *Cité Libre* (vol. xxvii, #2, Spring 1999), p. 87.

248 Stanley Aronowitz, "Technology and the Future of Work," *Culture on the Brink*, p. 22.

251 *The Book of SubGenius* (New York: Simon and Schuster, 1987), p. 64.

251 Stephen Duncombe, *Notes from Underground: Zines and the Politics of Alternative Culture* (London: Verso, 1997), p. 88.

252 Paul Levine, *Barbed Wire* webzine/CD-ROM.

253 Stephanie Nolen, "A Life of Laissez-faire Contentment," *The Globe and Mail* (March 27, 1999).

253 Zoe Whittal, "Hands Out," *She's Gonna Be*, ed. Ann Decter (Toronto: McGilligan Books, 1999), p. 87.

255 Duncombe, *Zines*, p. 77.

257 Jeannette Ordas, *Queen of the Universe*.

258   Shinan Govani, "Mystery Shoppers Keep Eye on The-
        atres," *National Post* (February 27, 1999).

258–59 Richard Foot, "600 Volunteer to Relive Lord of the Flies
        on TV," *National Post* (March 27, 1999), p. 1.

259–60 Clive Thompson, "Why Your Fabulous Job Sucks," *Shift*
        (March, 1999), p. 56.

261–62 Wilson Lee, *minute:thirty*.

262–63 Jeff Yamaguchi, *working for the man*, #3 vol. 2.

266   Aspiring poet, quoted in Diane Wright, "What We Do
        For Money," *Broken Pencil* (Spring 1999).

266   Brendan Bartholomew, "Thank You for Calling Sega,"
        from *Temp Slave!* reprinted in *Factsheet Five Zine Reader*,
        ed. R. Seth Friedman (New York: Crown, 1997), p. 150.

268   Kinko, quoted in *Johnny Can't Read*, #5.

269   Jeannette Ordas, *Queen of the Universe*, #4.

CHAPTER SEVEN

271   The Onion website, 1999.

273–74 Marshall McLuhan, *Understanding Media* (New York:
        McGraw-Hill, 1964), p. 207.

276   Guy Debord, quoted in Gareth Branwyn, *Jamming the
        Media* (San Francisco: Chronicle Books, 1997), p. 24.

276   James Barron, "Reading This Story Might Strain Your
        Eyes," *The New York Times* (November 15, 1998).

279   McLuhan, *Understanding Media*, p. 226.

281   John Heinzl, "Billboards Enjoy Boom Times," *The Globe
        and Mail* (June 16, 1999), M1.

281   Brenda Bouw, "Cashman Says He's Too Fat to Fly," *National Post* (July 24, 1999).

284   Jack Hitt, "Seven Days and Seven Nights Trapped Inside the West Edmonton Mall," *Saturday Night* (March, 1999), p. 64.

284   Mark Crispin Miller, *Boxed In* (Chicago: Northwestern University Press, 1988), pp. 12–13.

285   Jake Brooks, Nicholas Corman, Chuck Kapelke, Sara Smith, and Michelle Sullivan (eds.), *Nice Job! The Guide to Cool, Odd, Risky, and Gruesome Ways to Make a Living* (Berkeley: Ten Speed Press, 1999), p. 105.

285–86 Alexandra Ridge, "Accumulation By Design," *Metropolis* (August/September, 1998), p. 63.

286   Roland Barthes, *Mythologies*, trans. Annette Lavers (New York: Hill and Wang, 1972), p. 110.

287   "The Candy With a Certain Cachet," *National Post* (May 3, 1999).

287–89 Stacey Case, *Rivet*, #13.

288   Walter Kerr, *The Decline of Pleasure* (New York: Simon and Schuster, 1962), p. 112.

289   Carol Masciola, "Stolen Barbies, Unplayed With," *International Herald Tribune* (October 15, 1992).

294   "Heavy Brand News," *eye* (July 15, 1999), p. 7.

294–95 Mikala Folb, "Dollar Power," *Teen Tribute* (Summer 1999), p. 22.

295   Noel Carroll, *A Philosophy of Mass Art* (New York: Oxford University Press, 1998), p. 193.

297   McLuhan, *Understanding Media*, p. 198.

NOTES

297 Stuart Ewen, quoted in *New Internationalist* (July, 1999), p. 17.

298 Wade Rowland, *Ockham's Razor: A Search for Wonder in an Age of Doubt* (Toronto: Key Porter, 1999), p. 99.

302 Ben Bagdikian, *The Media Monopoly*, 4th edition (Boston: Beacon Press, 1992), Preface.

303–4 Kevin Kelly, "Zine Scene: Wordsmiths Launch a Cottage Industry," *St. Petersburg Times* (September 22, 1995), p. 22.

304 Michael L. Jones, "Zines: the Little Guys," *Louisville Magazine* (April 1, 1999), p. 42.

304 Simona Chiose, "Irony Meets Indulgence on the Zine Scene," *The Globe and Mail* (October 7, 1995), C7.

304 Antonia Zerbisias, "Zine Zone," *The Toronto Star* (August 11, 1996), B1.

304 Katherine Drouin, "Zines Look for a Niche," *Arizona Daily Sun* (December 10, 1994), A1.

304–5 Mark Ehrman, "Behind the Zines," *Los Angeles Times* (March 7, 1993), E1.

306 Rick Trembles, "Hoodwinked by a Hack," *Fish Piss* (#4, Winter 1998).

307 Jean Smith, "Rock Writing on the Pop Treadmill," *Broken Pencil* (Summer 1999), p. 17.

307 Antonia Zerbisias, "Stomping Grounds," *The Toronto Star* (February 28, 1998).

308 John Miller, *Yesterday's News* (Halifax: Fernwood, 1998), p. 191.

308 Stephen Duncombe, *Notes from Underground: Zines and the Politics of Alternative Culture* (London: Verso, 1997), p. 24.

309   McLuhan, *Understanding Media*, p. 235.

310   Scott Treleaven, *Salivation Army*.

311   Robert Barnard, Dave Cosgrave, Jennifer Welsh, *Chips &
       Pop* (Toronto: Malcolm Lester Books, 1998), p. 117.

312   John Turner, "Sell the Power," *Shift* (January, 1998), p. 46.

312   Betsy Powell, "Pop Turns to Focus Gurus," *The Toronto
       Star* (May 9, 1999), D16.

312–13 Shooting Gallery marketing director, quoted in Karen
       Hudes, "Independent Film, But With a Catch," *The New
       York Times* (November 15, 1998), p. 43.

313   McLuhan, *Understanding Media*, p. 199.

CONCLUSION

317   Wilson Lee, "The Message in the Medium," *Broken
       Pencil* (Winter 1999), p. 19.

ZINES AND INDEPENDENT CULTURE RESOURCES

a.d.i.d.a.s., Brandon Bain, 4318 Mitchell Ave., Niagara Falls, ON, L2E 6R5

Adbusters, 1243 West 7th Ave., Vancouver, BC, V6H 1B7

Artistamp News, Ed Varney, Box 3655, Vancouver, BC, V6B 3Y8

The Baffler, P.O. Box 378293 Chicago, IL 60637

Broken Pencil, P.O. Box 203, Station P, Toronto, ON, M5S 2S7

Cashiers du Cinemart, P.O. Box 2401, Riverview, MI 48192, U.S.A.

Deconstructing Beck/Negativland, Seeland Records, 1920 Monument Blvd., MF-1, Concord, CA 94520, U.S.A.

Essential Media, P.O. Box 661245, Los Angeles, CA 90066-1245, U.S.A.

Evolution Control Committee, Box 10391, Columbus, OH 43201, U.S.A.

Fish Piss, Louis Rastelli, Box 1232 Place d'Armes, Montreal, PQ, H2Y 3K2

Free Radio Berkeley, 1442 A Walnut St., #406, Berkeley, CA 94709, U.S.A.

Full of Hate, P.O. Box 32046, 901 Ste. Catherine E., Montreal, PQ, H2L 2E0

Guerrilla Media, 108–3495 Cambie Street, Vancouver, BC, V5Z 4R3

Happy Nightmare Baby, Angela Hysen, 1650 Lewes Way, Mississauga, ON, L4W 3L2

Heinous, Steve Mandich, P.O. Box 12065, Seattle, WA 98102, U.S.A.

I'm Johnny and I Don't Give a Fuck, Andy Healey, P.O. Box 21533, 1850 Commercial Dr., Vancouver, BC, V5N 4A0

In Grave Ink, Lindsay Tipping, #103–416 7th St. N.W., Calgary, AB, T2N 1S4

Johnny Can't Read, Shawn, P.O. Box 20105, Green Acres P.O., Thunder Bay, ON, P7E 6P2

Junkfood Architecture, Jeffrey Mackie, 5996 St. Urbain St., Montreal, PQ, H2T 2X5

King of the Fairies, Glendon McKinney, 91 Sackville St., Toronto, ON, M5A 3E6

minute:thirty, Wilson Lee, P.O. Box 265, Station C, Toronto, ON, M6J 3P4

Murder Can Be Fun, P.O. Box 640111, San Francisco, CA 94164, U.S.A.

Orgasm Death Gimmick, Kevin Pearce, 4476 Concord Place, Burlington, ON, L7L 1J4

Queen of the Universe, Jeannette Ordas, 1340 Woodland Drive, Vancouver, BC, V5L 3S3

Radio Free Elvis, Michael Comeau, 5 Parker Ct., Barrie, ON, L4N 2A6

Rivet, Stacey Case, 689 Queen St. West, Box 193, Toronto, ON, M6J 1E6

Salivation Army, Scott Treleaven, P.O. Box 67539, RPO Spadina Ave. W., Toronto, ON, M5T 3B8

Sockamagee, Steve Richards, 2037 Stainsbury Ave., Vancouver, BC, V5N 2M9

Sombre Souls on Prozac, Milena, RR #3, Caledon East, ON, L0N 1E0

Stay As You Are, Brad Yung, P.O. Box 30007, Parkgate P.O., North Vancouver, BC, V7H 2Y8

Stay Free, Carrie McLaren, P.O. Box 306, Prince St. Station, New York, NY 10012, U.S.A.

Temp Slave!, P.O. Box 8284, Madison, WI 53708-8284, U.S.A.

Under the Stars, Jennifer Brook, P.O. Box 34, Caledon East, ON, L0N 1E0

working for the man, Jeff Yamaguchi, P.O. Box 20403, Brooklyn, NY 11202, U.S.A.

ACKNOWLEDGMENTS

*This book is dedicated to my good friends
Hilary Clark and John Hodgins,
avowed lifestyle-culturites and
original members of the BP team.*

My thanks to all the artists, musicians, zinesters, slackers, and thinkers discussed in this book, not only for their boundless creative accomplishments but also for taking the time to answer my pestering questions. Bleek, Steve Mann, and the boys formerly known as Braino were particularly instrumental in that regard. Inspiration was also found in the thousands of zines sent to me over the years. My gratitude to everyone who gave me a chance to admire their work.

In the writing of this book, I am grateful to Christopher Frey for discussion and theorizing and for the depth of his knowledge in the field of pop culture arcana. Also, thanks to Hoge Day, Jon Elsberg, Orie Niedzviecki, Rob Teixeira, and Anne Collins for thoughts, opinions, and book-lending. Sam and Nina Niedzviecki housed me, fed me Pop-Tarts, gave me my first record, my first guitar, my first computer, and the chance—the need—to develop many of the ideas in this

ACKNOWLEDGMENTS

book. My agent, Jennifer Barclay, provided valuable guid-
ance. And, of course, I offer grateful acknowledgment to the
good people at Penguin Books Canada, particularly editor
Jackie Kaiser for the enthusiasm, commitment, and insight
she brought to this project.

Some of the ideas in this book were tried out in different
forms in different places. The following publications gave me
a place to explore my ideas: *Adbusters, Broken Pencil, Canadian Forum, Geist, The Globe and Mail, The London Free Press,
National Post, Realm* and *This Magazine.*

I am grateful to the Canada Council for the Arts for providing financial assistance in the course of the development
and writing of this book.

Finally, my humble thanks to Rachel Greenbaum. Her
keen mind, her compassionate heart, and her faith in the
human condition continue to inspire me.

Broken Pencil and Hal Niedzviecki
P.O. Box 203, Station P
Toronto, ON
Canada M5S 2S7

the broken pencil website is at:
www.brokenpencil.com

CREDITS

"Tires for Eyeballs" 1997 Braino, reprinted by permission.

"In Memoriam: A.H. Jr." 1996 David McGimpsey (ECW Press, Toronto), reprinted by permission.

"Georgia Lee" 1999 Tom Waits, reprinted by permission.

"Prozac Girl" 1998 Kathy Goldman, reprinted by permission.

"Temper, Temper" 1998 Sonja Ahlers (Insomniac Press, Toronto), reprinted by permission.

LIST OF ILLUSTRATIONS

LIST OF ILLUSTRATIONS